JavaScript

Study Guide

By

Kirupa Chinnathambi

FIRST EDITION 2017

ISBN : 978-93-8655-101-6

Reprinted in India under arrangement with Pearson Education Inc., USA

Authorized reprint from the English language edition, entitled JavaScript: Absolute Beginner's Guide, 1st Edition, 9780798758064 by Kirupa Chinnathambi, Published by Pearson Eduction, Inc., publishing as QUE Publishing,

LIMITS OF LIABILITY AND DISCLAIMER OF WARRANTY

Distributors:

BPB PUBLICATIONS
20, Ansari Road, Darya Ganj
New Delhi-110002
Ph: 23254990/23254991

DECCAN AGENCIES
4-3-329, Bank Street,
Hyderabad-500195
Ph: 24756967/24756400

MICRO MEDIA
Shop No. 5, Mahendra Chambers,
150 DN Rd. Next to Capital Cinema,
V.T. (C.S.T.) Station, MUMBAI-400 001
Ph: 22078296/22078297

BPB BOOK CENTRE
376 Old Lajpat Rai Market,
Delhi-110006
Ph: 23861747

COMPUTER BOOK CENTRE
12, Shrungar Shopping Centre,
M.G.Road, BENGALURU–560001
Ph: 25587923/25584641

Published by Manish Jain for BPB Publications, 20, Ansari Road, Darya Ganj, New Delhi-110002 and Printed at Repro India Pvt. Ltd, Mumbai

Accessing the Free Web Edition

Your purchase of this book in any format includes access to the corresponding Web Edition, which provides several special online-only features:

- The complete text of the book, with all the figures and code in full color
- Short videos by the author introducing each chapter
- Interactive quizzes to test your understanding of the material
- Updates and corrections as they become available

The Web Edition can be viewed on all types of computers and mobile devices with any modern web browser that supports HTML5.

To get access to the *JavaScript Absolute Beginner's Guide* Web Edition all you need to do is register this book:

1. Go to **www.quepublishing.com/register**.
2. Sign in or create a new account. www.quepublishing.com.
3. Enter ISBN: **9780789758064**.
4. Answer the questions as proof of purchase.
5. The Web Edition will appear under the Digital Purchases tab on your Account page. Click the Launch link to access the product.

Table of Contents

Dedication

To Meena!

(Who still laughs at the jokes found in these pages despite having read them a bazillion times!)

Acknowledgments

As I found out, getting a book like this out the door is no small feat. It involves a bunch of people in front of (and behind) the camera who work tirelessly to turn my ramblings into the beautiful pages that you are about see. To everyone at Pearson who made this possible, thank you!

With that said, there are a few people I'd like to explicitly call out. First, I'd like to thank Mark Taber for giving me this opportunity, Chris Zahn for patiently answering my numerous questions, and Loretta Yates for helping make the connections that made all of this happen. The technical content of this book has been reviewed in great detail by my long-time friends and online collaborators, Kyle Murray and Trevor McCauley. I can't thank them enough for their thorough (and occasionally, humorous!) feedback.

Lastly, I'd like to thank my parents for having always encouraged me to pursue creative hobbies like painting, writing, playing video games, and writing code. I wouldn't be half the rugged indoorsman I am today without you both.☺

About the Author

Kirupa Chinnathambi has spent most of his life trying to teach others to love web development as much as he does.

In 1999, before blogging was even a word, he started posting tutorials on **kirupa.com**. In the years since then, he has written hundreds of articles, written a few books (none as good as this one, of course!), and recorded a bunch of videos you can find on YouTube. When he isn't writing or talking about web development, he spends his waking hours helping make the Web more awesome as a Program Manager in Microsoft. In his non-waking hours, he is probably sleeping...or writing about himself in the third person.

INTRODUCTION

Have you ever tried learning to read, speak, or write in a language different from the one you grew up with? If you were anything like me, your early attempts probably looked something like the following:

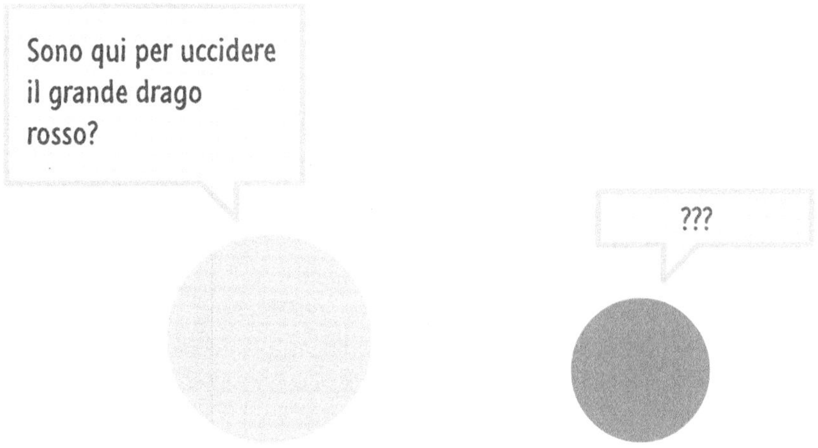

Sono qui per uccidere il grande drago rosso?

???

Unless you are Jason Bourne (or Roger Federer), you barely survived learning your first language. This is because learning languages is hard. It doesn't matter if you are learning your first language or a second or third. Being good at a language to a point where you are useful in a non-comical way takes a whole lotta time and effort.

It requires starting with the basics:

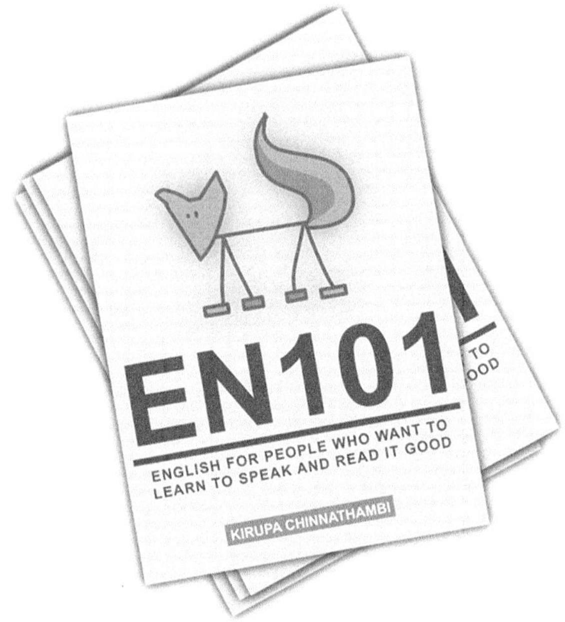

It requires a boatload of practice and patience. It's one of those few areas where there really aren't any shortcuts for becoming proficient.

Parlez-vous JavaScript?

Successfully learning a *programming* language is very similar to how you would approach learning a *real world* language. You start off with the basics. Once you've gotten good at that, you move on to something a bit more advanced. This whole process just keeps repeating itself, and it never really ends. None of us ever truly stop learning. It just requires starting somewhere. To help you with the "starting somewhere" part is where this book comes in. This book is filled from beginning to end with all sorts of good (and hilarious—I hope!) stuff to help you learn JavaScript.

Now, I hate to say anything bad about a programming language behind its back, but JavaScript is pretty dull and boring:

Why won't you answer my calls???!!

```
var count = 0;

function doingSomethingBoring() {
    count++;

    if (count > 10) {
        alert("Yaaaaaawwwnnnnnnnnn!");
    } else {
        alert("This one time, at band camp....");
    }
}
```

Dull

Boring!

There is no other way to describe it. Despite how boring JavaScript might most certainly be,[1] it doesn't mean that learning it has to be boring as well.

As you make your way through the book, hopefully you will find the very casual language and illustrations both informative as well as entertaining (infotaining!). All of this casualness and fun is balanced out by deep coverage of all the interesting things you need to know about JavaScript to become better at using it. *By the time you reach the last chapter, you will be prepared to face almost any JavaScript-related challenge head-on without breaking a sweat.*

1. FYI. All grammatical snafus are carefully and deliberately placed—most of the time!

Contacting Me/Getting Help

For non-technical questions, you can also send e-mail to **sales@bpbonline.com.** I love hearing from readers like you, and I make it a point to personally respond to every message I receive.

And with that, flip the page—it's time to get started!

IN THIS CHAPTER

- Learn why JavaScript is awesome
- Get your feet wet by creating a simple example
- Preview what to expect in subsequent chapters

1

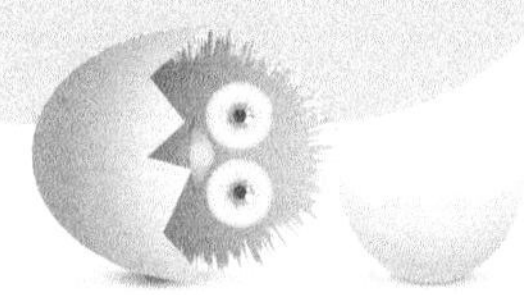

HELLO, WORLD!

HTML is all about displaying things. CSS is all about making things look good. Between the both of them, you can create some pretty nifty-looking stuff like the examples you see on CSS Zen Garden (**csszengarden.com**). Figure 1.1 shows one such example.

FIGURE 1.1

The CSS Zen Garden home page highlighting one layout designed entirely using only CSS.

Despite how nifty sites built using only CSS and HTML look, they will be pretty static. They don't adapt or react to what you are doing. With those two, it's almost like watching a rerun of a great ***Seinfeld*** episode over and over again. It's fun for a while, but it gets boring eventually. The web today isn't static. The sites that you use often (such as those in Figure 1.2) have a certain level of interactivity and personalization that goes well beyond what HTML and CSS by themselves can provide.

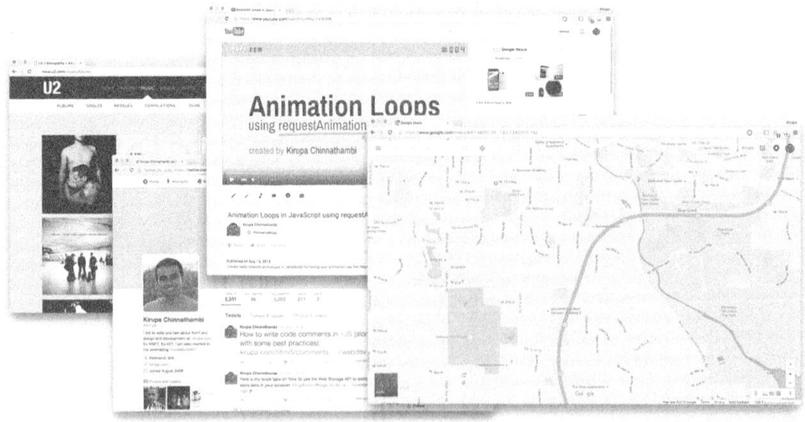

FIGURE 1.2

Examples of various web sites that rely heavily on JavaScript for their proper functioning.

To make your content come alive, you will need some outside help. What you need is JavaScript!

What Is JavaScript?

JavaScript is a modern-day programming language that is a peer of HTML and CSS. To be a bit vague, it basically enables you to add interactivity to your document. A short list of things you can do with JavaScript include the following:

- Listen to events like a mouse click and do something.
- Modify the HTML and CSS of your page after the page has loaded.
- Make things move around the screen in interesting ways.
- Create awesome games (like "Cut the Rope") that work in the browser.
- Communicate data between the server and the browser.
- Allow you to interact with a webcam, microphone, and other devices.

....and much MUCH more! The way you write JavaScript is pretty simple—sort of. You put together words that often resemble everyday English to tell your browser what to do. Here is an example:

```
var defaultName = "JavaScript";

function sayHello(name) {
    if (name === undefined) {
        alert("Hello, " + defaultName + "!");
    } else {
        alert("Hello, " + name + "!");
    }
}
```

Don't worry if you don't know what any of that means. Just pay attention to what the code looks like. Notice that you see a lot of English words like `function, if, else, alert, name`, and so on. In addition to the English words, you also have a lot of bizarre symbols and characters from the parts of your keyboard that you probably never notice. You'll be noticing them plenty enough really soon, and you'll fully understand what everything in this code does as well.

Anyway, that's enough background information for now. While you would expect me to now provide a history of JavaScript and the people and companies that make it work, I'm not going to bore you with stuff like that. *The only thing to know is that JavaScript is not related to Java.* And with that, we've covered the relevant history that matters. Instead, I want you to get your hands dirty by writing some JavaScript. By the end of this chapter, you will have created something sweet and simple that displays some text in your browser.

A Simple Example

Right now, you may feel a bit unprepared to start writing some code. This is especially true if you aren't all that familiar with programming in general. As you'll soon find out, JavaScript isn't nearly as annoying and complicated as it often pretends to be. It is simply just dull and boring. Big difference!

Code Editing Tools

Sorry to interrupt, but there is one more thing to call out before we go on. This entire book is written with no expectation that you use a fancy HTML authoring tool or a code editor. All you need is a basic editor (like Notepad!) that enables you to see HTML, CSS, and JavaScript. Now, that isn't to say that you won't be better off with a good code editor. They do make your life easier without taking away from the ruggedness of learning JavaScript with your bare hands.

Some of my favorite code editors are

- Atom
- Sublime Text
- Notepad++
- TextMate
- Coda
- Visual Studio Code

This book doesn't cover how to work with any particular code editor, nor does it make a big deal out of it. As long as you know how to create a new document, make some edits, save the document, and preview it in a browser, you know everything you need to follow along.

If you are new to code editors and are unsure how to proceed, then check out my playlist of short videos that shows how to use many of the editors listed here to work with HTML, CSS, and JavaScript: **http://www.kirupa.com/links/editors.htm**.

The HTML Document

The first thing you need is an HTML document. This document will host the JavaScript that you will be writing. You can use any blank HTML document that you want, but if you don't have an HTML page already created and/or want to follow closely along, create a blank HTML page and add the following content into it:

```
<!DOCTYPE html>
<html>

<head>
  <title>An Interesting Title Goes Here</title>

  <style>

  </style>
</head>

<body>

  <script>

  </script>
</body>

</html>
```

If you preview this document in your browser, you won't really see anything. That is totally expected, for this is (after all) a blank document that has nothing really going on. That's fine, for we'll fix that shortly starting with the `script` tag that you see toward the bottom of your example:

```
<script>

</script>
```

The `script` tag acts as a container where you can place any JavaScript you want to run. What we want to do is display the words *hello, world!* in a dialog box that appears when you load your HTML page. Depending on what browser you are using, Figure 1.3 shows what such a dialog box would look like.

FIGURE 1.3

Our dialog box displaying ***hello, world!***

Inside your script region, add the following (highlighted) line:

```
<script>
  alert("hello, world!");
</script>
```

Save your HTML file and open it in your browser. Once your page has loaded, you should see a dialog box with the words hello, world! displayed. It should look very similar to the screenshot you see in Figure 1.3.

If this is your first attempt at writing JavaScript, congratulations! You just crossed a giant hurdle. You created a working example using it. Now, let's look at what you did and try to make sense of what is going on.

Looking at the Code: Statements and Functions

What you just did is write a very simple JavaScript **statement**. A statement makes up the logical set of instructions that tell your browser what to do. A typical application will have many MANY statements. In our case, we just have one:

```
alert("hello, world!");
```

NOTE You can *usually* tell when something is a statement by looking at the last character in it. It is usually a semicolon (;) just like what you see in the earlier code snippet. Now, this is isn't a guaranteed way to identify a statement. JavaScript works fine in many cases without having a semicolon at the end of your statements, and some developers may even choose to omit them as part of the code they write.

Inside a statement, you will see all sorts of funky JavaScript jargon. Our code, despite being just one line, is no exception. You have this weird thing called `alert` that makes an appearance. This is an example of a common English word that behaves similarly in the JavaScript world to how it might in our everyday world. It is responsible for getting your attention by displaying some text.

To get more precise, the word `alert` is actually something known as a **function**. You will use functions all the time, for a function is basically a reusable chunk of code that does something. The *something* it does could be defined by you, defined by some third party library you are using, or it could be defined by the JavaScript framework itself. In our case, the code that gives your `alert` function the magical ability to display a dialog box with a message you pass to it lives deep inside the bowels of your browser. All you really need to know is that if you want to use the `alert` function, simply call it and pass in the text you want it to display. Everything else is taken care of for you.

Getting back to our example, the text you want to display is *hello, world!*. Notice how I am specifying it. I wrap the words inside quotation marks:

```
alert("hello, world!");
```

Whenever you are dealing with pieces of text (more commonly known as **strings**), you will always wrap them inside single or double quotation marks. I know that seems weird, but every programming language has its own quirks. This is one of the many quirks you will see as you explore JavaScript further. We'll look at strings in greater detail shortly, so for now, just enjoy the view from the outside.

Let's go one step further. Instead of displaying *hello, world!*, change the text you are displaying to show your first and last name instead. Here is an example of what my code looks like when I use my name—or the name I wish I had:

```
alert("Steve Holt!!!");
```

If you run your application, you will see your name appear in the dialog box. Pretty straightforward, right? You can replace the contents of your string with all sorts of stuff—the name of your pet, your favorite TV show, and so on. JavaScript will display it, and (best of all) it will not judge whether your favorite TV show happens to involve the day-to-day lives of the Kardashians...or meerkats.

THE ABSOLUTE MINIMUM

In this chapter, you created a simple example that helped get you familiar with writing some JavaScript code. As part of getting you familiar, I threw a lot of concepts and terms at you such as **statement, function, string**, and so on. We even used the alert function a bunch of times to get some text to display on screen:

```
alert("We just finished the first chapter!");
```

I certainly don't expect you to know or remember all of them now. In future chapters, we are going to take each interesting part of what you've seen so far and elaborate on it in nauseatingly vivid detail with (possibly) better examples. After all, I'm pretty sure you want to eventually do things in JavaScript that go beyond displaying some text in a ridiculously annoying dialog box.

Going forward, at the end of each chapter, you may even see a set of links to external resources written by me or others. These resources will give you more details or a different perspective on what you learned, along with opportunities to put your learning into practice with more involved examples. Think of what you see in this book as a jumping-off point for greater and more awesome things.

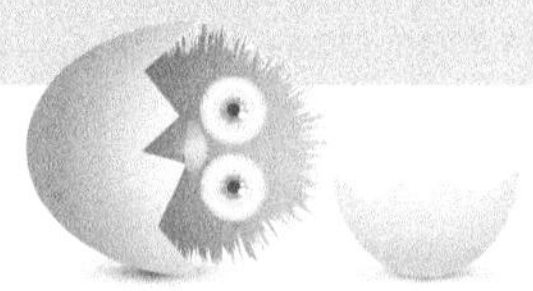

TIP Just a quick reminder for those of you reading these words in the print or e-book edition of this book: If you go to **www.quepublishing.com** and register this book, you can receive free access to an online Web Edition that not only contains the complete text of this book but also features a short, fun interactive quiz to test your understanding of the chapter you just read.

If you're reading these words in the Web Edition already and want to try your hand at the quiz, then you're in luck – all you need to do is scroll down!

IN THIS CHAPTER

- Learn how to use values to store data
- Organize your code with variables
- Get a brief look at variable naming conventions

2

VALUES AND VARIABLES

In JavaScript, every piece of data that you provide or use is considered to contain a value. In the example you saw from our introduction in the previous chapter, the words *hello, world!* might just be some words that you pass in to the `alert` function:

```
alert("hello, world!");
```

To JavaScript, these words and punctuation marks have a specific representation under the hood. They are considered **values**. You may not have thought much about that when you were typing those words in, but when you are in JavaScript country, every piece of data you touch is considered a value.

Now, why is knowing this important? It is important because you will be working with values a whole lot. Working with them in a way that doesn't drive you insane is a good thing. There are two things you need to simplify your life when working with values. You need to:

1. Easily identify them.
2. Reuse them throughout your application without unnecessarily duplicating the value itself.

Those two things are provided by what we are going to be spending the rest of our time on in this chapter: **variables**. Let's learn all about them here.

Onwards!

Using Variables

A variable is basically a name for a value. Instead of typing *hello, world!* every single time you want to use that phrase in your application, you can assign that phrase to a variable and use that variable whenever you need to use *hello, world!* again. This will make more sense in a few moments—I promise!

The way to use variables is by using the `var` keyword followed by the name you want to give your variable:

```
var myText;
```

In this line of code, we very successfully declared a variable called `myText`. Right now, your variable has simply been declared. It doesn't contain anything of value (ha!). It is merely an empty shell.

Let's fix that by initializing our variable to a value like—let's say—*hello, world!*:

```
var myText = "hello, world!";
```

You probably shouldn't be too surprised that I ended up using that phrase. Anyway, let's modify our original example that you saw earlier to use our newly declared (and initialized) variable:

```
var myText = "hello, world!";
alert(myText);
```

Notice that we are no longer passing in our *hello, world!* text to the `alert` function directly. Instead, we are passing in the variable name `myText`. The end result is the same. When this script runs, an alert with *hello, world!* will be shown.

What this change does is simple. It allows us to have one place in our code where *hello, world!* is being specified. If we wanted to change this text to *The dog ate my homework!*, all you would have to do is just make one change to the value specified by the `myText` variable:

```
var myText = "The dog ate my homework!";
alert(myText);
```

Throughout your code, wherever you referenced the `myText` variable, it is the new value that will be used. While this is hard to imagine for something as simple as what we have right now, for larger applications this convenience of having just one location where you can make a change that gets reflected everywhere is a major time saver. You'll see more, less-trivial cases of the value variables provide in subsequent examples and chapters.

More Variable Stuff

What you learned in the previous section will take you far in life—at least, in the part of your life that involves getting familiar with JavaScript. I am not going to go very deep into variables here; we'll do all of that as part of future chapters where the code is more complex and the importance of variables is more obvious. With that said, there are a few odds and ends that I want to cover before calling it a day.

Naming Variables

You have a lot of freedom in naming your variables however you see fit. Ignoring what names you should give things based on philosophical/cultural/stylistic preferences, from a technical point of view, JavaScript is very lenient about what characters (letters, numbers, and other stuff your keyboard can generate) can go into a variable name.

Basically, keep the following things in mind when naming them:

1. Your variables can be as short as one character, or they can be as long as you want. Think thousands and thousands…and thousands of characters.
2. Your variables can start with a letter, underscore (_), or the dollar sign ($) character. They can't start with a number.

3. Outside of the first character, your variables can be made up of any combination of letters, underscores, numbers, and **$** characters. You can also mix and match lowercase and uppercase to your heart's content.
4. Spaces are not allowed.

I've posted some examples of valid variable names in the following:

```
var myText;
var $;
var r8;
var _counter;
var $field;
var thisIsALongVariableName_butItCouldBeLonger;
var __$abc;
var OldSchoolNamingScheme;
```

To check whether your variable name is valid, check out the really awesome and simple *JavaScript Variable Name Validator* (**http://bit.ly/kirupaVariable**).

Outside of valid names that stop JavaScript from complaining, there are other things to focus on as well. There are things like naming conventions where you can spend hours debating what the proper variable name should look like. While we won't dwell on that topic here, a good starting point for understanding this space is Douglas Crockford's *Code Convention*: **http://bit.ly/kirupaCodeConvention**.

More on Declaring and Initializing Variables

One of the things you will learn about JavaScript is that it is a very forgiving and "easy to work with" language. That has some implications, but we'll ignore them for now and deal with the consequences later. For example, you don't have to use the **var** keyword to declare a variable. You could just do something as follows:

```
myText = "hello, world!";
alert(myText);
```

Notice the **myText** variable is being used without formally being declared with the **var** keyword. While not recommended, this is completely fine. The end result is that you will still have a variable called **myText**. The thing is, by declaring a variable this way, you are declaring it globally. Don't worry if the last sentence makes no sense. We'll look at what "globally" means when talking about variable scope in **Chapter 7**, "**Variable Scope**."

One more thing to call out. The thing you should know is that the declaration and initialization of a variable does not have to be part of the same statement. You can break it up across multiple statements:

```
var myText;
myText = "hello, world!";
alert(myText);
```

In practice, you will find yourself breaking up your declaration and initialization of variables all the time. You'll see some examples much later on where we do this, and it will totally make sense why at that point.

One more thing to call out—yes, this time I am not lying about this being the last thing. You can change the value of a variable whenever you want, to whatever you want:

```
var myText;
myText = "hello, world!";
myText = 99;
myText = 4 * 10;
myText = true;
myText = undefined;
alert(myText);
```

If you have experience working with languages that are more strict and don't allow variables to store a variety of data types, this leniency (and being over 21) makes JavaScript sorta cool.

THE ABSOLUTE MINIMUM

Values store data, and variables act as an easy way to refer to that data. There are a lot of interesting details about values, but those are details that you do not need to learn right now. Just know that JavaScript enables you to represent a variety of values such as text and numbers without a lot of fuss.

To make your values more memorable and reusable, you declare variables. You declare variables using the `var` keyword and a **variable name**. If you want to initialize the variable to a default value, you follow all of that up with an equal sign (=) and the value you want to initialize your variable with.

TIP Just a quick reminder for those of you reading these words in the print or e-book edition of this book: If you go to **www.quepublishing.com** and register this book, you can receive free access to an online Web Edition that not only contains the complete text of this book but also features a short, fun interactive quiz to test your understanding of the chapter you just read.

If you're reading these words in the Web Edition already and want to try your hand at the quiz, then you're in luck – all you need to do is scroll down!

IN THIS CHAPTER

- Learn how functions help you better organize and group your code
- Understand how functions make your code reusable
- Discover the importance of function arguments and how to use them

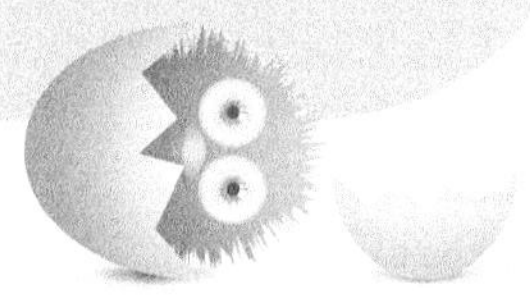

FUNCTIONS

So far, all of the code we've written contained virtually no structure. It was just...there:

```
alert("hello, world!");
```

There is nothing wrong with having code like this. This is especially true if your code is made up of a single statement. Most of the time, though, that will never be the case. Your code will rarely be this simple when you are using JavaScript in the real world for real-worldy things.

To highlight this, let's say we want to display the distance something has traveled (see Figure 3.1).

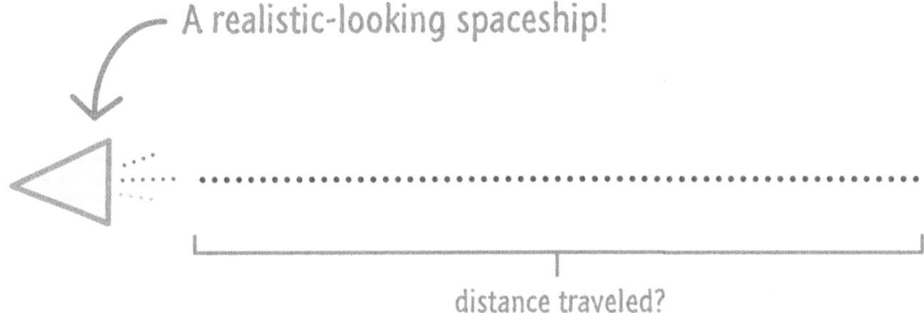

FIGURE 3.1

The distance something has traveled.

If you remember from school, distance is calculated by multiplying the speed something has traveled by how long it took as shown in Figure 3.2.

FIGURE 3.2

The formula for calculating distance.

The JavaScript version of that will look as follows:

```
var speed = 10;
var time = 5;
alert(speed * time);
```

We have two variables—**`speed`** and **`time`**—and they each store a number. The **`alert`** function displays the result of multiplying the values stored by the **`speed`** and **`time`** variables. Quick note: The `*` character (which I threw in there without warning) between two numbers indicates that a multiplication needs to take place. Anyway, as you can see, our JavaScript is a pretty literal translation of the distance equation you just saw.

Let's say we want to calculate the distance for more values. Using only what we've seen so far, our code would look as follows:

```
var speed = 10;
var time = 5;
alert(speed * time);
```

```
var speed1 = 85;
var time1 = 1.5;
alert(speed1 * time1);

var speed2 = 12;
var time2 = 9;
alert(speed2 * time2);

var speed3 = 42;
var time3 = 21;
alert(speed3 * time3);
```

I don't know about you, but this just looks (as Frank Caliendo impersonating Charles Barkley would say) *turrible.*[1] Our code is unnecessarily verbose and repetitive. As I mentioned earlier, when we looked at variables in the previous chapter, repetition makes your code harder to maintain. It also wastes your time.

This entire problem can be solved very easily by using what you'll be seeing a lot of here—**functions**:

```
function showDistance(speed, time) {
    alert(speed * time);
}

showDistance(10, 5);
showDistance(85, 1.5);
showDistance(12, 9);
showDistance(42, 21);
```

Don't worry too much about what this code does just yet. Just know that this smaller chunk of code does everything all those many lines of code did earlier without all of the negative side effects and calories. We'll learn all about functions, and how they do all the sweet things that they do, starting...right...now!

---

1. Frank Caliendo FTW: **http://bit.ly/kirupaFrankCB**.

What Is a Function?

At a very basic level, a function is nothing more than a wrapper for some code. A function basically

- Groups statements together
- Makes your code reusable

You will rarely write or use code that doesn't involve functions, so it's important that you become familiar with them and learn all about how well they work.

A Simple Function

The best way to learn about functions is to just dive right in and start using them, so let's start off by creating a very simple function. Creating a function is pretty easy and only requires understanding some little syntactical quirks like using weird parentheses and brackets.

The following is an example of what a very simple function looks like:

```
function sayHello() {
    alert("hello!");
}
```

Just having your function isn't enough, though. Your function needs to actually be *called*, and you can do that by adding the following line at the end of your code block:

```
function sayHello() {
    alert("hello!");
}
sayHello();
```

If you type all this in your favorite code editor and preview your page in your browser, you will see *hello!* displayed. The only thing that you need to know right now is that your code works. Let's look at *why* the code works by breaking it up into individual chunks and looking at them in greater detail.

First, you see the `function` keyword leading things off:

```
function sayHello()   {
    alert("hello!");
}
```

This keyword tells the JavaScript engine that lives deep inside your browser to treat this entire block of code as something to do with functions.

After the `function` keyword, you specify the actual name of the function followed by some opening and closing parentheses, `( )`:

```
function sayHello()    {
    alert("hello!");
}
```

Rounding out your function declaration are the opening and closing brackets that enclose any statements that you may have inside:

```
function sayHello()    {
    alert("hello!");
}
```

The final thing is the contents of your function—the statements that make your function actually...functional:

```
function sayHello()    {
    alert("hello!");
}
```

In our case, the content is the alert function that displays a dialog box with the word *hello!* displayed.

The last thing to look at is the function call:

```
function sayHello()    {
    alert("hello!");
}
sayHello();
```

The function call is typically the name of the function you want to call (or invoke) followed again by parentheses. Without your function call, the function you created doesn't do anything. It is the function call that wakes your function up and makes it do things.

Now, what you have just seen is a very simple function. In the next couple of sections, we are going to build on what you've just learned and look at increasingly more realistic examples of functions.

Creating a Function That Takes Arguments

Like I mentioned earlier, the previous **sayHello** example was quite simple:

```
function sayHello()    {
    alert("hello!");
}
```

You call a function, and the function does something. That simplification by itself is not out of the ordinary. All functions work just like that. There are differences, however, in the details on how functions get invoked, where they get their data from, and so on. The first such detail we are going to look at involves functions that take **arguments**.

Let's start with a simple example:

```
alert("my argument");
```

What we have here is your `alert` function. You've probably seen it a few (or a few dozen) times already. As you know, this function simply displays some text that you tell it to show (see Figure 3.3).

FIGURE 3.3

The text "my argument" is displayed as a result of the `alert` function.

Let's look at this a little closer. Between your opening and closing parentheses when calling the alert function, you specify the stuff that needs to be displayed. This "stuff" is more formally known as an argument. The `alert` function is just one of many functions that take arguments, and many functions you create will take arguments as well.

To stay local, within this chapter itself, another function that we briefly looked at that takes arguments is our **showDistance** function:

```
function showDistance(speed, time)    {
    alert(speed * time);
}
```

So, you can tell when a function takes arguments by looking at the function declaration itself:

```
function showDistance(speed, time) {
    ...
}
```

Functions that don't take arguments are easy to identify. They *typically* show up with empty parentheses following their name. Functions that take arguments aren't like that. Following their name and between the parentheses, these functions will contain some information about the quantity of arguments they need, along with some hints about what values your arguments will take.

For **showDistance**, you can infer that this function takes two arguments: the first corresponds to the **speed** and the second corresponds to the **time**.

You specify your arguments to the function as part of the function call:

```
function showDistance(speed, time) {
    alert(speed * time);
}
showDistance(10, 5);
```

In our case, we call **showDistance** and specify the values we want to pass to the function inside the parentheses.

```
showDistance(10, 5);
```

Functions that take arguments, however, contain some information about the quantity of arguments they need in the parentheses following their name, along with some hints about what values your arguments will take. To emphasize this, let's look at Figure 3.4.

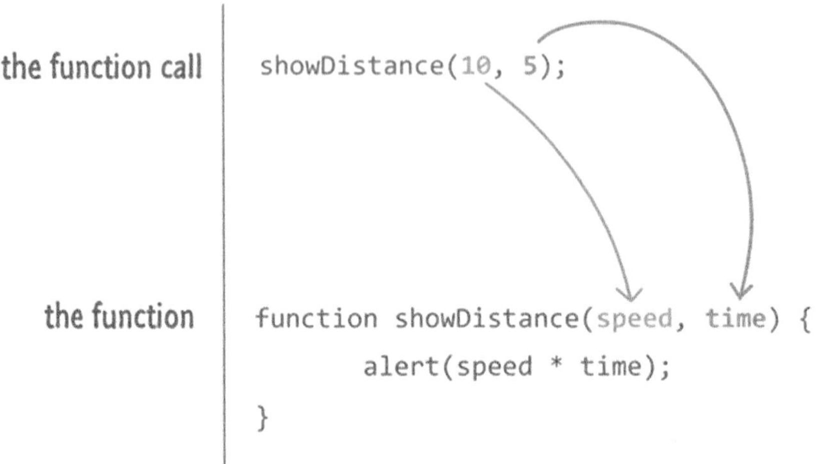

FIGURE 3.4

Order matters.

When the **showDistance** function gets called, the 10 corresponds to the **speed** argument, and the 5 corresponds to the **distance** argument. That mapping is entirely based on order.

Once the values you pass in as arguments reach your function, the names you specified for the arguments are treated just like variable names (see Figure 3.5).

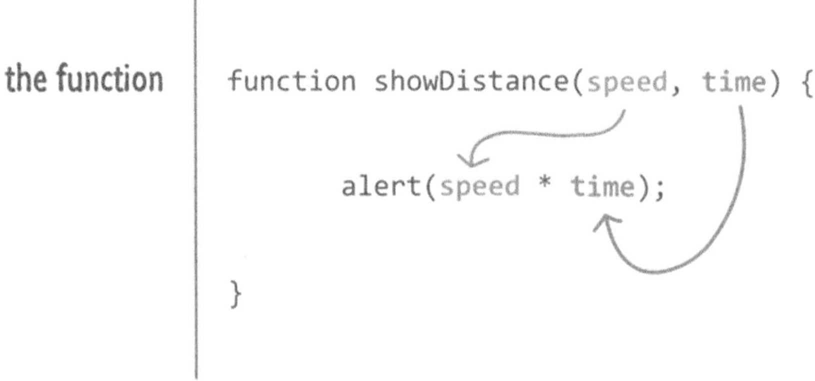

FIGURE 3.5

The names of the arguments are treated as variable names.

You can use these variable names to easily reference the values stored by the arguments inside your function.

NOTE If a function happens to take arguments and you don't provide any arguments as part of your function call, provide too few arguments, or provide too many arguments, things can still work. You can code your function defensively against these cases.

In general, to make the code you are writing clear, just provide the required number of arguments for the function you are calling. Don't complicate things unnecessarily.

Creating a Function That Returns Data

The last function variant we will look at is one that returns some data back to whatever called it. Here is what we want to do. We have our `showDistance` function, and we know that it looks as follows:

```
function showDistance(speed, time)   {
    alert(speed * time);
}
```

Instead of having our `showDistance` function calculate the distance and display it as an `alert`, we actually want to store that value for some future use. We want to do something like this:

```
var myDistance = showDistance(10, 5);
```

The `myDistance` variable will store the results of the calculation done by the `showDistance` function. There are just a few things you need to know about being able to do something like this.

The Return Keyword

The way you return data from a function is by using the `return` keyword. Let's create a new function called `getDistance` that looks identical to `showDistance` with the only difference being what happens when the function runs to completion:

```
function getDistance(speed, time)   {
    var distance = speed * time;
    return distance;
}
```

Notice that we are still calculating the distance by multiplying `speed` and `time`. Instead of displaying an alert, we return the distance (as stored by the `distance` variable).

To call the **getDistance** function, you can just call it as part of initializing a variable:

```
var myDistance = showDistance(10, 5);
```

When the **getDistance** function gets called, it gets evaluated and returns a numerical value that then becomes assigned to the **myDistance** variable. That's all there is to it.

Exiting the Function Early

Once your function hits the **return** keyword, it stops everything it is doing at that point, returns whatever value you specified to whatever called it, and exits:

```
function getDistance(speed, time)   {
    var distance = speed * time;
    return distance;

    if (speed < 0)   {
        distance *= -1;
    }
}
```

Any code that exists after your **return** statement will not be reached, such as the following highlighted lines:

```
function getDistance(speed, time) {
    var distance = speed * time;
    return distance;

    if (speed < 0) {
        distance *= -1;
    }
}
```

It will be as if that chunk of code never even existed. In practice, you will use the **return** statement to terminate a function after it has done what you wanted it to do. That function could return a value to the caller like you saw in the previous examples, or that function could simply exit:

```
function doSomething()   {
    // do something
    return;
}
```

Using the `return` keyword to return a value is optional. The `return` keyword can be used by itself as you see here to just exit the function.

THE ABSOLUTE MINIMUM

Functions are among a handful of things that you will use in almost every single JavaScript application. They provide the much sought-after capability to help make your code reusable. Whether you are creating your own functions or using the many functions that are built into the JavaScript language, you will simply not be able to live without them.

What you have seen so far are examples of how functions are commonly used. There are some advanced traits that functions possess that I did not cover here. Those uses will be covered in the future...a distant future. For now, everything you've learned will take you quite far when it comes to understanding how functions are used in the real world.

TIP Just a quick reminder for those of you reading these words in the print or e-book edition of this book: If you go to **www.quepublishing.com** and register this book, you can receive free access to an online Web Edition that not only contains the complete text of this book but also features a short, fun interactive quiz to test your understanding of the chapter you just read.

If you're reading these words in the Web Edition already and want to try your hand at the quiz, then you're in luck – all you need to do is scroll down!

IN THIS CHAPTER

- Use the popular if/else statement to help make a decision in code
- Learn about switch statements and when to use them

4

CONDITIONAL STATEMENTS: IF, ELSE, AND SWITCH

From the moment you wake up, whether you realize it or not, you start making decisions. Turn the alarm off. Turn the lights on. Look outside to see what the weather is like. Brush your teeth. Put on your robe and wizard hat. Basically...you get the point. By the time you step outside your door, you consciously or subconsciously will have made hundreds of decisions with each decision having a certain effect on what you ended up doing.

For example, if the weather looks cold outside, you might decide to wear a hoodie or a jacket. Independent of what you actually do, you can model this decision as shown in Figure 4.1.

FIGURE 4.1

An example of some of the choices you make everyday.

If the weather is cold, you do whatever falls into the *true* bucket. If the weather is not cold, then you do whatever is in the *false* bucket. Every decision you make can be modeled as a series of true and false statements. This may sound a bit chilly (ha!), but that's generally how we, others, and pretty much all living things go about making choices.

This generalization especially applies to everything your computer does. This may not be evident from the code we've written so far, but we are going to fix that. In this chapter, I will cover what is broadly known as **conditional statements**. These are the digital equivalents of the decisions we make where your code does something different depending on whether something is **true** or **false**.

Onwards!

The If/Else Statement

The most common conditional statement you will use in your code is the **if/else statement** or just the **if statement**. The way this statement works is shown in Figure 4.2.

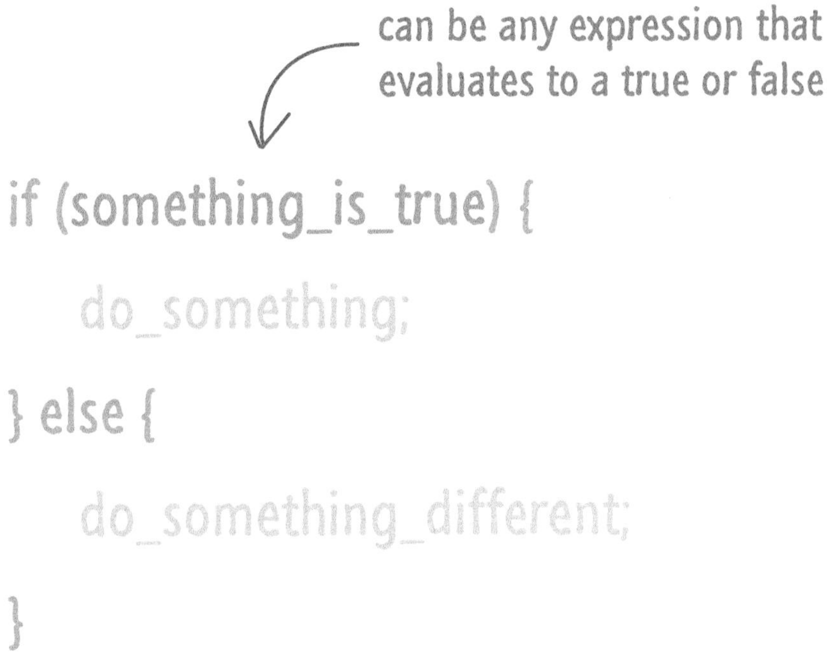

can be any expression that evaluates to a true or false

```
if (something_is_true) {
    do_something;
} else {
    do_something_different;
}
```

FIGURE 4.2

The anatomy of an if/else statement.

To make sense of this, let's take a look at a simple example of an **if statement** in action:

```
var safeToProceed = true;

if (safeToProceed) {
    alert("You shall pass!");
} else {
    alert("You shall not pass!");
}
```

If you put all of this code into an HTML document and run it, you will see an alert with the text *You shall pass!* This is because your expression (the thing following the word if that ultimately evaluates to **true** or **false**) is the variable `safeToProceed`. This variable is initialized to **true**, so the "true" part of your if statement kicks in.

Now, go ahead and change the value of the `safeToProceed` variable from **true** to **false**:

```
var safeToProceed = false;

if (safeToProceed) {
    alert("You shall pass!");
} else {
    alert("You shall not pass!");
}
```

This time when you run this code, you will see an alert with the text "You shall not pass!" This happens because your expression evaluates to **false**. So far, all of this should seem pretty simple. That's good. Hopefully you'll feel the same way in a few more sections!

Meet the Conditional Operators

In most cases, your expression will rarely be a simple variable that is set to **true** or **false** like it was in our earlier example. Your expression will involve what are known as **conditional operators** that help you to compare between two or more things to establish a **true** or **false** outcome.

The general format of such expressions is as shown in Figure 4.3.

```
if (expression operator expression) {
    do_something;
} else {
    do_something_different;
}
```

FIGURE 4.3

A more general look at what your if/else statements look like.

The conditional operator defines a relationship between the expressions. The end goal is to return a **true** or a **false** so that our **if statement** knows which block of code to execute. This may not make much sense yet, but bear with me. Let's look at the conditional operators first before diving into more examples where we tie everything together.

The conditional operators are listed in Table 4.1.

TABLE 4.1 Conditional Operators in JavaScript

Operator	When It Is True
==	If the first expression evaluates to something that is equal to the second expression.
>=	If the first expression evaluates to something that is greater than or equal to the second expression
>	If the first expression evaluates to something that is greater than the second expression
<=	If the first expression evaluates to something that is lesser than or equal to the second expression
<	If the first expression evaluates to something that is less than the second expression
!=	If the first expression evaluates to something that is not equal to the second expression
&&	If the first expression and the second expression both evaluate to true
||	If either the first expression or the second expression evaluate to true
==	If the first expression evaluates to something that is equal to the second expression
>=	If the first expression evaluates to something that is greater or equal to the second expression
>	If the first expression evaluates to something that is greater than the second expression
!== and ===	Just know that these exist. We'll look at these in a future chapter.

Let's take our fuzzy understanding of conditional operators and make them unfuzzy by looking at an example:

```
var speedLimit = 55;

function amISpeeding(speed) {
    if (speed >= speedLimit) {
```

```
        alert("Yes. You are speeding.");
    } else {
        alert("No. You are not speeding. What's wrong with you?");
    }
}

amISpeeding(53);
amISpeeding(72);
```

Take a moment to understand what exactly is going on. We have a variable called `speedLimit` that is initialized to 55. We then have a function called `amISpeeding` that takes an argument named `speed`. Inside this function, you have an `if` statement whose expression checks whether the passed in `speed` value is greater than or equal (using >=) to the value stored by the `speedLimit` variable:

```
function amISpeeding(speed) {
    if (speed >= speedLimit) {
        alert("Yes. You are speeding.");
    } else {
        alert("No. You are not speeding. What's wrong with you?");
    }
}
```

The last thing (well, actually the first thing) our code does is actually call the `amISpeedingfunction` by passing in a few values for `speed`:

```
amISpeeding(53);
amISpeeding(72);
```

When we call this function with a speed of **53**, the `speed >= speedLimit` expression evaluates to **false**. The reason is that **53** is not greater than or equal to the stored value of `speedLimit`, which is **55**. This will result in an alert showing the "you are not speeding" message.

The opposite happens when you call `amISpeeding` with a speed of **72**. In this case, you are speeding and the conditional expression evaluates to **true**. An alert telling you that you are speeding will also appear.

Creating More Complex Expressions

The thing you need to know about these expressions is that they can be as simple or as complex as you can make them. They can be made up of variables, function calls, or raw values. They can even be made up of *combinations* of variables, function calls, or raw values all separated using any of the operators you saw earlier. The only thing that you need to ensure is that your expression ultimately evaluates to **true** or **false**.

Here is a slightly more involved example:

```
var xPos = 300;
var yPos = 150;

function sendWarning(x, y) {
    if ((x < xPos) && (y < yPos)) {
        alert("Adjust the position");
    } else {
        alert("Things are fine!");
    }
}

sendWarning(500, 160);
sendWarning(100, 100);
sendWarning(201, 149);
```

Notice what your condition inside `sendWarning`'s `if` statement looks like:

```
function sendWarning(x, y) {
    if ((x < xPos) && (y < yPos)) {
        alert("Adjust the position");
    } else {
        alert("Things are fine!");
    }
}
```

There are three conditions being tested here. The first one is whether `x` is less than `xPos`. The second one is whether `y` is less than `yPos`. The third is seeing whether the *first statement and the second statement* both evaluate to **true** to allow the `&&` operator to return a **true** as well. You can chain many series of conditional statements together depending on what you are doing. The tricky thing, besides learning what all the operators do, is to ensure that each condition and subcondition is properly insulated using parentheses.

All of what I am describing here and in the previous section falls under the umbrella of **Boolean Logic**. If you are not familiar with this topic, I recommend that you glance through the excellent quirksmode article on this exact topic: **http://www.quirksmode.org/js/boolean.html**.

Variations on the If/Else Statement

We are almost done with the `if` statement. The last thing we are going to is look at some of its relatives.

The if-only Statement

The first one is the solo `if` statement that doesn't have an `else` companion:

```
if (weight > 5000) {
    alert("No free shipping for you!");
}
```

In this case, if the expression evaluates to true, then great. If the expression evaluates to false, then your code just skips over the alert and moves on to wherever it needs to go next. The else block is completely optional when working with if statements. To contrast the if-only statement, we have our next relative...

The Dreaded If/Else-If/Else Statement

Not everything can be neatly bucketed into a single `if` or `if/else` statement. For those kinds of situations, you can chain `if` statements together by using the `else if` keyword. Instead of explaining this further, let's just look at an example:

```
if (position < 100) {
    alert("Do something!");
} else if ((position >= 100) && (position < 300)) {
    alert("Do something else!");
} else {
    alert("Do something even more different!");
}
```

If the first `if` statement evaluates to **true**, then your code branches into the first `alert`. If the first `if` statement is **false**, then our code evaluates the `else if` statement to see if the expressions in it evaluate to **true** or **false**. This repeats until your code reaches the end. In other words, your code simply navigates down through each `if` and `else if` statement until one of the expressions evaluates to **true**:

```
if (condition) {
    ...
} else if (condition) {
    ...
} else if (condition) {
    ...
```

```
} else if (condition) {
    ...
} else if (condition) {
    ...
} else if (condition) {
    ...
} else {
    ...
}
```

If none of the statements have expressions that evaluate to **true**, the code inside the `else` block (if it exists) executes. Between the more complex expressions and `if/else if` statements, you can represent pretty much any decision that your code might need to evaluate.

Phew

And with this, you have learned all there is to know about the `if` statement. It's time to move on to a different conditional statement...

Switch Statements

In a world filled with beautiful `if`, `else`, and `else if` statements, the need for yet another way of dealing with conditionals may seem unnecessary. However, people with more battered keyboards than you and me disagreed, so we have what are known as **switch statements**. In this section, putting my initial snarkastic comments aside, you'll learn all about them and why they are useful.

Let's get started!

Using a Switch Statement

The basic structure of a `switch` statement is as follows:

```
switch (expression) {
    case value1:
        statement;
        break;
    case value2:
        statement;
        break;
```

```
    case value3:
        statement;
        break;
    default:
        statement;
}
```

The thing to never forget is that a **switch** statement is nothing more than a conditional statement that tests whether something is *true* or *false*. That "something" is a variation of whether the *result of evaluating the expression equals a case value.* Now, I do realize that this probably makes no sense if you have never worked with **switch** statements before. I have worked with **switch** statements, and what I wrote barely makes sense to me either!

Let's make this explanation stick by looking at a better example:

```
var color = "green";

switch (color) {
    case "yellow":
        alert("yellow color");
        break;
    case "red":
        alert("red color");
        break;
    case "blue":
        alert("blue color");
        break;
    case "green":
        alert("green color");
        break;
    case "black":
        alert("black color");
        break;
    default:
        alert("no known color specified");
}
```

In this simple example, I have a variable called `color` whose value is set to green:

```
var color = "green";
```

This `color` variable is what gets passed in to our `switch` statement, and it is here that things get interesting!

Our `switch` statement contains a collection of case blocks. Only one of these blocks will get hit with their code getting executed. The way this chosen one gets picked is by matching a block's case value with the result of evaluating the expression. In our case, because our expression evaluates to a value of **green**, the code inside the case block whose case value is also **green** gets executed:

```
var color = "green";

switch (color) {
    case "yellow":
        alert("yellow color");
        break;
    case "red":
        alert("red color");
        break;
    case "blue":
        alert("blue color");
        break;
    case "green":
        alert("green color");
        break;
    case "black":
        alert("black color");
        break;
    default:
        alert("no known color specified");
}
```

Note that *only* the code inside the `green` case block gets executed. This is thanks to the `break` keyword that ends that block. When your code hits the `break`, it exits the entire `switch` block and continues executing the code that lies below it. If you did not specify the `break` keyword, you will still execute the code inside the green case block. The difference is that you will then move to the next case block (the `black` one in our example) and execute any code that is there. Unless you hit another **break** keyword, your code will just move through every single case block until it reaches the end. You almost never want that.

With all of this said, if you were to run this code, you will see an `alert` dialog box that displays the words **green color!**

You can alter the value for the `color` variable to other valid values to see the other case blocks execute. Sometimes, no case block's value will match the result of evaluating an expression. In those cases, your switch statement will just do nothing. If you wish to specify a default behavior, add a `default` block as highlighted below:

```
switch (color) {
    case "yellow":
        alert("yellow color");
        break;
    case "red":
        alert("red color");
        break;
    case "blue":
        alert("blue color");
        break;
    case "green":
        alert("green color");
        break;
    case "black":
        alert("black color");
        break;
    default:
        alert("no known color specified");
}
```

Note that the `default` block looks a bit different than your other case statements. More specifically, it doesn't actually contain the word `case`. You should remember this detail in case it comes up during trivia night. You never know!

Similarity to an If/Else Statement

At the beginning, I mentioned that a `switch` statement is used for evaluating conditions—just like an `if/else` statement. Given that this is a major accusation, let's explore this in further detail by first looking at how an `if` statement would look if it were to be literally translated into a `switch` statement.

Let's say we have an `if` statement that looks as follows:

```
var number = 20;

if (number > 10) {
  alert("yes");
} else {
  alert("nope");
}
```

Because the value of our number variable is *20*, our `if` statement will evaluate to *true*. Seems pretty straightforward. Now, let's turn this into a `switch` statement:

```
switch (number > 10) {
  case true:
    alert("yes");
    break;
  case false:
    alert("nope");
    break;
}
```

Notice that our conditional expression is `number > 10`. The case value for the case blocks is set to *true* or *false*. Because `number > 10` evaluates to *true*, the code inside the *true* case block gets executed. While your expression in this case wasn't as simple as reading a color value stored in a variable as in the previous section, our view of how `switch` statements work still hasn't changed. Your expressions can be as complex as you would like. If they evaluate to something that can be matched inside a case value, then everything is golden—like a fleece!

Now, let's look at a slightly more involved example doing the opposite of what we just did. This time, let's convert our earlier `switch` statement involving colors into equivalent `if/else` statements. The `switch` statement we used earlier looks as follows when converted into a series of `if/else` statements:

```
var color = "green";

if (color == "yellow") {
    alert("yellow color");
} else if (color == "red") {
    alert ("red color");
```

```
} else if (color == "blue") {
    alert ("blue color");
} else if (color == "green") {
    alert ("green color");
} else if (color == "black") {
    alert ("black color");
} else {
    alert ("no color specified");
}
```

As you can see, `if/else` statements are very similar to `switch` statements and vice versa. The `default` case block becomes an `else` block. The relationship between the expression and the case value in a `switch` statement is combined into `if/else` conditions in an `if/else` statement. Everything translates nicely!

Deciding Which to Use

In the previous section, you saw how interchangeable `switch` statements and `if/else` statements are. When you have two ways of doing something very similar, it is only natural to want to know when it is appropriate to use one over the other. In a nutshell, and this is totally not helpful, use whichever one you prefer. There are many arguments on the web about when to use `switch` versus an `if/else`, and the one thing that is clear is that they are all inconclusive. For once, the Internet has failed to provide a clear answer on a complicated debate.

My personal preference is to go with whatever is more readable. If you look at the comparisons earlier between `switch` and `if/else` statements, you'll notice that if you have a lot of conditions, your `switch` statement tends to look a bit cleaner. It is certainly less verbose and a bit more readable. What your cut off mark is for deciding when to switch (ha!) between using a `switch` statement and an `if/else` statement is entirely up to you. I tend to draw the line at around four or five conditions.

Second, a `switch` statement works best when you are evaluating an expression and matching the result to a value. If you are doing something more complex involving weird conditions, value checking, and other shenanigans, you probably want to use something different. That "something different" is probably an `if` statement. You may find other tricks as you progress further through the book that may be more appropriate.

To reiterate, use whatever you like. For every person who agrees with what I've written, you'll find someone who can convincingly provide a counter argument. If you are part of a team with coding guidelines, then follow them. Whatever you do, just be consistent. It makes your life, as well as the life of anybody else who will be working on your code, a little bit easier.

For what it is worth, I've personally never been in a situation where I had to use a `switch` statement, but I've been in many situations where I was looking at someone else's code that used a lot of `switch` statements. Your mileage may vary.

THE ABSOLUTE MINIMUM

While creating true artificial intelligence goes beyond the scope of this book (:P), you *can* write code to help your application make choices. This code will almost always take the form of an if/else statement where you provide the browser with a set of choices it needs to make:

```
var loginStatus = false;

if (name == "Admin") {
    loginStatus = true;
}
```

These choices are fed by conditions that need to evaluate to *true* or *false*.

In this chapter, we learned the mechanics of how to work with if/else statements and their (sortof) related cousins, the switch statements. In future chapters, you'll see us using these statements very casually, as if we've known them for years, so you'll be very familiar with how to write these statements by the time you reach the end of this book.

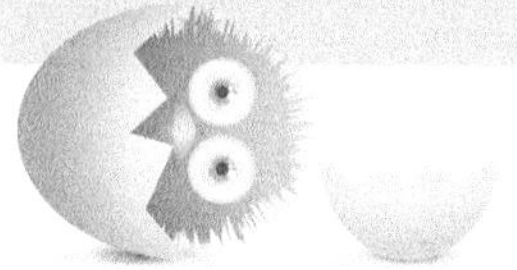

TIP Just a quick reminder for those of you reading these words in the print or e-book edition of this book: If you go to **www.quepublishing.com** and register this book, you can receive free access to an online Web Edition that not only contains the complete text of this book but also features a short, fun interactive quiz to test your understanding of the chapter you just read.

If you're reading these words in the Web Edition already and want to try your hand at the quiz, then you're in luck – all you need to do is scroll down!

IN THIS CHAPTER

- Learn how to have some code run repeatedly
- Work with **for**, **while**, and **do...while** loops

5

MEET THE LOOPS: FOR, WHILE, AND DO...WHILE!

When you are coding something, there will be times when you want to repeat an action or run some code multiple times. For example, let's say we have a function called `saySomething` that we want to repeatedly call 10 times.

One way we could do this is by simply calling the function 10 times using copy and paste:

```
saySomething();
saySomething();
saySomething();
saySomething();
saySomething();
saySomething();
saySomething();
saySomething();
saySomething();
saySomething();
```

This works and accomplishes what we set out to do, but you shouldn't do something like this. Duplicating code is never a good idea.

Now, even if you decide to duplicate some code a few times manually, this approach doesn't really work in practice. You will often never know the number of times you need to run your code. The number of times will vary based on some external factor such as the number of items in a collection of data, some result from a web service call, the number of letters in a word, and various other things that will keep changing. It won't always be a fixed number like 10. More than likely, the number of times you want to repeat some code could be very VERY large. You don't want to copy and paste something a few hundred or thousand times to repeat something. That would be terrible.

What we need is a generic solution for repeating code with control over how many times the code repeats. In JavaScript, this solution is provided in the form of something known as a **loop**. There are three kinds of loops you can create:

- `for` loops
- `while` loops
- `do...while` loops

Each of these three loop variations enable you to specify the code you want to repeat (aka loop) and a way to stop the repetition when a condition is met. In the following sections, you'll learn all about how to use them.

Onwards!

The for Loop

One of the most common ways to create a loop is by using the `for` statement to create what is known as a `for` loop. A `for` loop allows you to repeatedly run some code until an expression you specify returns **false**. That probably doesn't make a whole lot of sense, so to help clarify this definition, let's look at an example.

If we had to translate our earlier `saySomething` example using `for`, it would look as follows:

```
var count = 10;

function saySomething() {
    document.writeln("hello!");
}

for (var i = 0; i < count; i++) {
    saySomething();
}
```

If you were to enter this code inside some `script` tags and preview it in your browser, you will see something similar to what is shown in Figure 5.1.

FIGURE 5.1

The word hello! will be repeated ten times across your page.

NOTE The words are printed to the browser because we used `document.writeln`. This is another method we will use (besides `alert`) that will help us quickly test something out. The `document.writeln` method takes whatever you want to print as arguments, and when it runs, it replaces everything in the page with the content you were interested in displaying.

This is made possible thanks to the `for` loop, so we are gonna thank it by learning all about how it works. First, let's look at our star:

```
for (var i = 0; i < count; i++) {
    saySomething();
}
```

This is a `for` loop. It probably looks very different from other statements you've seen so far, and that's because, well, it is very different. To understand the differences, let's generalize a `for` loop into the form shown in Figure 5.2.

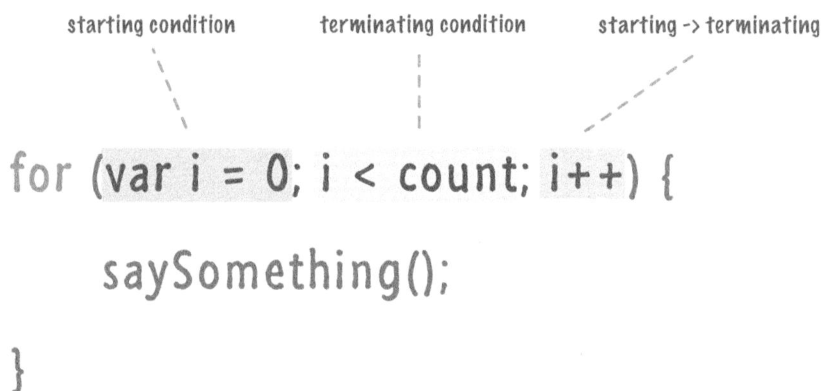

FIGURE 5.2

Our `for` loop and the three regions that we will focus on.

These three differently shaded regions each play a very important role in how your loop functions. In order to use a `for` loop well, we must know what each region accomplishes. That brings us to…

The Starting Condition

In the first region, we define a *starting condition*. A common starting condition usually involves declaring and initializing a variable. In our example, I create a new variable called `i` and initialize it to the number **0**:

```
for (var i = 0; i < count; i++) {
    saySomething();
}
```

In case you are wondering, the variable name in these cases is traditionally a single letter, with *i* being the most common. The value you initialize this variable to is also traditionally *0*. There is one really good reason for using *0*, and I'll explain that reason a bit later.

Terminating Condition (aka Are we done yet?)

Once we define our starting point, in the next region we determine the *terminating condition*. That is basically a fancy way of saying how long to keep looping. This is handled by a conditional expression (just like what you say in the previous chapter!) that returns either **true** or **false**. In our example, the condition is that our `i` variable is less than the value of `count`—which is *10*:

```
for (var i = 0; i < count; i++) {
    saySomething();
}
```

If our `i` variable is less than **10**, this expression evaluates to **true** and our loop continues to run. If our `i` variable becomes equal to or greater than **10**, the condition is **false**, and our loop terminates. Now, you may be wondering what causes our `i` variable to actually change from its starting value of **0**. Well, that is covered next...

Reaching the End

So far, we've looked at our starting point. We also looked at the expression that needs to evaluate to **false** if we want to break our loop. What is missing is the final region where we describe how to go f*rom your starting point to the terminating point*:

```
for (var i = 0; i < count; i++) {
    saySomething();
}
```

In our example, at each iteration of our loop, we increment our `i` variable by **1**. In case you aren't familiar with this syntax, the ++ after `i` means you increase whatever value the `i` variable had by **1**. Each time our loop runs, whatever you specified here will execute. In this case, our `i` value will increment.

Putting It All Together

Okay, now that we looked at each part of the `for` statement in great detail, let's run through it all once more to make sure we totally got this. Our full example, repeated from earlier, is as follows:

```
var count = 10;

for (var i = 0; i < count; i++) {
    saySomething();
}

function saySomething() {
    document.writeln("hello!");
}
```

When our `for` loop is initially hit, the `i` variable is created and initialized to *0*. Next, our code checks if the value of `i` is less than the value referenced by `count`...which is *10*. At this point, everything is green and whatever code is inside the loop executes. In our case, that is the `saySomething` function. Once the statements inside your loop have executed, the last part of the `for` statement kicks in. The `i` variable is incremented by *1*.

Now, the loop starts all over again except the variable `i` isn't re-initialized. Its value is set to the incremented value of *1*, and that means it still passes the `i < count` test. The `saySomething` function is called again, and the value of `i` is incremented again. Now, the `i` variable's value is *2*.

This whole process repeats until the value of `i` equals *10*. At this point, the `i < count` test will fail and the loop will exit after having successfully executed the `saySomething` function *10* times.

Some `for` Loop Examples

In the previous section, we dissected a simple `for` loop and labeled all of its inner workings. The thing about `for` loops, and most everything in JavaScript, is that a simple example doesn't always cover everything you might need. The best solution is to look at some more examples of `for` loops, and that's what we are going to be doing in the next few sections.

Stopping a Loop Early

Sometimes, you may want to end your loop before it reaches completion. The way you end a loop is by using the `break` keyword. Below is an example:

```
for (var i = 0; i < 100; i++) {
    document.writeln(i);

    if (i == 45) {
        break;
    }
}
```

When the value of `i` equals *45*, the `break` keyword stops the loop from continuing further. While this example was just a little bit contrived, when you do run into a real-world case for ending your loop, you now know what to do.

Skipping an Iteration

There will be moments when you want your loop to skip its current iteration and move on to the next one. That is cleverly handled by the `continue` keyword:

Unlike `break` where your loop just stops and goes home, `continue` tells your loop to stop and move on to the next iteration. You'll often find yourself using `continue` when handling errors where you just want the loop to move on to the next item.

```
var floors = 28;

for (var i = 1; i <= floors; i++) {
    if (i == 13) {
        // no floor here
        continue;
    }

    document.writeln("At floor: " + i + "<br>");
}
```

Going Backwards

There is no reason for why you have to start at 0 and then increment upward:

```
for (var i = 25; i > 0; i--) {
    document.writeln("hello");
}
```

You can just as easily start high and then decrement until your loop condition returns a **false**.

You may have heard that doing something like this increases your loop's performance. The jury is still out on whether decrementing is actually faster than incrementing, but feel free to experiment and see if you notice any performance benefits.

You Don't Have to Use Numbers

When filling out your `for` loop, you don't have to only use numbers or do a traditional increment/decrement operation:

```
for (var i = "a"; i !="aaaaaaaa"; i += "a") {
    document.writeln("hmm...");
}
```

You can use anything you want as long as your loop will eventually hit a point where it can end. Notice that in this example, I am using the letter `a` as my currency for running this loop. When you "add" letters together as we are doing, the result is `a`, `aa`, `aaa`, `aaaa`, `aaaaa`, and so on!

Array! Array! Array!

I know we haven't looked at arrays in detail yet, but one of the greatest love stories of all time is that between a data structure known as an array and the `for` loop. The bulk of your time, you will be using loops to travel through all of the data stored in an array, so just glance through the following code and explanation. I'll rehash this information in greater detail when we formally talk about arrays really soon in **Chapter 15, Arrays**.

```
var myArray = ["one", "two", "three"];

for (var i = 0; i < myArray.length; i++) {
    document.writeln(myArray[i]);
}
```

The TL; DR version is as follows: An array is a collection of items. The way to enumerate and access all of the items in an array requires some sort of a loop, and the `for` loop is usually the chosen one.

Anyway, I figured I would introduce you to the array and `for` loop pair. Just like two seemingly random characters at the beginning of a Quentin Tarantino movie, their actual contribution to the story seems irrelevant at this point in time.

Oh No He Didn't!

Oh yes! Yes I did. I went there, took a picture, posted on Facebook, and came back:

```
var i = 0;
var yay = true;

for (; yay;) {
    if (i == 10) {
        yay = false;
    }
    i++;
    document.writeln("weird");
}
```

You don't have to fill out the three sections of your `for` loop to make it work. As long as, in the end, you manage to satisfy the loop's terminating condition, you can do whatever you want—just like I did. Now, just because you can do something doesn't mean you should. This example falls clearly in the "You shouldn't do this!" bucket.

The Other Loops

Living in the shadow of the beloved `for` loop are the `while` and `do...while` loop variants. These two loop variants clearly serve a purpose, but I've never quite found what that purpose is. Despite that, in the interest of completeness and to familiarize you with code you will encounter in the wild, let's quickly look at both of them.

The `while` Loop

The **`while`** loop repeats some code until its test condition (another expression) returns **false**:

```
var count = 0;

while (count < 10) {
    document.writeln("looping away!");

    count++;
}
```

In this example, the condition is represented by the `count<10` expression. With each iteration, our loop increments the count value by *1*. Once the value of `count` becomes *10*, the loop stops because the `count<10` expression will return **false**. That's all there is to the **`while`** loop.

The `do...while` Loop

Now, we get to the Meg Griffin of the loop variants. That would be the **`do...while`** loop whose purpose is even less defined than **`while`**. Where the **`while`** loop had its conditional expression first before the loop would execute, the **`do...while`** loop has its conditional expression at the end.

Here is an example:

```
var count = 0;

do {
    count++;

    document.writeln("I don't know what I am doing here!");
} while (count < 10);
```

The main difference between a **`while`** loop and a **`do...while`** loop is that the contents of a **`while`** loop could never get executed if its conditional expression is **false** from the very beginning:

```
while (false) {
    document.writeln("Can't touch this!");
}
```

With a `do...while` loop, because the conditional expression is evaluated only after one iteration, your loop's contents are guaranteed to run at least once:

```
do {
    document.writeln("This code will run once!");
} while (false);
```

Yaaawwn! Anyway, there is just one last bit of information I need to tell you before we move on. The `break` and `continue` statements that we saw earlier as part of the awesome `for` loop also work similarly when used inside the `while` and `do...while` loop variants.

THE ABSOLUTE MINIMUM

So there you have it—a look at `for` loops and how you can use them along with very basic coverage of the `while` and `do...while` loops. Right now, you may not see yourself using loops a whole lot. As we start getting into more involved situations involving collections of data, HTML elements in your document, text manipulation, and other complex situations, loops will be one of the natural components you will rely on frequently.

TIP Just a quick reminder for those of you reading these words in the print or e-book edition of this book: If you go to **www.quepublishing.com** and register this book, you can receive free access to an online Web Edition that not only contains the complete text of this book but also features a short, fun interactive quiz to test your understanding of the chapter you just read.

If you're reading these words in the Web Edition already and want to try your hand at the quiz, then you're in luck – all you need to do is scroll down!

IN THIS CHAPTER

- Learn how to delay when your code runs
- Figure out several ways to run your code repeatedly without blocking your entire app

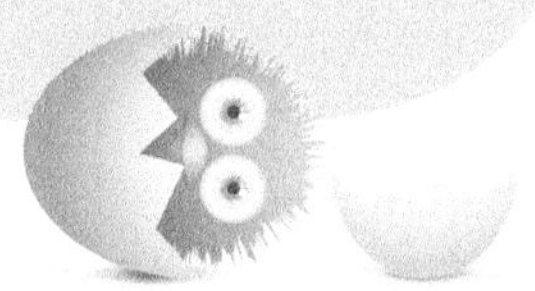

TIMERS

By default, your code runs synchronously. That is a fancy of way of saying that when a statement needs to execute, it executes immediately. There are no *ifs*, *ands*, or *buts* about it. The concept of delaying execution or deferring work to later isn't a part of JavaScript's default behavior. That doesn't mean the ability to delay work to a later time doesn't exist! If you swerve just slightly off the main road, there are three functions that allow you to mostly do just that (and more). Those functions are `setTimeout`, `setInterval`, and `requestAnimationFrame`.

In this chapter, we look at what each of these function do and other good stuff that comes along with learning more about some of the basic components JavaScript provides for helping your code do interesting things.

Onwards!

Meet the Three Timers

Like you saw a few pixels ago, the main suspects of this chapter are going to be the `setTimeout`, `setInterval`, and `requestAnimationFrame` functions. In the following sections, let's look at each of these functions in greater detail and figure out a reason for their existence.

Delaying with setTimeout

The `setTimeout` function enables you to delay executing some code. The way you use it is pretty simple. This function makes it possible for you to specify what code to execute and how many milliseconds (aka 1/1000 of a second) to wait before the code you specified executes.

Putting that into JavaScript, it looks something like this:

```
var timeID = setTimeout(someFunction, delayInMilliseconds);
```

Going a bit more example-ish, if I wanted to call a function called `showAlert` after 5 seconds, the `setTimeout` declaration would look as follows:

```
function showAlert() {
  alert("moo");
}

var timeID = setTimeout(showAlert, 5000);
```

Pretty simple, right? Now, let's talk about something less interesting that I cover just for completeness. That something has to do with the `timeID` variable that is initialized to our `setTimeout` function. It isn't there by accident. If you ever wanted to access this `setTimeout` timer again, you need a way to reference it. By associating a variable with our `setTimeout` declaration, we can easily accomplish that.

Now, you may be wondering why we would ever want to reference a timer once we've created it. There aren't too many reasons. The only reason I can think of would be to cancel the timer. For `setTimeout`, that is conveniently accomplished using the `clearTimeout` function and passing the timeout ID as the argument:

```
clearTimeout(timeID);
```

If you are never planning on cancelling your timer, you can just use `setTimeout` directly without having it be part of the variable initialization.

Anyway, moving past the technical details on how to use `setTimeout`, let's talk about when you would commonly use it in the real world. As you will find out eventually, especially if you are doing front-end/user interface (UI) development, deferring some action to a later time is more common than you might think. Here are some examples that I ran into just in the recent past:

1. A menu slides in, and after a few seconds of the user no longer playing with the menu, the menu slides away.
2. You have a long running operation that is unable to complete, and a `setTimeout` function interrupts that operation to return control back to the user.
3. My favorite is where you use the setTimeout function to detect whether a user is inactive or not (See: **http://bit.ly/kirupaDetectIdle**).

If you do a search for **setTimeout** on this site or Google, you'll see many more real-world cases where `setTimeout` proves very useful.

Looping with `setInterval`

The next timer function we are going to look at is `setInterval`. The `setInterval` function is similar to `setTimeout` in that it also enables you to execute code after a specified amount of time. What makes it different is that it doesn't just execute the code once. It keeps on executing the code in a loop forever.

Here is how you would use the `setInterval` function:

```
var intervalID = setInterval(someFunction, delayInMilliseconds);
```

Except for the function name, the way you use `setInterval` is even identical to `setTimeout`. The first argument specifies the inline code or function you would like to execute. The second argument specifies how long to wait before your code loops again. You can also optionally initialize the `setInterval` function to a variable to store an interval ID—an ID that you can later use to do exciting things like cancel the looping.

OK! Now that we've seen all that, here is an example of this code at work for looping a function called `drawText` with a delay of 2 seconds between each loop:

```
function drawText() {
  document.querySelector("p").textContent += "#\n";
}

var intervalID = setInterval(drawText, 2000);
```

Just make sure you have a p element somewhere in your page that will act as the target our code will add the # character to.

If you wish to cancel the looping, you can use the appropriately named clearInterval function:

```
clearInterval(intervalID);
```

Its usage is similar to its clearTimeout equivalent. You pass in the ID of the setInterval timer instance that you optionally retrieved while setting up your setInterval in the first place.

Here is some interesting trivia. For the longest time, setInterval was the primary function you had for creating animations in JavaScript. To get something running at 60 frames a second, you would do something that looks as follows:

```
// 1000 divided 60 is the millisecond value for 60fps
window.setInterval(moveCircles, 1000/60);
```

Towards the end of this chapter, you'll see some links to examples and articles I've written on the web where setInterval is part of a larger, more realistic example.

Animating Smoothly with requestAnimationFrame

Now, we get to one of my favorite functions ever: requestAnimationFrame. The requestAnimationFrame function is all about synchronizing your code with a browser repaint event. What this means is pretty simple. Your browser is busy juggling a billion different things at any given time - fiddling with layout, reacting to page scrolls, listening for mouse clicks, displaying the result of keyboard taps, executing JavaScript, loading resources, and more. At the same time your browser is doing all of this, it is also redrawing the screen at 60 frames per second...or at least trying its very best to.

When you have code that is designed to animate something to the screen, you want to ensure your animation code runs properly without getting lost in the shuffle of everything else your browser is doing. Using the setInterval function mentioned earlier doesn't guarantee that frames won't get dropped when the browser is busy optimizing for other things. To avoid your animation code from being treated like any other generic piece of code, you have the requestAnimationFrame function. This function gets special treatment by the browser. This special treatment allows it to time its execution perfectly to avoid dropped frames, avoid unnecessary work, and generally steer clear of other side effects that plague other looping solutions.

The way you use this function starts off a bit similar to `setTimeout` and `setInterval`:

```
var requestID = requestAnimationFrame(someFunction);
```

The only real difference is that you don't specify a duration value. The duration is automatically calculated based on the current frame rate, whether the current tab is active or not, whether your device is running on battery or not, and a whole host of other factors that go beyond what we can control or understand.

Anyway, this usage of the `requestAnimationFrame` function is merely the textbook version. In real life, you'll rarely make a single call to `requestAnimationFrame` like this. Key to all animations created in JavaScript is an animation loop, and it is this loop that we want to throw `requestAnimationFrame` at. The result of that throw looks something as follows:

```
function animationLoop() {
  // animation-related code

  requestAnimationFrame(animationLoop);
}

// start off our animation loop!
animationLoop();
```

Notice that our `requestAnimationFrame` calls the `animationLoop` function fully from within the `animationLoop` function itself. That isn't a bug in the code. While this kind of circular referencing would almost guarantee a hang, `requestAnimationFrame`'s implementation avoids that. Instead, it ensures the `animationLoop` function is called just the right amount of times needed to ensure things get drawn to the screen to create smooth and fluid animations. It does so without freezing the rest of your application functionality up.

To stop a `requestAnimationFrame` function, you have the `cancelAnimationFrame` function:

```
cancelAnimationFrame(requestID);
```

Just like you've seen several times with functions of this sort, `cancelAnimation-Frame` takes the ID value of our `requestAnimationFrame` function that is returned when you call it. If you plan on using cancelAnimationFrame, then you can modify our earlier animationLoop example as follows:

```
var requestID;

function animationLoop() {
```

```
  // animation-related code

  requestID = requestAnimationFrame(animationLoop);
}

// start off our animation loop!
animationLoop();
```

Notice that our call to `requestAnimationFrame` always sets the value of `requestID`, and you can use `requestID` as the argument to `cancelAnimationFrame` to stop our loop.

THE ABSOLUTE MINIMUM

If you think that timers fall under a more niche category compared to some of the other more essential things like the if/else statements and loops we looked at earlier, you would probably be right in thinking that. You can build many awesome apps without ever having to rely on `setTimeout`, `setInterval`, or `requestAnimationFrame`. That doesn't mean it isn't essential to know about them, though. There will be a time when you'll need to delay when your code executes, loop your code continuously, or create a sweet animation using JavaScript. When that time arrives, you'll be prepared...or at least know what to Google for.

To see these timer functions used in the wild, check out these optional articles and examples that may help you out:

- **Creating Animations Using requestAnimationFrame**
  http://bit.ly/kirupaAnimationsJS
- **Creating a Sweet Content Slider**
  http://bit.ly/sliderTutorial
- **Creating an Analog Clock**
  http://bit.ly/kirupaAnalogClock
- **The Seizure Generator**
  http://bit.ly/kirupaSeizureGenerator

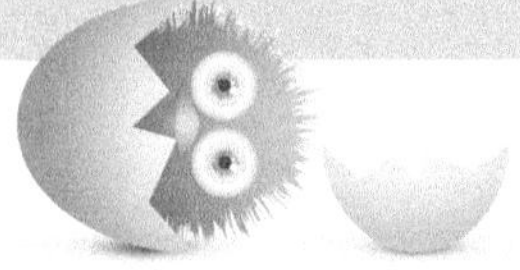

TIP Just a quick reminder for those of you reading these words in the print or e-book edition of this book: If you go to **www.quepublishing.com** and register this book, you can receive free access to an online Web Edition that not only contains the complete text of this book but also features a short, fun interactive quiz to test your understanding of the chapter you just read.

If you're reading these words in the Web Edition already and want to try your hand at the quiz, then you're in luck – all you need to do is scroll down!

IN THIS CHAPTER

- Understand global scope
- Familiarize yourself with the various techniques available for using local scope
- Learn about some quirks that might cause your code to behave unpredictably

7

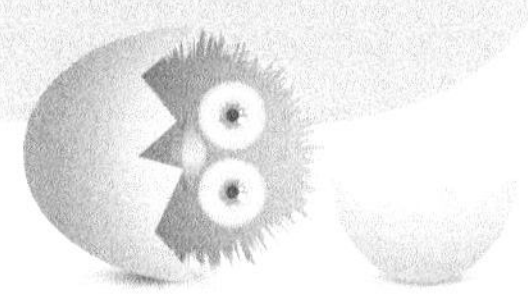

VARIABLE SCOPE

Let's revisit something relating to variables that we saw in **Chapter 2, "Values and Variables."** Each variable you declare has a certain level of visibility that determines when you can actually use it. In human-understandable terms, what this means is simple: just because you declare a variable doesn't mean that it can be accessed from anywhere in your code. There are some basic things you need to understand, and this whole area of understanding falls under a topic known as **variable scope**.

In this chapter, I explain variable scope by looking at common cases that you've (mostly) already seen. This is a pretty deep topic, but we are just going to scratch the surface here. You'll see variable scope creep up in many subsequent chapters where we will expand on what you will learn here.

Onwards!

Global Scope

We are going to start our exploration of scope at the very top with what is known as **global scope**. In real life, when we say that something can be heard globally, it means that you can be anywhere in the world and still be able to hear that...something (see Figure 7.1).

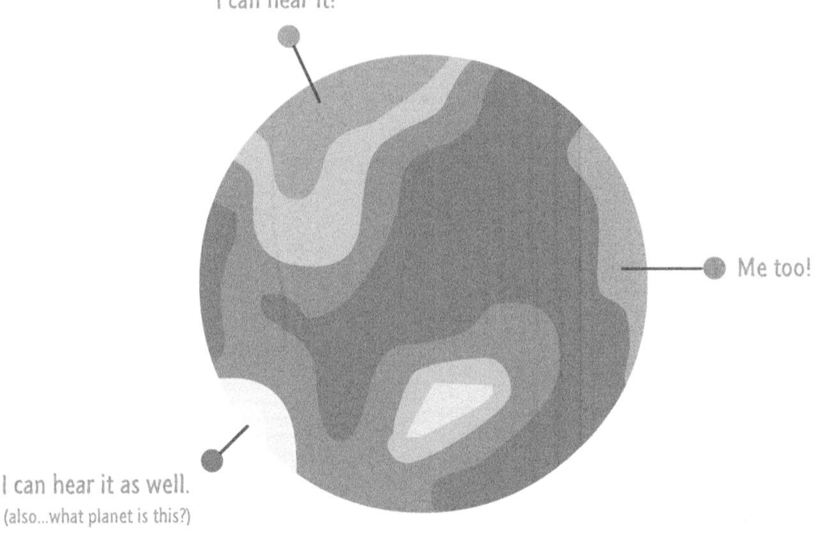

FIGURE 7.1

Something that is global can be accessed and heard from anywhere.

In JavaScript, much the same applies. If we say, for example, that a variable is available globally, it means that any code on your page has access to read and modify this variable. The way you make something apply globally is by declaring it in your code completely outside of a function.

To illustrate this, let's take a look at the following example:

```
<script>
var counter = 0;
</script>
```

Here, I am simply declaring a variable called **counter** and initializing it to *0*. By virtue of this variable being declared directly inside the **script** tag without being placed inside a function, the counter variable is considered to be global. What this distinction means is that your counter variable can be accessed by any code that lives in your document.

The code that follows highlights this:

```
var counter = 0;

function returnCount() {
    return counter;
}
```

In this example, the **counter** variable is declared outside of the **returnCount** function. Despite that, the **returnCount** function has full access to the **counter** variable.

At this point, you are probably wondering why I am pointing out what seems very obvious. After all, you've been using global variables all this time without really noticing it. All I am doing here is formally introducing you to a guest that has been hanging around your party for a while, a guest that has the potential for causing a lot of mayhem if you aren't careful.

NOTE I've been pretty vague in defining what **global** exactly means. This is deliberate, as formally describing it will involve a whole lot more backstory to make sense of everything. If you are familiar enough with JavaScript (or are feeling adventurous), read on. If not, feel free to skip this note and move on to the next section. We'll revisit this later.

Anyway, something is considered global in JavaScript when it is a direct child of your browser's **window** object. That is a more precise way of saying "declared outside of a function." You can verify this pretty easily by checking if **counter** and **window.counter** point to exactly the same thing:

```
alert(window.counter == counter);
```

The answer is going to be **true**. The reason is that you are referring to the exact same thing.

Realizing that global variables live under your **window** object should help you understand why you can access a global variable from anywhere in your document. All your code (for everything you'll see in this book) lives under the umbrella of your **window** object.

Local Scope

Now, things get a little interesting when we look at things that aren't globally declared. This is where understanding scope really helps you out. As you saw earlier, a variable declared globally is accessible inside a function:

```
var counter = 0;

function returnCount() {
    return counter;
}
```

The opposite doesn't hold true. A variable declared inside a function will not work when accessed outside of the function:

```
function setState() {
    var state = "on";
}
setState();

alert(state) // nooooooooooo
```

In this example, the `state` variable is declared inside the `setState` function, and accessing the `state` variable outside of that function doesn't work. The reason is that the scope for your `state` variable is local to the `setState` function itself. A more generic way of describing this is by saying that your `state` variable is just local.

NOTE Let's clarify something that I briefly mentioned when looking at variables. Continuing our earlier example, if we declare the `state` variable without using the `var` keyword, the scoping behavior is drastically different:

```
function setState() {
    state = "on";
}
setState();
alert(state); // on
```

In this case, even though your `state` variable makes its appearance inside the `setState` function first, not including the `var` keyword makes this variable live globally.

Keep in mind that a variable that is used without being declared using the `var` keyword will always live globally.

Miscellaneous Scoping Shenanigans

Since we are talking about JavaScript here, things would be too easy if we just left everything with variable scope as it stands now. In the following sections, I am going to highlight some quirks that you need to be familiar with.

Declarations Using `var` Do Not Support Block Scoping

Before I attempt to explain this, take a look at the following code:

```
function checkWeight(weight) {
    if (weight > 5000) {
        var text = "No free shipping for you!";
        alert(text);
    }
    alert(text); // how did it know??!
}

checkWeight(6000);
```

I've highlighted the relevant lines that you should focus on. Inside the `if` statement, we declare a variable called `text`. When this code is run, the `alert` function directly below it displays *No free shipping for you!* That makes sense. What might make less sense is that the second alert that is outside of the `if` statement also displays *No free shipping for you!*.

Here is what is going on. Your `text` variable is declared inside what is known as a **block**. A block is anything that appears within the open and close brackets - `{` and `}`. In many programming languages, variables declared inside a block are part of that block's own scope. That means those variables are local and can't be accessed outside of the block.

JavaScript is not like those many "other" programming languages. *JavaScript doesn't support block scoping.* For the code you just saw, despite the `text` variable being declared inside a block, from JavaScript's point of view, it might as well have been declared at the top of your `checkWeight` function itself as follows:

```
function checkWeight(weight) {
    var text;
```

```
    if (weight > 5000) {
        text = "No free shipping for you!";
        alert(text);
    }
    alert(text);
}

checkWeight(6000);
```

The behavior of this **checkWeight** function is identical compared to what you saw a few moments earlier.

To repeat, there are only two scopes you need to keep track of. The first is the global scope where what you are declaring is completely outside the grip of a function. The second is the local scope where what you are declaring is enclosed by whatever function you are inside.

NOTE The latest version of JavaScript (part of the ECMAScript 6/ES2015 improvements) introduces support for the `let` keyword that allows you to declare variables that are block scoped:

```
var x = 100;

function blockScoping() {
    if (true) {
        let x = 350;
        alert(x) // 350
    }
    alert(x); // 100;
}
blockScoping();
```

How JavaScript Processes Variables

If you thought the earlier block scoping logic was weird, wait till you see this one. Take a look at the following code:

```
var foo = "Hello!";

function doSomethingClever() {
    alert(foo);
```

```
    var foo = "Good Bye!";
    alert(foo);
}

doSomethingClever();
```

Examine the code in detail. What do you think is shown in the two highlighted `alert` function calls? Given what is going on, you may answer *Hello!* and *Good Bye!* However, if you test this code out, what you will actually see is undefined and *Good Bye!* Let's look at what is going on here.

At the very top, we have our `foo` variable that is instantiated to *Hello!*. Inside the `doSomethingClever` function, the first thing we have is an `alert` that should show the value stored by the `foo` variable. A few lines below that, we re-declare the `foo` variable with a new value of *Good Bye!*:

```
var foo = "Hello!";

function doSomethingClever() {
    alert(foo);

    var foo = "Good Bye!";
    alert(foo);
}

doSomethingClever();
```

Because our first `alert` comes before the `foo` variable re-declaration, the logical assumption is that `foo`'s original value of *Hello!* will be what gets shown. As you saw earlier, that isn't the case. The value of `foo` when it hits the first `alert` is actually `undefined`. The reason for this has to do with how JavaScript deals with variables.

When JavaScript encounters a function, one of the first things it does is scan the full body of the code for any declared variables. When it encounters them, it initializes them by default with a value of `undefined`. Because the `doSomethingClever` function is declaring a variable called `foo`, before the first `alert` even hits, an entry for `foo` is created with a value of `undefined`. Eventually, when our code hits `var foo = "Good Bye!"`, the value of `foo` is properly initialized. That doesn't help our first `alert` function, but it does help the second one that follows the re-declaration of `foo`. All of this has a name. It is known as **hoisting** or **variable hoisting**!

Keep this little quirk in mind if you ever run into a situation where you are re-declaring variables into a local scope like this simple example highlighted. Tracking down why your variables aren't behaving as expected isn't fun, and hopefully this tidbit of knowledge will come in handy.

Closures

No conversation about variable scope can be wrapped up without discussing **closures**. That is, until right now. I am not going to explain closures here, for it is important and involved enough to require its own chapter. That chapter...is coming up next!

Given that this section is titled "Closures," I'll just do my usual closing song and dance here itself:

> *Well, that concludes this topic of variable scopes. This topic seems very simple on the surface, but as you can see, there are some unique characteristics that take some time and practice to fully understand.*

I am not good at conclusions...or singing and dancing. I get that, and they are all on my bucket list. I swear!

THE ABSOLUTE MINIMUM

Where your variables live has a major impact on where they can be used. Variables declared globally are accessible to your entire application. Variables declared locally will only be accessible to whatever scope they are found in. Within the range of global and local variables, JavaScript has a lot going on up its sleeve.

This chapter gave you an overview of how variable scope can affect your code, and you'll see some of these concepts presented front-and-center in the near future.

TIP Just a quick reminder for those of you reading these words in the print or e-book edition of this book: If you go to **www.quepublishing.com** and register this book, you can receive free access to an online Web Edition that not only contains the complete text of this book but also features a short, fun interactive quiz to test your understanding of the chapter you just read.

If you're reading these words in the Web Edition already and want to try your hand at the quiz, then you're in luck – all you need to do is scroll down!

IN THIS CHAPTER

- Understand what closures are
- Tie together everything you've learned about functions, variables, and scope

8

CLOSURES

By now, you probably know all about functions and all the fun ***functioney*** things that they do. An important part of working with functions, with JavaScript, and (possibly) life in general is understanding the topic known as **closures**. Closures touch upon a gray area where functions and variable scope intersect (see Figure 8.1).

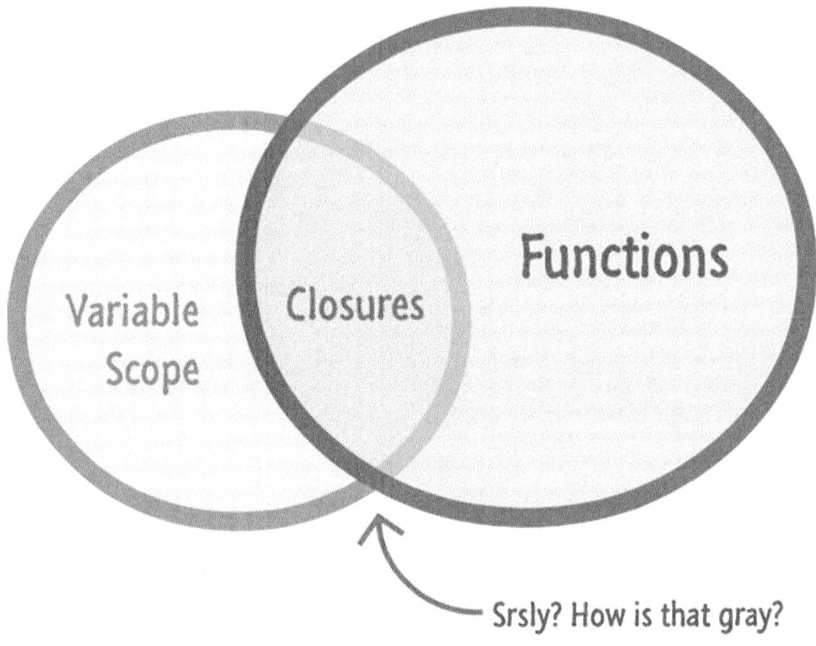

FIGURE 8.1

The intersection of functions and variable scope.

Now, I am not going to say any thing more about closures, as this is something best explained by seeing the actual code. Any words I add right now to define or describe closures will only serve to confuse things. In the following sections, we'll start off in familiar territory and then slowly venture into hostile areas where closures can be found.

Onwards!

Functions within Functions

The first thing we are going to do is really drill down on what happens when you have functions within functions...and the inner function gets returned. As part of that, let's do a quick review of functions.

Take a look at the following code:

```
function calculateRectangleArea(length, width) {
    return length * width;
}
```

```
var roomArea = calculateRectangleArea(10, 10);
alert(roomArea);
```

The `calculateRectangleArea` function takes two arguments and returns the multiplied value of those arguments to whatever called it. In this example, the "whatever called it" part is played by the `roomArea` variable.

After this code has run, the `roomArea` variable contains the result of multiplying 10 by 10...which is simply 100. Figure 8.2 visualizes this situation:

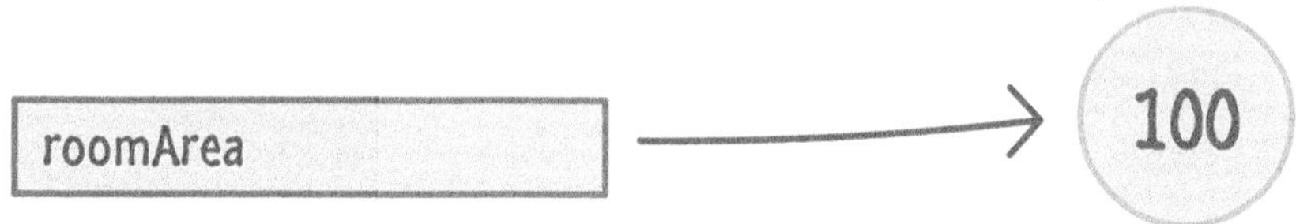

FIGURE 8.2

*Nobody knows why `roomArea` is a rectangle and the **100** value is a circle :-(*

As you know, what a function returns can pretty much be anything. In this case, we returned a number. You can very easily return some text (aka a `String`), the `undefined` value, a custom object, and so on. As long as the code that is calling the function knows what to do with what the function returns, you can do pretty much whatever you want. You can even return another function. Let me rathole on this a bit.

Below is a very simple example of what I am talking about:

```
function youSayGoodbye() {

    alert("Goodbye!");

    function andISayHello() {
        alert("Hello!");
    }

    return andISayHello;
}
```

You can have functions that contain functions inside them. In this example, we have our **youSayGoodbye** function that contains an alert and another function called **andISayHello**:

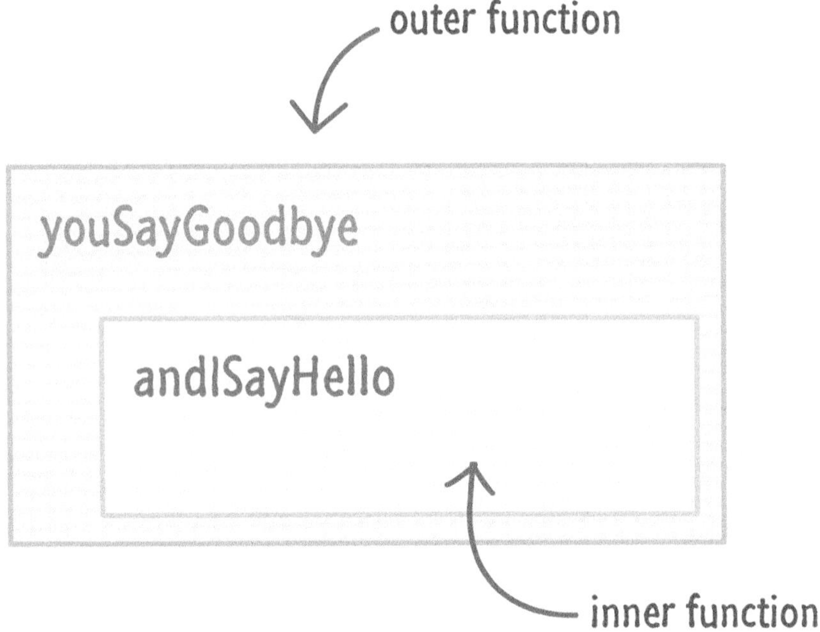

The interesting part is what the **youSayGoodbye** function returns when it gets called. It returns the **andISayHello** function:

```
function youSayGoodbye() {

    alert("Goodbye!");

    function andISayHello() {
        alert("Hello!");
    }

    return andISayHello;
}
```

Let's go ahead and play this example out. To call this function, initialize a variable that points to **youSayGoodbye**:

```
var something = youSayGoodbye();
```

The moment this line of code runs, all of the code inside your `youSayGoodbye` function will get run as well. This means, you will see a dialog box (thanks to the `alert`) that says *Good Bye!* The `andISayHello` function gets returned. The important thing to note is that the `andISayHello` function does not get run yet, for we haven't actually called it. We simply return a reference to it.

At this point, your `something` variable only has eyes for one thing, and that thing is the `andISayHello` function:

The `youSayGoodbye` outer function, from the something variable's point of view, simply goes away. Because the `something` variable now points to a function, you can invoke this function by just calling it using the open and close parentheses like you normally would:

```
var something = youSayGoodbye();
something();
```

When you do this, the returned inner function (aka `andISayHello`) will execute. Just like before, you will see a dialog box appear, but this dialog box will say *Hello!*—which is what the `alert` inside this function specified.

Okay, we are getting close to the promised hostile territory. In the next section, we will expand on what we've just learnt by taking a look at another example with a slight twist.

When the Inner Functions Aren't Self-Contained

In the previous example, your `andISayHello` inner function was self-contained and didn't rely on any variables from the outer function:

```
function youSayGoodbye() {

    alert("Goodbye!");
```

```
    function andISayHello() {
        alert("Hello!");
    }

    return andISayHello;
}
```

In many real scenarios, very rarely will you run into a case like this. You'll often have variables and data that is shared between the outer function and the inner function. To highlight this, take a look at the following:

```
function stopWatch() {
    var startTime = Date.now();

    function getDelay() {
        var elapsedTime = Date.now() - startTime;
        alert(elapsedTime);
    }

    return getDelay;
}
```

This example shows a very simple way of measuring the time it takes to do something. Inside the `stopWatch` function, you have a `startTime` variable that is set to the value of `Date.now()`:

```
function stopWatch() {
    var startTime = Date.now();

    function getDelay() {
        var elapsedTime = Date.now() - startTime;
        alert(elapsedTime);
    }

    return getDelay;
}
```

NOTE The `Date.now()` function is something we haven't seen before, so let's quickly take a look at it. What this function does is return a really large number that represents the current time. More specifically, the really large number is the number of milliseconds that have elapsed since *1 January 1970 00:00:00 UTC*.

You also have an inner function called `getDelay`:

```
function stopWatch() {
    var startTime = Date.now();

    function getDelay() {
        var elapsedTime = Date.now() - startTime;
        alert(elapsedTime);
    }

    return getDelay;
}
```

The `getDelay` function displays a dialog box containing the difference in time between a new call to `Date.now()` and the `startTime` variable declared earlier.

Getting back to the outer `stopWatch` function, the last thing that happens is that it returns the `getDelay` function before exiting. As you can see, the code you see here is very similar to the earlier example. You have an outer function, you have an inner function, and you have the outer function returning the inner function.

Now, to see the `stopWatch` function at work, add the following lines of code:

```
var timer = stopWatch();

// do something that takes some time
for (var i = 0; i < 1000000; i++) {
    var foo = Math.random() * 10000;
}

// call the returned function
timer();
```

If you run this example, you'll see a dialog box displaying the number of milliseconds it took between your timer variable getting initialized, your `for` loop running to completion, and the `timer` variable getting invoked as a function.

Basically, you have a stopwatch that you invoke, run some long-running operation, and invoke again to see how long the long-running operation took place.

Now that you can see our little stopwatch example working, let's go back to the `stopWatch` function and see what exactly is going on. Like I mentioned a few lines ago, a lot of what you see is similar to the `youSayGoodbye/andISayHello` example. There is a twist that makes this example different, and the important part to note is what happens when the `getDelay` function is returned to the `timer` variable.

Here is an incomplete visualization of what this looks like:

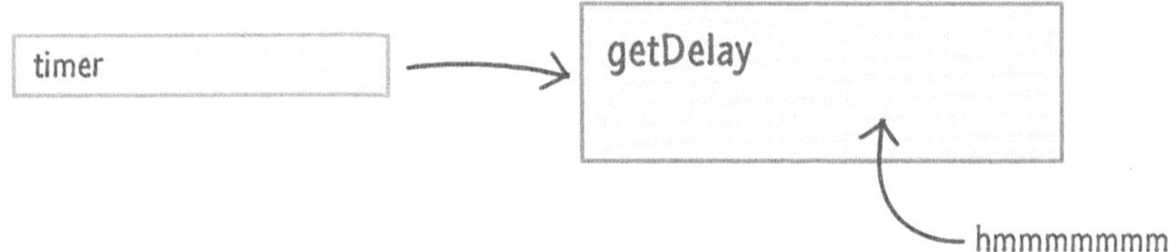

The `stopWatch` outer function is no longer in play, and the `timer` variable is still tied to the `getDelay` function. Now, here is the twist. The `getDelay` function relies on the `startTime` variable that lives in the scope of the outer `stopWatch` function:

```
function stopWatch() {
    var startTime = Date.now();

    function getDelay() {
        var elapsedTime = Date.now() - startTime;
        alert(elapsedTime);
    }

    return getDelay;
}
```

When the outer `stopWatch` function runs and disappears once `getDelay` is returned to the `timer` variable, what happens in the following line?

```
function getDelay() {
    var elapsedTime = Date.now() - startTime;
    alert(elapsedTime);
}
```

In this context, it would make sense if the `startTime` variable is actually `undefined`, right? But, the example obviously worked, so something else is going on here. That something else is the shy and mysterious **closure**. Here is a look at what happens to make our `startTime` variable actually store a value and not be `undefined`.

The JavaScript runtime that keeps track of all of your variables, memory usage, references, and so on is really clever. In this example, it detects that the inner function (`getDelay`) is relying on variables from the outer function (`stopWatch`). When that happens, the runtime ensures that any variables in the outer function that are needed are still available to the inner function *even if the outer function goes away.*

To visualize this properly, here is what the `timer` variable looks like:

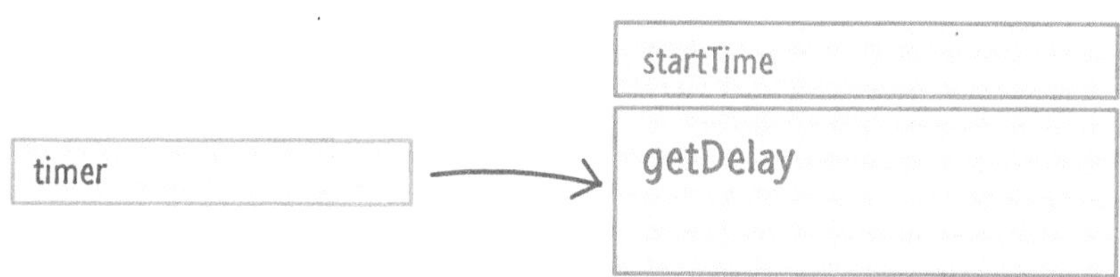

It is still referring to the `getDelay` function, but the `getDelay` function also has access to the `startTime` variable that existed in the outer `stopWatch` function. This inner function, because it *enclosed* relevant variables from the outer function into its bubble (aka scope), is known as a **closure**:

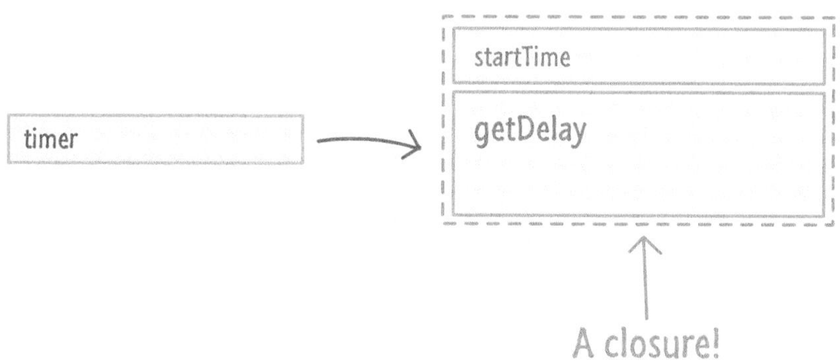

To define the closure more formally, it is a *newly created function that also contains its variable context*:

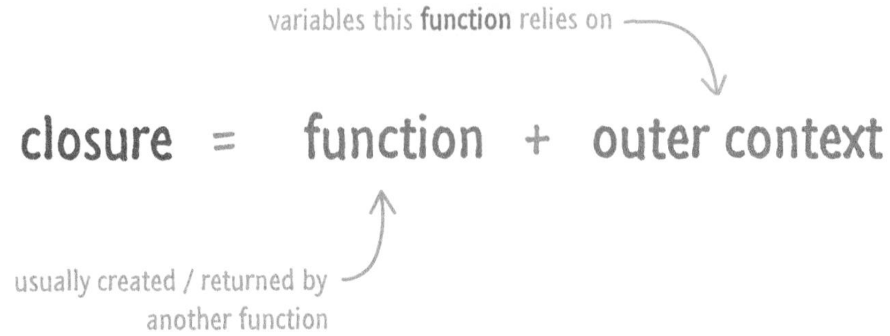

To review this one more time using our existing example, the `startTime` variable gets the value of `Date.now` the moment the `timer` variable gets initialized and the `stopWatch` function runs. When the `stopWatch` function returns the inner `getDelay` function, the `stopWatch` function is no longer active. You can sort of say that it goes away. What doesn't go away are any shared variables inside `stopWatch` that the inner function relies on. Those shared variables are not destroyed. Instead, they are enclosed by the inner function aka the closure.

THE ABSOLUTE MINIMUM

By looking at closures through examples first, you really missed out on a lot of boring definitions, theories, and hand waving. In all seriousness, closures are very common in JavaScript. You will encounter them in many subtle and not-so-subtle ways.

If there is only thing you take out of all of this, remember the following: The *most important thing closures do is allow functions to keep on working even if their environment drastically changes or disappears.* Any variables that were in scope when the function was created are enclosed and protected to ensure the function still works. This behavior is essential for a very dynamic language like JavaScript where you often create, modify, and destroy things on the fly. Happy days!

TIP Just a quick reminder for those of you reading these words in the print or e-book edition of this book: If you go to **www.quepublishing.com** and register this book, you can receive free access to an online Web Edition that not only contains the complete text of this book but also features a short, fun interactive quiz to test your understanding of the chapter you just read.

If you're reading these words in the Web Edition already and want to try your hand at the quiz, then you're in luck – all you need to do is scroll down!

IN THIS CHAPTER

- Learn about the various places your code can live
- Understand the pros and cons of the various approaches

WHERE SHOULD YOUR CODE LIVE?

Let's take a break from our regularly scheduled...programming (ha!). Instead of looking at what goes into our code, in this chapter, we are going to go a bit higher and look at something really basic. We are going to look at where exactly the code you write should live.

Onwards!

The Options on the Table

So far, all of the code we have been writing has been contained fully inside an HTML document as shown in Figure 9.1.

FIGURE 9.1

All of our code so far has been located in the same document as our HTML and CSS.

In this world, the only thing that protects your HTML document from JavaScript is just a couple of script tags. Now, your JavaScript does not have to live inside your HTML document. You have another option, which involves creating a separate file where all of your JavaScript will instead live as illustrated in Figure 9.2.

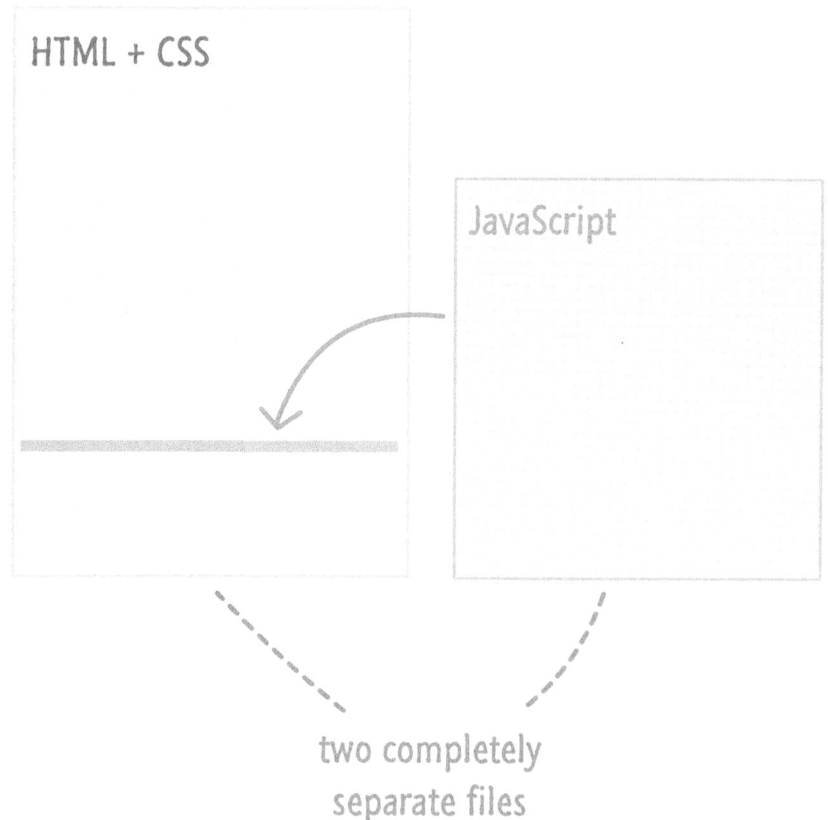

FIGURE 9.2

You can put your JavaScript into a separate file.

In this approach, you don't have any real JavaScript inside your HTML document. You still have your script tag, but this tag simply points to the JavaScript file instead of containing line after line of actual JavaScript code.

Of course, none of these approaches are mutually exclusive. You can mix both approaches into an HTML document and have a hybrid approach where you have both an external JavaScript file as well as lines of JavaScript code inside your HTML document as shown in Figure 9.3.

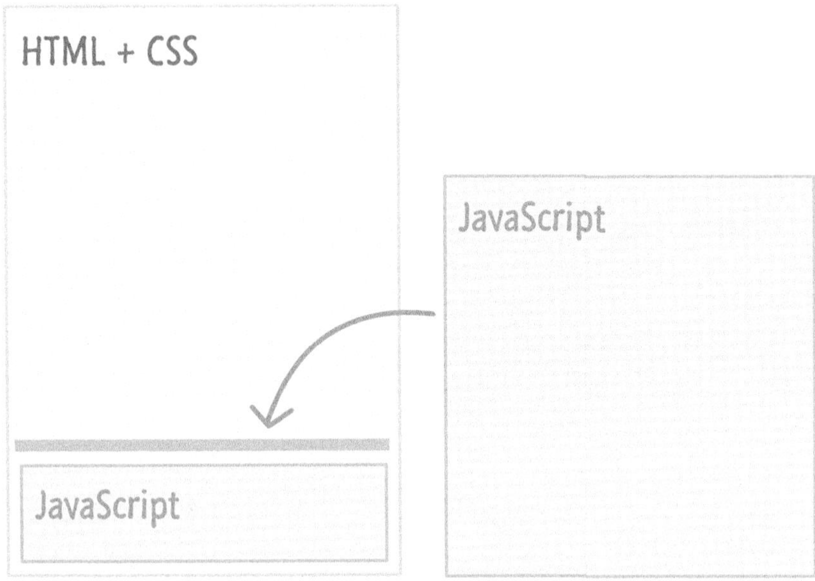

FIGURE 9.3

A hybrid approach where your JavaScript lives both externally as well as inside your HTML document.

To make things more interesting, you also have variations on the two approaches such as having multiple script sections in a HTML document, having multiple JS files, and so on. In the following sections, we'll look at both these approaches in greater detail and discuss when you would choose one approach over the other.

By the end of this short chapter, you will have a good understanding of the pros and cons of each approach so that you can do the right thing with the JavaScript in your web pages and applications.

Approach #1: All the Code Lives in Your HTML Document

The first approach we will look at is the one that we've been using all along so far. This is the approach where all of your JavaScript lives inside a `script` tag alongside the rest of your HTML document:

```
<!DOCTYPE html>
<html>
<body>
```

```
        <h1>Example</h1>

        <script>
            function showDistance(speed, time) {
                alert(speed * time);
            }

            showDistance(10, 5);
            showDistance(85, 1.5);
            showDistance(12, 9);
            showDistance(42, 21);
        </script>
    </body>
    </html>
```

When your browser loads the page, it goes through and parses every line of HTML from top to bottom. When it hits the **script** tag, it will go ahead and execute all the lines of JavaScript as well. Once it has finished executing your code, it will continue to parse the rest of your document.

Approach #2: The Code Lives in a Separate File

The second approach is one where your main HTML document doesn't contain any JavaScript content. Instead, all of your JavaScript lives in a separate document. There are two parts to this approach. The first part deals with the JavaScript file. The second part deals with referencing this JavaScript file in the HTML. Let's look at both of these parts in greater detail.

The JavaScript File

The key to making this approach work is the separate file that contains your JavaScript code. It doesn't matter what you name this file, but its extension should be **.js**. For example, my JavaScript file is called **example.js**:

Inside this file, you will only have JavaScript:

```
function showDistance(speed, time) {
    alert(speed * time);
}

showDistance(10, 5);
showDistance(85, 1.5);
showDistance(12, 9);
showDistance(42, 21);
```

Everything you would normally put inside a **script** tag in the HTML will go here. Nothing else will go into this file. Putting anything else like arbitrary pieces of HTML and CSS isn't allowed, and your browser will complain if you try to sneak some non-JavaScript content inside it.

Referencing the JavaScript File

Once you have your JavaScript file created, the second (and final) step is to reference it in the HTML page. This is handled by your **script** tag. More specifically, it is handled by your `script` tag's `src` attribute that points to the location of your JavaScript file:

```
<!DOCTYPE html>
<html>
<body>
    <h1>Example</h1>

    <script src="example.js"></script>
</body>
</html>
```

In this example, if your JavaScript file is located in the same directory as your HTML document, you can use a relative path and just reference the file name directly. If your JavaScript file lives in another folder, you should alter your path accordingly:

```
<!DOCTYPE html>
<html>
<body>
    <h1>Example</h1>

    <script src="/some/other/folder/example.js"></script>
</body>
</html>
```

In this case, our script file starts looking at the root of your site and walks through folders with the name **some**, **other**, and **folder**. You can completely avoid relative paths and use an absolute path if you want:

```
<!DOCTYPE html>
<html>
<body>
    <h1>Example</h1>

    <script src="http://www.kirupa.com/js/example.js"></script>
</body>
</html>
```

Either a relative path or absolute path will work just fine. For situations where the path between your HTML page and the script you are referencing will vary (such as inside a template, a server-side include, a third-party library, and so on), you'll be safer using an absolute path.

SCRIPTS, PARSING, AND LOCATION IN DOCUMENT

A few sections earlier, I briefly described how scripts get executed. Your browser parses your HTML page starting at the top and then moves down line by line. When a `script` tag gets hit, your browser starts executing the code that is contained inside the `script` tag. This execution is also done line-by-line starting at the top. Everything else that your page might be doing takes a backseat while the execution is going on. If the `script` tag references an external JavaScript file, your browser first downloads the external file before starting to execute its contents.

This behavior where your browser linearly parses your document has some interesting side effects that affect where in your document you want to place your `script` tags. Technically, your `script` tag can live anywhere in your HTML document. There is a preferred place you should specify your scripts, though. Because of how your browser parses the page and blocks everything while your scripts are executing, *you want to place your `script` tags toward the bottom of your HTML document after all of your HTML elements.*

If your `script` tag is towards the top of your document, your browser will block everything else while the script is running. This could result in users seeing a partially loaded and unresponsive HTML page if you are downloading a large script file or executing a script that is taking a long time to complete. Unless you really have a good reason to force your JavaScript to run before your full document is parsed, ensure your `script` tags appear towards the end of your document as shown in almost all of the earlier examples. There is one other advantage to placing your scripts at the bottom of your page, but I will explain that much later when talking about the DOM and what happens during a page load.

So...Which Approach to Use?

You have two main approaches around where your code should live:

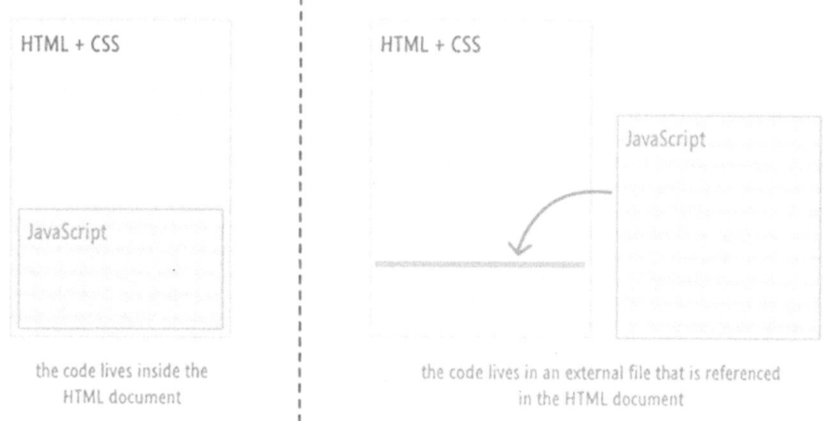

The approach you end up choosing depends on your answer to the following question: *Is the identical code going to be used across multiple HTML documents?*

Yes, My Code Will Be Used on Multiple Documents!

If the answer is *yes*, then you probably want to put the code in an external file and then reference it across all of the HTML pages in which you want it executing. The first reason you want to do this is to avoid having code repeated across multiple pages:

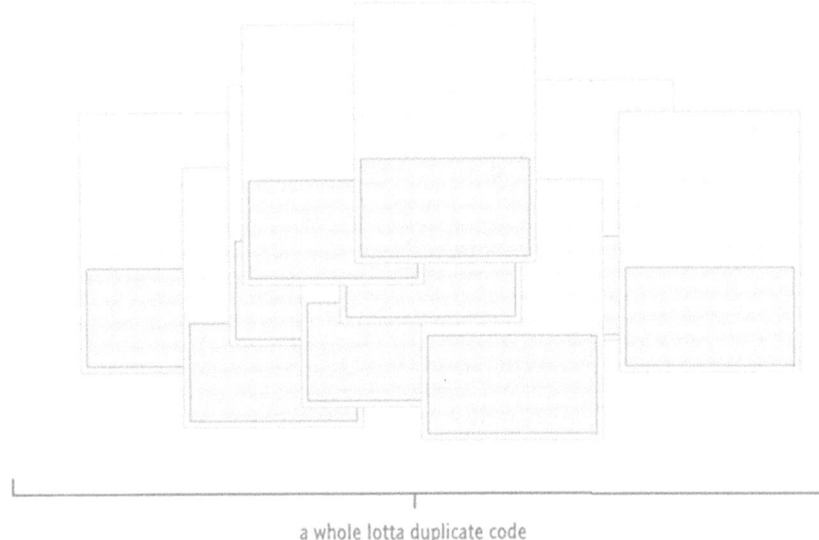

Duplicates make maintenance a nightmare where a change to your script will require you updating every single HTML document with the exact change. If you are employing some sort of templating or SSI (server-side includes) logic where there is only one HTML fragment containing your script, then the maintenance issue is less of a problem.

The second reason has to do with file size. When you have your script duplicated across many HTML pages, each time a user loads one of those HTML pages, they are downloading your script all over again. This is less of a problem for smaller scripts, but once you have more than a few hundred lines of code, the size starts adding up.

When you factor all our code into a single file, you don't have the issues I just outlined:

Your code is easily maintainable because you update your code inside one single file. Any HTML document that references this JavaScript file automatically receives the most recent version when it loads. By having all of your code in one file, your browser will download the code only once and deliver the cached version of the file on subsequent accesses.

No, My Code Is Used Only Once, on a Single HTML Document!

If you answered *no* to the earlier question regarding whether your code is going to be used in multiple HTML documents, then you can do whatever you want. You can still choose to put your code into a separate file and reference it in your HTML document, but the benefits of doing that are less than what you saw earlier with my example involving many documents.

Placing your code entirely inside your HTML document is also fine for this situation. Most of the examples you will see in this site have all of the code within the HTML document itself. Our examples aren't really going to be used across multiple pages, and they aren't going to be so large where readability is improved by putting all of the code in a separate location.

THE ABSOLUTE MINIMUM

As you can see, even something as seemingly simple as determining where your code should live ends up taking many pages of explanation and discussion. Welcome to the world of HTML and JavaScript where nothing is really black and white. Anyway, getting back to the point of this article, a typical HTML document will contain many script files loaded from an external location. Some of those files will be your own; some, however, will be created by a third party and included into your document.

Also, do you remember the hybrid approach I showed at the very beginning where your HTML document contains both a reference to a separate JavaScript file as well as actual code within the document? Well, that approach is pretty common as well. Ultimately, the approach you end up using is entirely up to you. Hopefully, this chapter gave you a taste of the information needed to make the right choice. In Chapter 32, "Page Load Events and Other Stuff," we take a deeper look at what you saw here by looking at page loading-related events and certain special attributes that complicate things. Don't worry about them for now.

TIP Just a quick reminder for those of you reading these words in the print or e-book edition of this book: If you go to **www.quepublishing.com** and register this book, you can receive free access to an online Web Edition that not only contains the complete text of this book but also features a short, fun interactive quiz to test your understanding of the chapter you just read.

If you're reading these words in the Web Edition already and want to try your hand at the quiz, then you're in luck – all you need to do is scroll down!

IN THIS CHAPTER

- Learn the importance of code comments
- Familiarize yourself with the JavaScript syntax for writing comments
- Understand good commenting practices

10

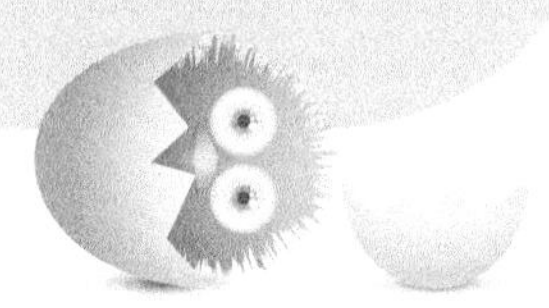

COMMENTING YOUR CODE

We are almost done with our break. Just one more topic left, and it is a good one! See, here is the thing—everything you write in your code editor might *seem* like it is intended for your browser's eyes only:

```
var xPos = -500;

function boringComputerStuff() {
  xPos += 5;

  if (xPos > 1000) {
    xPos = -500;
  }

  requestAnimationFrame(boringComputerStuff);
}
```

As you will soon find out, that isn't the case. There is another audience for your code. *That audience is made up of human beings.*

Your code is often used or scrutinized by other people. This is especially true if you are working in a team with other JavaScript developers. You'll often be looking at your teammates' code, and they'll often be looking at your's. You need to ensure your code makes sense when someone new is looking at it. If you are working solo, this applies to you as well. That brilliant function that makes sense to you today might be gibberish when looked at next week.

There are many ways of solving this problem. One of the best ways is by using something known as **comments**. In this short article, we will learn what comments are, how to specify them in JavaScript, and learn some good practices on how to use them.

Onwards!

What Are Comments?

Comments are the things you write in your code that communicate something to humans:

```
// This is for not inviting me to your birthday party!
var blah = true;

function sweetRevenge() {
  var blah = true;

  while (blah) {
    // Infinite dialog boxes! HAHAHA!!!!
    alert("Hahahaha!");
  }
}
sweetRevenge();
```

In this example, the comments are marked by the // character, and they provide some not-so-useful information about the code at hand.

The thing to keep in mind about comments is that they don't run and get executed like all the other code you write. *JavaScript ignores your comments.* It doesn't like you. It doesn't care what you have to say, so you don't have to worry about proper syntax, punctuation, spelling, and everything else you need to keep in mind when writing normal code. Comments exist only for us to help understand what a piece of code is doing.

There is one other purpose comments serve. You can use comments to mark lines of code that you don't want executed:

```
function insecureLogin(input) {
  if (input == "password") {
    //var key = Math.random() * 100000;
    //processLogin(key);
  }
  return false;
}
```

In this example, the following two lines can be seen in your code editor, but they won't run:

```
//var key = Math.random() * 100000;
//processLogin(key);
```

You'll often find yourself using the code editor as a scratchpad, and comments are a great way to keep track of things you've tried in making your code work without affecting how your application ultimately runs.

Single Line Comments

There are several ways to specify comments in your code. One way is by specifying **single line comments** using the // mark followed by what you want to communicate. This is the comment variation you've seen several times already.

You can specify these comments in their own dedicated line:

```
// Return the larger of the two arguments
function max(a, b) {
  if (a > b) {
    return a;
  } else {
    return b;
  }
}
```

You can also specify these comments on the same line as a statement:

```
var zorb = "Alien"; // Annoy the planetary citizens
```

Where you specify them is entirely up to you. Choose a location that seems appropriate for the comment you are writing.

As you know well by now, your comments don't run as part of your application. Only you, me, and possibly Dupree can see them. If that last line made no sense, what you are telling me is that you did not see one of the greatest comedies of our generation. I highly encourage you to put this book down and take a few hours to rectify that.

Multi-line Comments

The problem with single line comments is that you have to specify the // characters in front of every single line you want to comment. That can get really tiring - especially if you are writing a long comment or commenting out a large chunk of code.

For those situations, you have another way of specifying comments. You have the /* and */ characters to specify the beginning and ending of what are known as **multi-line comments**:

```
/*
var mouseX = 0;
var mouseY = 0;

canvas.addEventListener("mousemove", setMousePosition, false);

function setMousePosition(e) {
  mouseX = e.clientX;
  mouseY = e.clientY;
}
*/
```

Instead of adding // marks in front of each line like an animal, we can use the /* and */ characters to save us a lot of time and frustration.

In most applications, you'll use a combination of single line and multi-line comments depending on what you are trying to document. This means you need to be familiar with both of these commenting approaches.

JSDOC STYLE COMMENTS

When you are writing some code that you want used by others, you probably want an *easier way* to communicate what your code does beyond having people rummage through source code. That *easier way* exists, and it is made possible by a tool known as **JSDoc**! With JSDoc, you slightly modify how you write your comments:

```
/**
 * Shuffles the contents of your Array.
 *
 * @this {Array}
 * @return {Array} A new array with the contents fully shuffled.
 */
Array.prototype.shuffle = function() {
  var input = this;

  for (var i = input.length - 1; i >= 0; i--) {

    var randomIndex = Math.floor(Math.random() * (i + 1));
    var itemAtIndex = input[randomIndex];

    input[randomIndex] = input[i];
    input[i] = itemAtIndex;
  }
  return input;
}
```

Once you have commented your files, you can use the JSDoc tool to export the relevant parts of your comments into an easily browsable set of HTML pages. This allows you to spend more time writing JavaScript while giving your users an easy way to understand what your code does and how to use various parts of it.

If you want to learn more on how to use JSDoc, check out their awesome **Getting Started page** for more details.

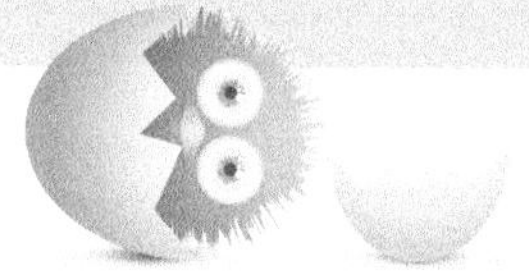

Commenting Best Practices

Now that we have a good idea of what comments are and the several ways we have to write them in JavaScript, let's talk a bit about how to properly use comments to make your code easy to read:

1. *Always comment your code as you are writing it.* Writing comments is dreadfully boring, but it is an important part of writing code. It is much more time efficient for you (and others) to understand what your code does from reading a comment as opposed to reading line after line of boring JavaScript.
2. *Don't defer comment writing for later.* Related to the previous point, deferring comment writing for a later time is the grown-up equivalent of procrastinating on a chore. If you don't comment your code as you are writing it, you'll probably just skip commenting entirely. That's not a good thing.
3. *Use more English and less JavaScript.* Comments are one of the few places when writing JavaScript that you can freely use English (or whatever language you prefer communicating in). Don't complicate your comments unnecessarily with code. Be clear. Be concise. Use words.
4. *Embrace whitespace.* When scanning large blocks of code, you want to ensure your comments stand out and are clear to follow. That involves being liberal with your Spacebar and Enter/Return key. Take a look at the following example:

```
function selectInitialState(state) {
  var selectContent = document.querySelector("#stateList");
  var stateIndex = null;


  /*
      For the returned state, we would like to ensure that
      we select it in our UI. This means we iterate through
      every state in the drop-down until we find a match.
      When a match is found, we ensure it gets selected.
  */


  for (var i = 0; i < selectContent.length; i++) {

    var stateInSelect = selectContent.options[i].innerText;

    if (stateInSelect == state) {
```

```
            stateIndex = i;
          }
        }

        selectContent.selectedIndex = stateIndex;
      }
```

Notice that our comment is appropriately spaced to distinguish it from the rest of the code. If your comments are strewn about in arbitrary locations where they are difficult to identify, that just unnecessarily slows you and whoever is reading your code down.

5. *Don't comment obvious things.* If a line of code is self-explanatory, don't waste time explaining what it does unless there is some subtle behavior you need to call out as a warning. Instead, invest that time in commenting the less obvious parts of your code.

The best practices you see here will take you far in ensuring you write properly commented code. If you are working on a larger project with other people, I can assure you that your team already has some established guidelines on what proper commenting looks like. Take some time to understand those guidelines and follow them. You'll be happy. Your team will be happy.

THE ABSOLUTE MINIMUM

Comments are often viewed as a necessary evil. After all, would you rather take a few minutes documenting what *you* clearly already know, or would you rather implement the next cool piece of functionality? The way I like to describe comments is as follows: *It is a long-term investment.*

The value and benefit of comments is often not immediately obvious. It becomes obvious when you start having other people looking over your code, and it becomes obvious when you have to revisit your own code after you've forgotten all about it and how it works. Don't sacrifice long-term time savings for a short-term kick. Invest in single line (//) and multi-line (/* and */) comments now before it is too late.

TIP Just a quick reminder for those of you reading these words in the print or e-book edition of this book: If you go to **www.quepublishing.com** and register this book, you can receive free access to an online Web Edition that not only contains the complete text of this book but also features a short, fun interactive quiz to test your understanding of the chapter you just read.

If you're reading these words in the Web Edition already and want to try your hand at the quiz, then you're in luck – all you need to do is scroll down!

IN THIS CHAPTER

- Understand what all this fuss about **Objects** is about
- Learn about the basic types you'll run into in JavaScript
- Find out that pizza has an educational value beyond just being deliciously awesome

11

OF PIZZA, TYPES, PRIMITIVES, AND OBJECTS

It's time to get serious. Srsly! In the past few chapters, we've been working with various kinds of values. You've worked with strings, numbers, booleans (aka *true* and *false*), functions, and various other built-in things that are part of the JavaScript language.

Below are some examples to jog your memory:

```
var someText = "hello, world!";
var count = 50;
var isActive = true;
```

Unlike other languages, JavaScript makes it really easy to specify and use these built-in things. You don't even have to think about or plan ahead to use any of them. Despite how simple it is to use these different kinds of built-in things, there is a lot of detail that is hidden from you. Knowing these details is important because it will not only help you make sense of your code more easily, it may even help you to more quickly pinpoint what is going wrong when things aren't working the way they should.

Now, as you can probably guess, "built-in-things" isn't the proper way to describe the variety of values that you can use in JavaScript. There is a more formal name for the variety of values you can use in your code, and that name is **types**. In this chapter, you are going to get a gentle introduction to what they are.

Onwards!

Let's First Talk About Pizza

No, I haven't completely lost it. Since I am always eating something (or thinking about eating something), I am going to try to explain the mysterious world of types by first explaining the much simpler world of pizza.

In case you haven't had pizza in a while, this is what a typical pizza looks like:

A pizza doesn't just magically appear looking like this. It is made up of other ingredients—some simple and some not so simple as illustrated in Figure 11.1.

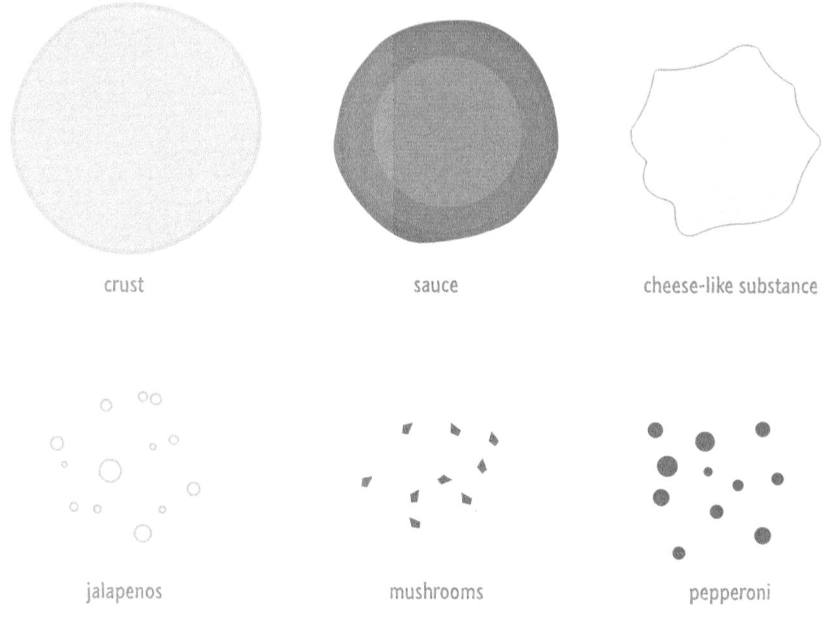

FIGURE 11.1

A pizza is made up of many smaller ingredients.

The simple ingredients are easy to spot. These would be your mushrooms and jalapeños. The reason these are simple is that you can't break these ingredients apart any further:

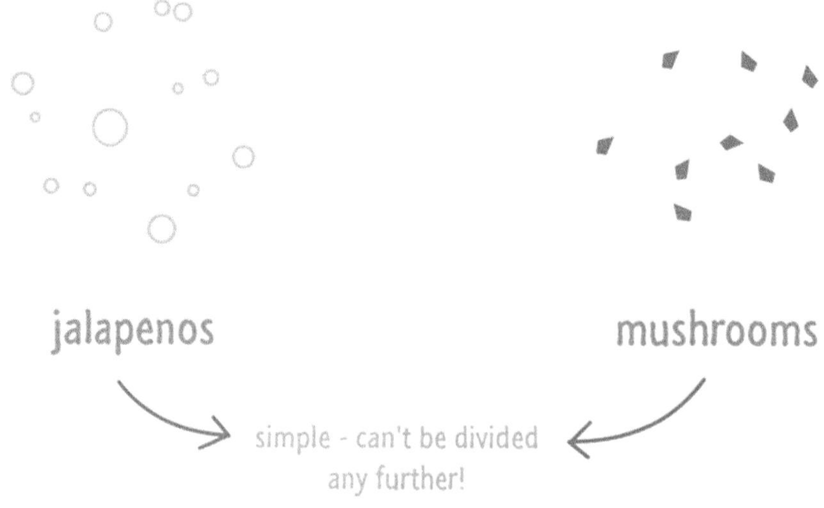

They aren't prepared. They aren't made up of other simple ingredients. Just like the dude, they abide.

The not-so-simple, complex ingredients would be your *cheese*, *sauce*, *crust*, and the *pepperoni*. These are more complex for all the reasons the simple ones are… um…simple. These complex ingredients are made up of *other ingredients*:

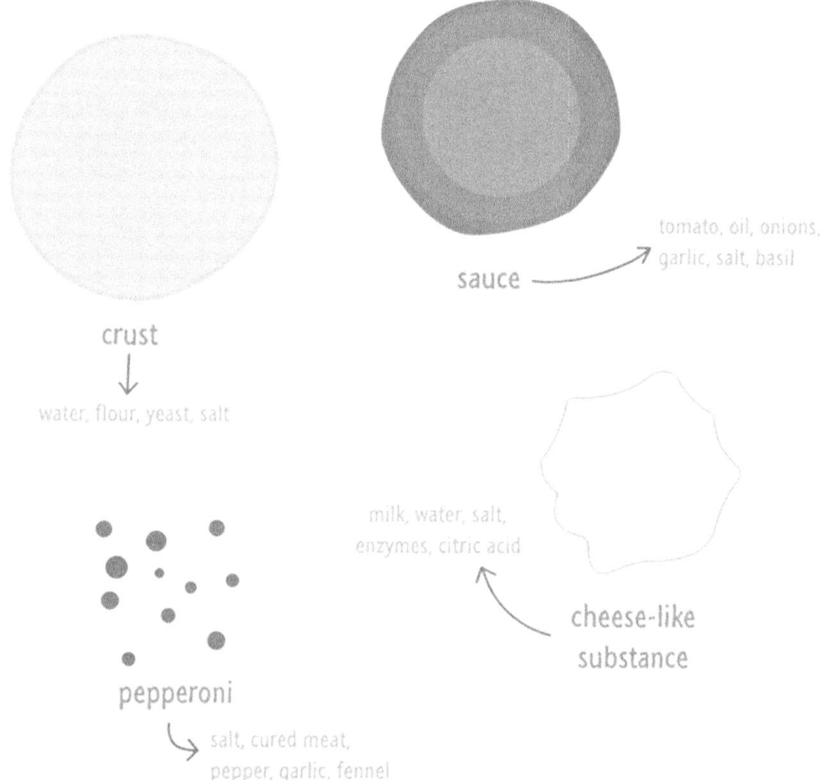

Unfortunately for all of us, there is no one ingredient called cheese or pepperoni out there. You need to combine and prepare and add some more ingredients to make up some of the complex ingredients you see here. There is a subtle point that needs to be noted about complex ingredients. Their composition isn't limited to just simple ingredients. Complex ingredients can themselves be made up of other complex ingredients. How scandalous?!!

From Pizza to JavaScript

While this may be hard to believe, everything you learned about pizzas in the previous section was there for a purpose. The description of the simple and complex ingredients very neatly applies to types and JavaScript. Each individual ingredient could be considered a counterpart to a type that you can use:

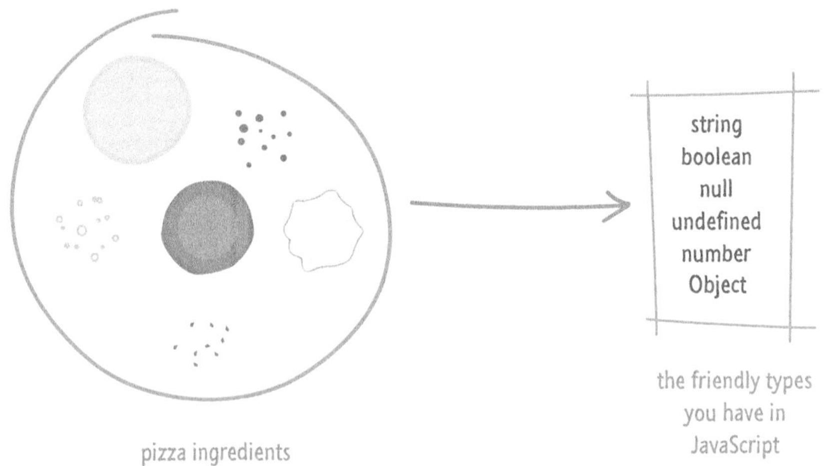

Just like the cheese, sauce, pepperoni, mushrooms, and bacon in our version of a pizza, the basic types in JavaScript are **String**, **Number**, **Boolean**, **Null**, **Undefined**, and **Object**. Some of these types may be very familiar to you already, and some of them may not be. While we will look at all of these types in much greater detail in future chapters, Table 11.1 provides a very brief summary of what they do.

TABLE 11.1 Basic JavaScript Types

Type	What It Does
`String`	The basic structure for working with text
`Number`	As you can guess, it allows you to work with numbers
`Boolean`	Comes alive when you are using true and false
`Null`	Represents the digital equivalent of nothing...or **moo** :P
`Undefined`	While sorta similar to null, this is returned when a value should exist but doesn't...like when you declare a variable but don't assign anything to it
`Object`	Acts as a shell for other types including other objects

Now, while each of these types is pretty unique in what it does, there is a simple grouping they fall under. Just like with your pizza's simple and complex ingredients, your types can be simple or complex as well. Except, in JavaScript terminology involving types, simple and complex are more formally known as **primitive** and **object** respectively. Another way of saying this is that your types in JavaScript are known as **primitive types** (or just **primitives**) and **object types** (or just **objects**).

The next two paragraphs are going to be really boring, and I don't expect you to memorize what I am about to say. Your primitive types are your `String`, `Number`, `Boolean`, `Null`, and `Undefined` types. Any values that fall under this umbrella can't be divided any further. They are the jalapeños and mushrooms of the JavaScript world. Anything that you create or use that is an `Object`, under the covers, is potentially made up of other primitive types or other `Objects`. `Objects` can also be empty, but we'll cover all those details eventually.

As you can see, primitives are pretty easy to understand. There is no depth to them, and you pretty much get what you see when you encounter one. Your `Object` types are a bit more mysterious, and so they are the last thing I want to cover before unleashing details about all of these types is what `Objects` in JavaScript actually are.

What Are Objects?

The concept of objects in a programming language like JavaScript maps nicely to its real-world equivalents. In the real world, you are literally surrounded by objects. Your computer is an object. A book on a shelf is an object. A potato is (arguably) an object. Your alarm clock is an object. The autographed Cee Lo Green poster you got on eBay is also an object! I could go on forever, but (for everyone's sake :P) I'm going to stop here.

Some objects like a paperweight don't do much:

They just sit there. Other objects, like a television, go above and beyond the call of mere existence and do a lot of things:

A typical television takes input, allows you to turn it on or off, change the channel, adjust the volume, and do all sorts of television-y things.

The thing to realize is that objects come in different shapes, sizes, and usefulness. Despite the variations, objects are all the same at a high level. They are an **abstraction**. They provide an easy way for you to use them without having to worry about what goes on under the covers. Even the simplest objects hide a certain level of complexity that you simply don't have to worry about.

For example, it doesn't matter what goes on inside your TV, how the wires are connected, or what type of glue is used to hold everything together. Those are unnecessary details. All that you care about is that the TV does what it is told. When you want it to change the channel, the channel should change. When you adjust the volume, the volume should adjust. Everything else is just noise.

Basically, think of an object as a black box. There are some predefined/documented things it does. How it does them is something you can't easily see. How it does its magic is also something you don't really care about as long as it works. We'll change that notion later when we learn to actually create the insides of an object, but let's relish this simple and happy world for now.

The Predefined Objects Roaming Around

Besides the built-in types you saw earlier, you also have a handful of predefined objects in JavaScript that you can use out of the box. These objects allow you to work with everything from collections of data to dates to even text and numbers. Table 11.2 presents some of these objects along with, just like before, a short blurb on what they do.

TABLE 11.2 Some Pre-defined JavaScript Objects

Type	What It Does
Array	Helps store, retrieve, and manipulate a collection of data
Boolean	Acts as a wrapper around the `boolean` primitive; still very much in love with true and false
Date	Allows you to more easily represent and work with dates
Function	Allows you to invoke some code among other esoteric things
Math	The nerdy one in the group that helps you better work with numbers
Number	Acts as a wrapper around the `number` primitive
RegExp	Provides a lot of functionality for matching patterns in text
String	Acts as a wrapper around the `string` primitive

The way you use these built-in objects is slightly different from how you use primitives. Each object has its own quirk regarding how you can use them as well. Explaining each object and how it is meant to be used is something that I will defer to for later, but here is a very short snippet of commented code to show you what is possible:

```
// an array
var names = ["Jerry", "Elaine", "George", "Kramer"];
var alsoNames = new Array("Dennis", "Frank", "Dee", "Mac");

// a round number
var roundNumber = Math.round("3.14");

// today's date
var today = new Date();

// a boolean object
var booleanObject = new Boolean(true);
```

```
// infinity
var unquantifiablyBigNumber = Infinity;

// a string object
var hello = new String("Hello!");
```

One thing that you may find puzzling is the existence of the Object-form of the `string`, `boolean`, and `number` primitives. On the surface, the Object-form and primitive-form of these types look very similar. Here is an example:

```
var movie = "Pulp Fiction";
var movieObj = new String("Pulp Fiction");


alert(movie);
alert(movieObj);
```

What you will see printed will be identical. Below the surface, though, both `movie` and `movieObj` are very different. One is literally a primitive of type `string`, and the other is of type `Object`. This leads to some interesting (and possibly incomprehensible) behavior that I will gradually touch upon as we explore the handful of built-in types that you've seen so far.

THE ABSOLUTE MINIMUM

If this feels like a movie that abruptly ended just as things were getting interesting, I don't blame you for thinking that way. The main takeaway is that your primitives make up the most basic types that you can use in your code. Your objects are a bit more complex and are made up of other primitives or objects. We'll see more of that in a little bit when we dive deeper. Beyond that, we learned the names for the common built-in types and some basic background material about all of them.

What you are going to see in subsequent chapters is a deeper look at all of these types and the nuances of working with them. Think of this chapter as the gentle on-ramp that suddenly drops you onto the rails of a crazy rollercoaster.

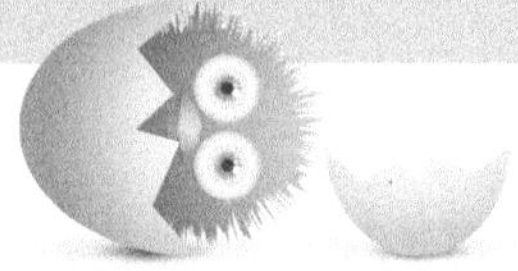

TIP Just a quick reminder for those of you reading these words in the print or e-book edition of this book: If you go to **www.quepublishing.com** and register this book, you can receive free access to an online Web Edition that not only contains the complete text of this book but also features a short, fun interactive quiz to test your understanding of the chapter you just read.

If you're reading these words in the Web Edition already and want to try your hand at the quiz, then you're in luck – all you need to do is scroll down!

IN THIS CHAPTER

- Understand how text is treated in JavaScript
- Learn how to perform common string operations
- Look at the various string properties

12

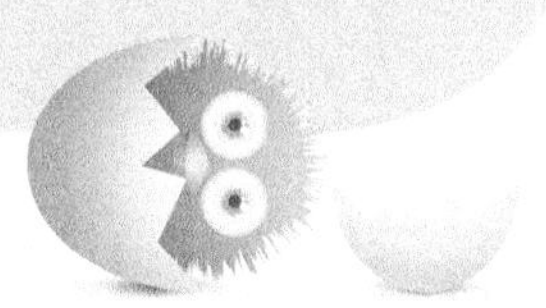

STRINGS

I have a hunch that you are a human being. As a human, you probably relate really well with words. You speak them. You write them. You also tend to use a lot of them in the things you program. As it turns out, JavaScript likes words a whole lot as well. The letters and funny-looking symbols that make up your (and my) language have a formal name. They are known as **strings**:

That image may not be very representative of what I am talking about. In fact, that image has nothing to do what I am talking about...

Anyway, strings in JavaScript are nothing more than a series of characters. Despite how boring that sounds, accessing and manipulating these characters is a skill that you must be familiar with. That's where this chapter comes in.

Onwards!

The Basics

The way you can work with strings is by just using them in your code. Just make sure to enclose them in single or double quotes. Below are some examples:

```
var text = "this is some text";
var moreText = 'I am in single quotes!';

alert("this is some more text");
```

Besides just listing strings, you'll often combine a couple of strings together. You can easily do that by just using the + operator:

```
var initial = "hello";
alert(initial + " world!");

alert("I can also " + "do this!");
```

In all of these examples, you are able to see the string. The only reason I point out something this obvious is that, when you can see the contents of your string as literally as you do, these strings are more appropriately known as **string literals**. That doesn't change the fact that the resulting structure is still a built-in primitive type called a **string** (you know...a basic pizza ingredient from the previous chapter).

If you had to visualize what the `text` and `moreText` strings look like, they would look as shown in Figure 12.1.

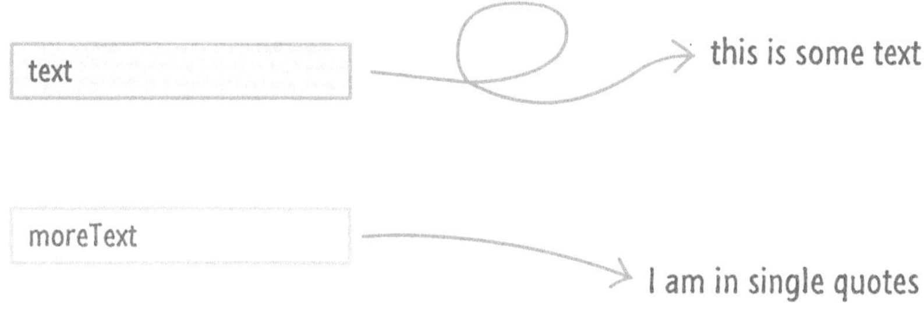

FIGURE 12.1

What our code looks like as visualized by weird lines and colorful boxes!

You just have your two variables pointing to some literal chunks of text. There isn't anything else that is going on. If you are wondering why I wasted this space in visualizing something so obvious, the visualizations will get more complex once we move into `Object` territory. You'll see hints of that in this chapter itself.

Anyway, all of this isn't particularly important...yet. The only important thing to keep in mind is that you need to wrap your string literals in either quotation marks (`"`) or apostrophes (`'`) to designate them as a region of text. If you don't do that, bad things happen and your code probably won't run.

That's all there is to the basics. The fun stuff comes from using all of the functionality JavaScript provides for working with strings. We'll look at that and more in the following sections.

String Properties and Methods

When you are working with strings, the underlying `String` object implementation contains a lot of properties that make working with text (usually) easier. In the following sections, instead of going over every property and boring both of us to death, I'll just focus on the important ones in the context of tasks you will be doing.

Accessing Individual Characters

While a string looks like one cohesive unit, it is actually made up of a series of characters. You can access each character in several ways. The most common way is by using array/bracket notation and passing in a number that corresponds to the index position of the character:

```
var vowels = "aeiou";
alert(vowels[2]);
```

In this example, I will see the **i** character because it is the item at the second index position. If you have no idea what just happened, Figure 12.2 may help.

FIGURE 12.2

How the index positions map to the string character.

Here is something you should keep in mind when the word **index** is thrown around. Index positions in JavaScript start at 0 and move up from there. That is why your index position is 2, but the count of the element at that position is actually 3. This gets less weird the more you work with JavaScript and other languages that don't contain the words **Visual** and **Basic**.

To go one step further, you can access all characters in your string by just looping through the index positions. The start of the loop will be 0, and the end of your loop will be determined by the length of your string. The length of your string (aka a count of the number of characters) is returned by the `length` property.

Here is an example of the preceding paragraph in action:

```
var vowels = "aeiou";

for (var i = 0; i < vowels.length; i++) {
    alert(vowels[i]);
}
```

While you may not be looping through a string all the time, it is very common to use the length property to get a count of the number of characters in your string.

If you don't get along with the array/bracket notation, you also have the `charAt` method that returns a character at a specified index position:

```
var vowels = "aeiou";
alert(vowels.charAt(2));
```

The end result is identical to what you see using the array notation. I wouldn't really use this method unless you care about really old browsers like Internet Explorer 7. Yep, I didn't think you did either.

WAIT...WHAT?

If you are wondering where in the world string primitives have the ability to access properties only available to `String` objects, suspend your curiosity for a few moments until the next chapter where we'll look at this in much greater detail.

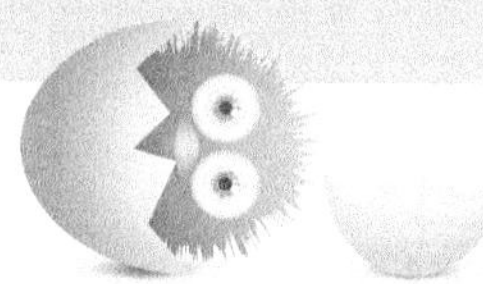

Combining (aka Concatenating) Strings

To combine two strings together, you can just use the + or += operators and just add them like you would a series of numbers:

```
var stringA = "I am a simple string.";
var stringB = "I am a simple string, too!";

alert(stringA + " " + stringB);
```

Notice that, in the third line, we add both `stringA` and `stringB` together. Between them, we specify an empty space character (" ") to ensure there is a space between each of the individual strings. You can mix and match string literals with string primitives and string objects and still get your text all combined together.

For example, this is all valid:

```
var textA = "Please";
var textB = new String("stop!");
var combined = textA + " make it " + textB;

alert(combined);
```

Despite all of the mixing going on, the type of the `combined` variable is simply a **string** primitive.

For combining strings, you also have the `concat` method. You can call this method from any string and specify a sequence of string primitives, literals, and objects that you want to combine into one…megastring:

```
var foo = "I really";
var blah = "why anybody would";
var blarg = "do this";

var result = foo.concat(" don't know", " ", blah, " ", blarg);

alert(result);
```

For the most part, just use the + and += approach for combining strings. It is faster than the `concat` approach. With everything else being equal, who wouldn't want some extra speed in their code?

Making Substrings out of Strings

Sometimes, what you are interested in is a sequence of characters somewhere in the middle of your string. The two properties that help satisfy this interest are `slice` and `substr`. Let's say we have the following string:

```
var theBigString = "Pulp Fiction is an awesome movie!";
```

Let's mess with this string for a bit.

The `slice` Method!

The **slice** method allows you to specify the start and end positions of the part of the string that you want to extract:

```
var theBigString = "Pulp Fiction is an awesome movie!";
alert(theBigString.slice(5, 12));
```

In this example, we extract the characters between index positions 5 and 12. The end result is that the word **Fiction** is what will get returned.

The start and end position values do not have to be positive. If you specify a negative value for the end position, the end position for your string is what is left when you count backwards from the end:

```
var theBigString = "Pulp Fiction is an awesome movie!";
alert(theBigString.slice(0, -6));
```

If you specify a negative start position, your start position is the count of whatever you specify starting from the end of the string:

```
var theBigString = "Pulp Fiction is an awesome movie!";
alert(theBigString.slice(-14, -7));
```

You just saw three variations of how the `slice` method can be used. I've never used anything but the first version with a positive start and end position, and you'll probably fall in a similar boat.

The `substr` Method!

The next approach we will look at for splitting up your string is the `substr` method. This method takes two arguments as well:

```
var newString = substr(start, length);
```

The first argument is a number that specifies your starting position, and the second argument is a number that specifies the length of your substring. This makes more sense when we look at some examples:

```
var theBigString = "Pulp Fiction is an awesome movie!";


alert(theBigString.substr(0, 4)); // Pulp
```

We start the substring at the zeroth position and count four characters up. That is why **Pulp** is returned. If you want to just extract the word **Fiction**, this is what your code would look like:

```
var theBigString = "Pulp Fiction is an awesome movie!";

alert(theBigString.substr(5, 7)); // Fiction
```

If you don't specify the length, the substring that gets returned is the string that goes from the start position to the end:

```
var theBigString = "Pulp Fiction is an awesome movie!";

alert(theBigString.substr(5)); // Fiction is an awesome movie!
```

There are a few more variations of values you can pass in for `substr`, but these are the big ones.

Splitting a String/`split`

That which you can concatenate, you can also split apart. I am pretty sure a wise person once said that. Another way you can split apart a string is by using the `split` method. Calling this method on a string returns an array of substrings. These substrings are separated by a character or Regular Expression (aka RegEx) that you use to determine when to split apart your string.

Let's look at a simple example where this makes more sense:

```
var inspirationalQuote = "That which you can concatenate, you can
  also split apart.";

var splitWords = inspirationalQuote.split(" ");
alert(splitWords.length); // 10
```

In this example, we are splitting the `inspirationalQuote` text on the space character. Every time a space character is encountered, what is left of the string before it is removed and made an item in the array that gets returned by this method.

Here is another example:

```
var days = "Monday,Tuesday,Wednesday,Thursday,Friday,
  Saturday,Sunday";

var splitWords = days.split(",");
alert(splitWords[6]); // Sunday
```

We have the `days` variable, which stores a string of days separated only by a comma. If we wanted to separate out each day, we could use the `split` method with the separator character being the comma. The end result is an array of seven items where each item is the day of the week from the original string.

You'll be surprised at how often you will find yourself using the `split` method to break apart a sequence of characters that can be as simple as a sentence or something more complex like data returned from a web service.

Finding Something Inside a String

If you ever need to find a character or characters inside a string, you can use the `indexOf`, `lastIndexOf`, and `match` methods. Let's look at the `indexOf` method first.

What the `indexOf` method does is take the character(s) you are looking for as its argument. If what you are looking for is found, it returns the index position in the string where the first occurrence...occurs. If no matches are found, this method gifts you with a *–1*. Let's look at an example:

```
var question = "I wonder what the pigs did to make these birds so
  angry?";


alert(question.indexOf("pigs")); // 18
```

I am trying to see if pigs exist in my string. Because what I am looking for does exist, the `indexOf` method lets me know that the first occurrence of this word occurs at the 18th index position. If I look for something that doesn't exist, like the letter **z** in this example, a *–1* gets returned for:

```
var question = "I wonder what the pigs did to make these birds so
  angry?";


alert(question.indexOf("z")); // -1
```

The `lastIndexOf` method is very similar to `indexOf`. As you can guess by the name, `lastIndexOf` returns the last occurrence of what you are looking for:

```
var question = "How much wood could a woodchuck chuck if a
  woodchuck could chuck wood?";


alert(question.lastIndexOf("wood")); // 65
```

There is one more argument you can specify to both `indexOf` and `lastIndexOf`. In addition to providing the characters to search for, you can also specify an index position on your string to start your search from:

```
var question = "How much wood could a woodchuck chuck if a
  woodchuck could chuck wood?";

alert(question.indexOf("wood", 30)); // 43
```

The last thing to mention about the `indexOf` and `lastIndexOf` methods is that you can match any instance of these characters appearing in your string. These functions do not differentiate between whole words or what you are looking for being a substring of a larger set of characters. Be sure to take that into account.

Before we wrap this up, let's look at the `match` method. With the `match` method, you have a little more control. This method takes a Regex as its argument:

```
var phrase = "There are 3 little pigs.";
var regexp = /[0-9]/;

var numbers = phrase.match(regexp);

alert(numbers[0]); // 3
```

What gets returned is also an array of matching substrings, so you can use your Array ninja skills to make working with the results a breeze. Learning how to work with regular expressions is something that we'll look at much later.

Upper and Lower Casing Strings

Finally, let's end this coverage on Strings with something easy that doesn't require anything complicated. To uppercase or lowercase a string, you can use the appropriately named `toUpperCase` and `toLowerCase` methods. Let's look at this example:

```
var phrase = "My name is Bond. James Bond.";

alert(phrase.toUpperCase()); // MY NAME IS BOND. JAMES BOND.
alert(phrase.toLowerCase()); // my name is bond. james bond.
```

See, told you this was easy!

THE ABSOLUTE MINIMUM

Strings are one of the handful of basic data types you have available in JavaScript, and you just saw a good overview of the many things you can do using them. One issue that I skirted around is where your string primitives seem to mysteriously have all of these properties that are common only to Objects. We'll look at that one in the next chapter!

Some additional resources and examples:

- **The Devowelizer: http://bit.ly/kirupaDeVowelize**
- **Capitalize the First Letter of a String: http://bit.ly/kirupaCapLetter**
- **10 Ways to Reverse a String: http://bit.ly/kirupaWaysToReverseString**

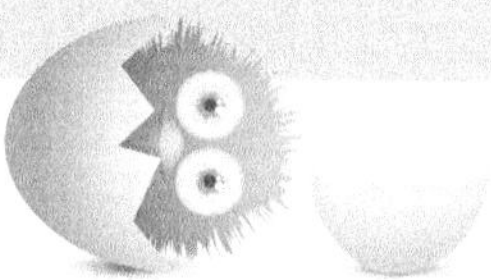

TIP Just a quick reminder for those of you reading these words in the print or e-book edition of this book: If you go to **www.quepublishing.com** and register this book, you can receive free access to an online Web Edition that not only contains the complete text of this book but also features a short, fun interactive quiz to test your understanding of the chapter you just read.

If you're reading these words in the Web Edition already and want to try your hand at the quiz, then you're in luck – all you need to do is scroll down!

IN THIS CHAPTER

- Get a deeper understanding of how primitives and objects work
- Understand that even primitives have object-like traits
- Wonder how JavaScript ever got to being so popular

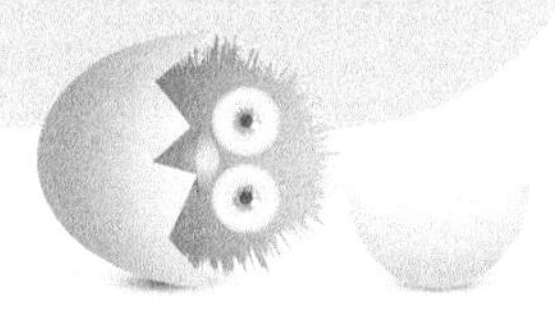

WHEN PRIMITIVES BEHAVE LIKE OBJECTS

In the previous chapter (**Chapter 12, "Strings"**) and less so in the **"Of Pizza, Types, Primitives, and Objects"** chapter (Chapter 11), you got a sneak peek at something that is probably pretty confusing. I've stated many times that primitives are very plain and simple. Unlike Objects, they don't contain properties that allow you to fiddle with their values in interesting (or boring) ways. Yet, as clearly demonstrated by all the stuff you can do with strings, your primitives seem to have a mysterious dark side to them:

```
var greeting = "Hi, everybody!!!";
var shout = greeting.toUpperCase(); // where did toUpperCase
  come from?
```

As you can see from this brief snippet, your `greeting` variable, which stores a primitive value in the form of text, seems to have access to the `toUpperCase` method. How is this even possible? Where did that method come from? Why am I here? Answers to confusing existential questions like this will make up the bulk of what you see in this page. Also, I apologize for writing that previous sentence in passive voice. Happen again it won't.

Strings Aren't the Only Problem

Because of how cute they are, it's easy to pick on strings as the main perpetrator of this primitive/Object confusion. As it turns out, many of the built-in primitive types are involved in this racket as well. Table 13.1 presents the built-in `Object` types with the guilty parties that also exist as primitives highlighted.

TABLE 13.1 Object Types that also Exist as Primitives

Type	What It Does
`Array`	helps store, retrieve, and manipulate a collection of data
`Boolean`	acts as a wrapper around the `boolean` primitive; still very much in love with true and false
`Date`	allows you to more easily represent and work with dates
`Function`	allows you to invoke some code among other esoteric things
`Math`	the nerdy one in the group that helps you better work with numbers
`Number`	acts as a wrapper around the `number` primitive
`RegExp`	provides a lot of functionality for matching patterns in text
`String`	acts as a wrapper around the `string` primitive

Whenever you are working with boolean, number, or string primitives, you have access to properties their Object equivalent exposes. In the following sections, you'll see what exactly is going on.

Let's Pick on Strings Anyway

Just as you were taught by your parents growing up, you typically use a string in the literal form:

```
var primitiveText = "Homer Simpson";
```

As you saw in the table earlier, strings also have the ability to be used as objects. There are several ways to create a new object, but the most common way to create an object for a built-in type like our string is to use the `new` keyword followed by the word `String`:

```
var name = new String("Homer Simpson");
```

The `String` in this case isn't just any normal word. It represents what is known as a constructor function whose sole purpose is to be used for creating objects. Just like there are several ways to create objects, there are several ways to create String objects as well. The way I see it, knowing about one way that you really shouldn't be creating them with is enough.

Anyway, the main difference between the primitive and object forms of a string is the sheer amount of additional baggage the object form carries with it. Let's bring our silly visualizations back. Your `primitiveText` variable and its baggage looks as shown in Figure 13.1.

FIGURE 13.1

What primitiveText looks like.

There really isn't much there. Now, don't let the next part scare you, but if we had to visualize our `String` object called `name`, it would look like what you see in Figure 13.2.

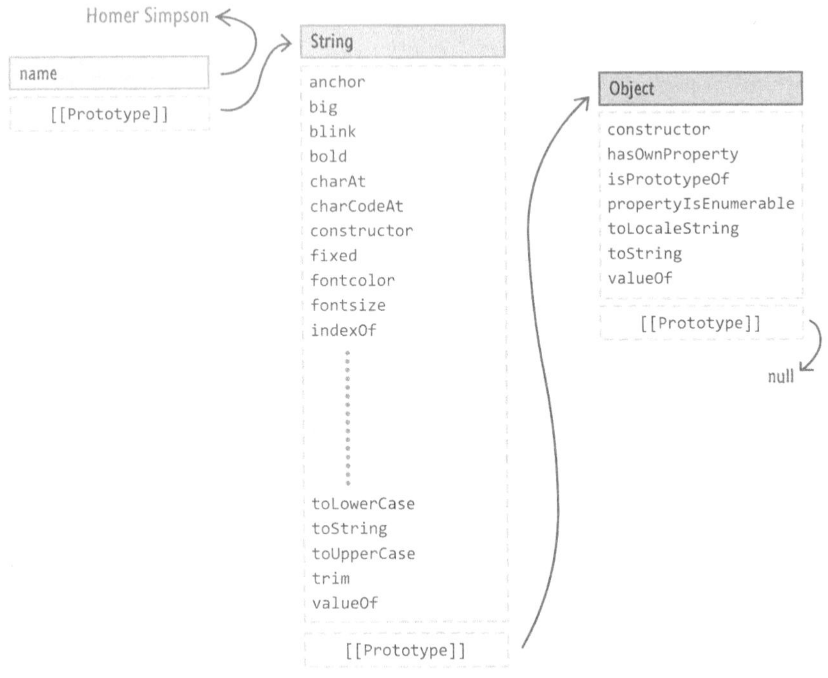

FIGURE 13.2

It is a bit more complex, right?

You have your **name** variable containing a pointer to the text, *Homer Simpson*. You also have all of the various properties and methods that go with the **String** object - things you may have used like **indexOf**, **toUpperCase**, and so on. You'll get a massive overview of what exactly this diagram represents in **Chapter 16, "A Deeper Look at Objects,"** so don't worry yourself too much about what you see here. Just know that the object form of any of the primitives carries with it a lot of functionality.

Why This Matters

Let's go back to our earlier point of confusion. Our string is a primitive. How can a primitive type allow you to access properties on it? The answer has to do with JavaScript being really weird. Let's say you have the following string:

```
var game = "Dragon Age: Origins";
```

The game variable is very clearly a string primitive that is assigned to some literal text. If I want to access the length of this text, I would do something as follows:

```
var game = "Dragon Age: Origins";
alert(game.length);
```

As part of evaluating game.length, *JavaScript will convert your primitive string into an object*. For a brief moment, your lowly primitive will become a beautiful object to figure out what the length actually is. The thing to keep in mind is that all of this is temporary. Because this temporary object isn't grounded or tied to anything after it serves its purpose, it goes away and you are left with the result of the length evaluation (a number) and the game variable (still a string primitive).

This transformation only happens for primitives. If you ever explicitly create a String object, then what you create is permanently kept as an object. Let's say you have the following:

```
var gameObject = new String("Dragon Age:Origins");
```

In this case, our gameObject variable very clearly points to something whose type is Object. This variable will continue to point to an Object type unless you modify the string or do something else that causes the reference to be changed. The primitive morphing into an object and then morphing back into a primitive is something unique to primitives. Your objects don't partake in such tomfoolery.

You can easily verify everything I've said by examining the type of your data. That is done by using the typeof keyword. Here is an example of me using it to confirm everything I've just told you about:

```
var game = "Dragon Age: Origins";
alert("Length is: " + game.length);

var gameObject = new String("Dragon Age:Origins");

alert(typeof game); // string
alert(typeof game.length); // number
alert(typeof gameObject); // Object
```

Now, aren't you glad you learned all this?

THE ABSOLUTE MINIMUM

Hopefully, this brief explanation helps you to reconcile why your primitives behave like objects when they need to. At this point, you might have a different question around why anybody would have designed a language that does something this bizarre. After all, if a primitive turns into an object when it needs to do something useful, why not just stay an object always? The answer has to do with memory consumption.

As you saw from my discussion and illustrations on how much extra baggage the object form of a primitive carries when compared to just a primitive, all of those pointers to additional functionality cost resources. The solution in JavaScript is a compromise. All literal values like text, numbers, and booleans are kept as primitives if they are declared and/or used as such. Only when they need to are they converted to their respective Object forms. To ensure your app continues to keep a low memory footprint, these converted objects are quickly discarded (aka **garbage collected**) once they've served their purpose.

TIP Just a quick reminder for those of you reading these words in the print or e-book edition of this book: If you go to **www.quepublishing.com** and register this book, you can receive free access to an online Web Edition that not only contains the complete text of this book but also features a short, fun interactive quiz to test your understanding of the chapter you just read.

If you're reading these words in the Web Edition already and want to try your hand at the quiz, then you're in luck – all you need to do is scroll down!

IN THIS CHAPTER

- Use arrays to handle lists of data
- Learn how to perform common tasks using the various Array properties

14

ARRAYS

Let's imagine you are jotting down a list on a piece of paper. Let's call the piece of paper "groceries." Now, on this sheet of paper, you write a numbered list starting with zero with all the items that belong there such as what you see in Figure 14.1.

0. Milk

1. Eggs

2. Frosted Flakes

3. Salami

4. Juice

FIGURE 14.1

An example of a grocery list.

By simply creating a list of things, what you have right now is a real-world example of an **array**! The piece of paper called "groceries" would be your array. The items that you need to purchase are known as **array values** (or **array elements**).

In this chapter, you will learn all about what I like to go grocery shopping for. You may indirectly get an introduction to the very common built-in type, the array.

Onwards!

Creating an Array

The popular way in which all the cool kids create arrays these days is to use an open and close bracket. The example that follows is our groceries variable that is initialized to an empty array:

```
var groceries = [];
```

You have your variable name on the left, and you have a pair of brackets on the right that initializes this variable as an empty array. This ***bracket-y*** approach for creating an array is better known as the **array literal notation**.

Now, you will commonly want to create an array with some items inside it from the very beginning. To create these non-empty arrays, place the items you want inside the brackets and separate them by commas:

```
var groceries = ["Milk", "Eggs", "Frosted Flakes", "Salami",
  "Juice"];
```

Notice that my groceries array now contains *Milk*, *Eggs*, *Frosted Flakes*, *Salami*, and *Juice*. I just have to reiterate how important the commas are. Without the commas, you'll just have one giant item. All right, now that you've learned how to declare an array, let's look at how you can actually use it to store and work with data.

Accessing Array Values

One of the nice things about arrays is that you not only have easy access to the array, but you also have easy access to the array values...similar to highlighting an item on your grocery list as shown in Figure 14.2.

0. Milk

1. Eggs

2. Frosted Flakes

3. Salami

4. Juice

FIGURE 14.2

Eggs are highlighted. Must be important.

The only thing you need to know is the procedure for accessing an individual item.

Inside an array, each item is assigned a number (formally known as an **index value**) starting with zero just like you saw with characters inside a string earlier. In the above example, *Milk* would have an index value of 0, *Eggs* would have an index value of 1, *Frosted Flakes* the index value of 2, and so on.

Let's say that our groceries array is declared as follows:

```
var groceries = ["Milk", "Eggs", "Frosted Flakes", "Salami",
  "Juice"];
```

If I wanted to access an item from the array, all I need to do is specify the index value of the item I am interested in:

```
groceries[1];
```

The index value is specified using square brackets. In this example, you are referring to the *Eggs* value because the index value 1 refers to it. If you specified a 2, you would return *Frosted Flakes*. You can keep specifying a larger index value until you have no more entries in the array left that map to it.

The number you can use as your index value goes all the way from 0 to one less than your array's length. The reason is that, as shown in the diagram earlier, your index values start with a value of 0. If your array only has 5 items, trying to display `grocery[6]` or `grocery[5]` will result in a message of *undefined.*

Let's go one step further. In most real-world scenarios, you will want to programmatically go through your array as opposed to accessing each item individually.

You can take what I explained in the previous paragraph and use a `for` loop to accomplish this:

```
for (var i = 0; i < groceries.length; i++) {
    var item = groceries[i];
}
```

Notice the range of your loop starts at 0 and ends just one before your array's full length (as returned by the `length` property). This works because, like I mentioned earlier, your array index values go from 0 to one short of the value returned for the array's length. And yes, the `length` property returns a count of all the items in your array! (To be precise, the `length` property returns the number of index values in your array, and that can sometimes not equal the number of actual items your array is storing. That is a nitpicky detail we'll deal with another time.)

Adding Items to Your Array

Rarely will you leave your array in the state you initialized it in originally. You will want to add items to it. To add items to your array, you will use the `push` method:

```
groceries.push("Cookies");
```

The `push` method is called directly on your array, and you pass in the data you want to add to it. By using the `push` method, your newly added data will always find itself at the end of the array.

For example, after running the code on our initial array, you will see Cookies added to the end of your groceries array as shown in Figure 14.3.

0. Milk
1. Eggs
2. Frosted Flakes
3. Salami
4. Juice
5. Cookies

FIGURE 14.3

Our newly added item was placed at the end.

If you want to add data to the beginning of your array, you use the `unshift` method:

```
groceries.unshift("Bananas");
```

When data is added to the beginning of your array, the index value for all of the existing items increases to account for the newly inserted data as shown in Figure 14.4.

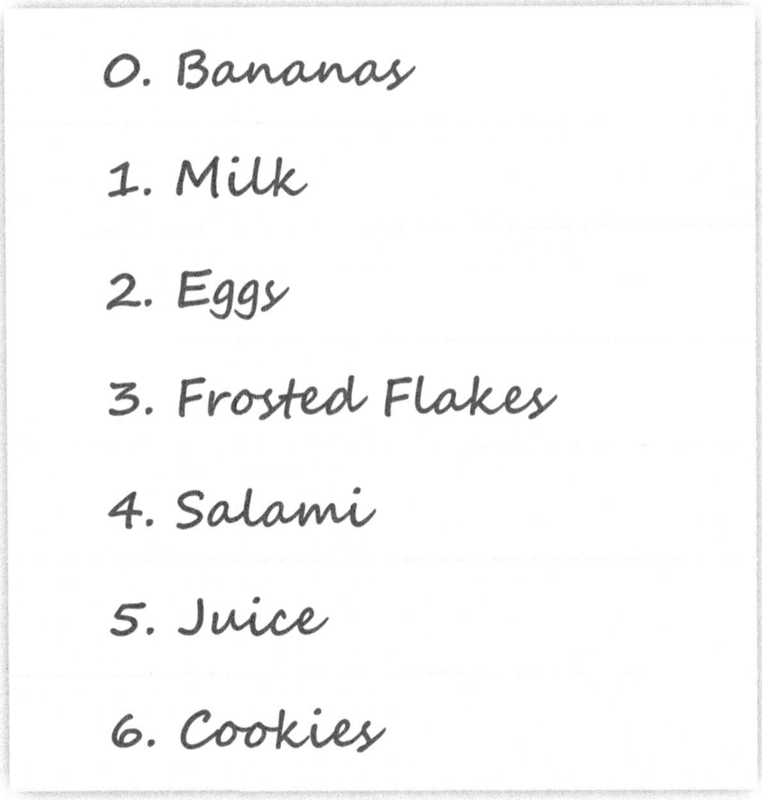

0. Bananas
1. Milk
2. Eggs
3. Frosted Flakes
4. Salami
5. Juice
6. Cookies

FIGURE 14.4

This time, our newly added item was placed at the beginning.

The reason is that the first item in your array will always have an index value of 0. This means that the space originally occupied by the zeroth item needs to push itself and everything below it out to make room for the new data.

Both the `push` and `unshift` methods, besides adding the elements to the array when you use them, return the new length of the array as well:

```
alert(groceries.push("Cookies")); // returns 6
```

Not sure why that is useful, but keep it under your hat in case you do need it.

Removing Items from the Array

To remove an item from the array, you can use the `pop` or `shift` methods. The `pop` method removes the last item from the array and returns it:

```
var lastItem = groceries.pop();
```

The `shift` method does the same thing on the opposite end of the array. Instead of the last item being removed and returned, the shift method removes and returns the first item from the array:

```
var firstItem = groceries.shift();
```

When an item is removed from the beginning of the array, the index position of all remaining elements is decremented by 1 to fill in the gap:

Note that, when you are adding items to your array using `unshift` or `push`, the returned value from that method call is the new length of your array. That is not what happens when you call the `pop` and `shift` methods, though! When you are removing items using `shift` and `pop`, the value returned by the method call is the removed item itself!

We are almost done talking about removing things. The last method we are going to look at is `slice`:

```
var newArray = groceries.slice(1, 4);
```

The `slice` method allows you copy a portion of an array and return a new array with just those copied items. In this snippet, we copy all items between the second and fifth items in our array and return them to a new array we call...`newArray`! When you are using `slice`, your original array is never modified. No items are actually removed. They are simply copied over.

Finding Items in the Array

To find items inside your array, you have two built-in methods called `indexOf` and `lastIndexOf`. These methods work by scanning your array and returning the index position of the matching element.

The `indexOf` method returns the index value of the first occurrence of the item you are searching for:

```
var groceries = ["milk", "eggs", "frosted flakes", "salami",
  "juice"];
var resultIndex = groceries.indexOf("eggs", 0);


alert(resultIndex); // 1
```

Notice that the `resultIndex` variable stores the result of calling `indexOf` on our `groceries` array. To use `indexOf`, I pass in the element I am looking for along with the index position to start from:

```
groceries.indexOf("eggs", 0);
```

The value returned by `indexOf` in this case will be 1.

The `lastIndexOf` method is similar to `indexOf` in how you use it, but it differs a bit on what it returns when an element is found. Where `indexOf` finds the first occurrence of the element you are searching for, `lastIndexOf` finds the last occurrence of the element you are searching for and returns that element's index position.

When you search for an element that does not exist in your array, both `indexOf` and `lastIndexOf` return a value of −1.

Merging Arrays

The last thing we are going to do is look at how to create a new array that is made up of two separate arrays. Let's say you have two arrays called good and bad:

```
var good = ["Mario", "Luigi", "Kirby", "Yoshi"];
var bad = ["Bowser", "Koopa Troopa", "Goomba"];
```

To combine both of these arrays into one array, use the `concat` method on the array you want to make bigger and pass the array you want to merge into it as the argument. What will get returned is a new array whose contents are both good and bad:

```
var goodAndBad = good.concat(bad);
alert(goodAndBad);
```

In this example, because the concat method returns a new array, the goodAndBad variable ends up becoming an array that stores the results of our concatenation operation. The order of the elements inside goodAndBad is good first and bad second:

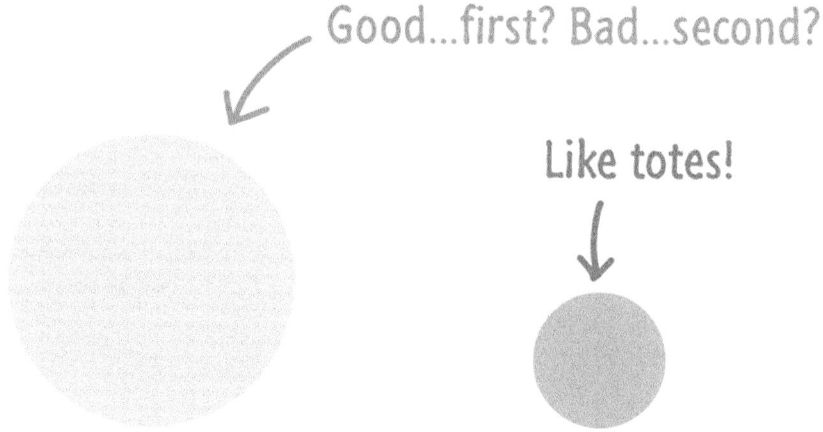

THE ABSOLUTE MINIMUM

That is almost all there is to know about arrays...well, at least the things you will use them for most frequently. At the very least, you will have learned how to use them to create a grocery list!

Some additional resources and examples:

- **Shuffling an Array: http://bit.ly/kirupaArrayShuffle**
- **Picking a Random Item from an Array: http://bit.ly/kirupaRandomItemArray**
- **Removing Duplicates from an Array: http://bit.ly/kirupaRemoveDuplicates**
- **Hashtables vs. Arrays: http://bit.ly/kirupaHvA**

TIP Just a quick reminder for those of you reading these words in the print or e-book edition of this book: If you go to **www.quepublishing.com** and register this book, you can receive free access to an online Web Edition that not only contains the complete text of this book but also features a short, fun interactive quiz to test your understanding of the chapter you just read.

If you're reading these words in the Web Edition already and want to try your hand at the quiz, then you're in luck – all you need to do is scroll down!

IN THIS CHAPTER

- Make sense of numbers
- Learn about the variety of numerical values you will encounter
- Meet the Math object and the various mathematical things you can do

15

NUMBERS

When you are not dealing with strings, a large part of your time in JavaScript will be spent dealing with numbers. Even if you aren't working with numbers directly, you'll indirectly encounter them when doing even the most basic of tasks such as keeping count of something, working with arrays, and so on.

In this chapter, I will provide an introduction to numbers in JavaScript by looking at how you can use them to accomplish many common tasks. Along the way, we will dive a little bit beyond the basics to broadly explore some interesting number-related things you might find useful.

Onwards!

Using a Number

In order to use a number, all you have to do is...well, use it. Below is a simple example of me declaring a variable called **stooges** that is initialized to the number **3**:

```
var stooges = 3;
```

That is it. There are no hoops to jump through. If you want to use more complex numbers, just use them as if nothing is different:

```
var pi = 3.14159;
var color = 0xFF;
var massOfEarth = 5.9742e+24;
```

In the above example, I am using a decimal value, a hexadecimal value, and a really large value using exponents. In the end, your browser will automatically do the right thing. Note that the "right thing" doesn't just exist in the positive space. You can use negative numbers easily as well. To use negative numbers, just place a minus (-) character before the number you want to turn into a negative value:

```
var temperature = -42;
```

What you've seen in this section makes up the bulk of how you will actually use numbers. In the next couple of sections, let's go a little bit deeper and look at some of the other interesting things you can do with numbers.

TRIVIA: NUMBERS IN JAVASCRIPT

If you are curious why working with numbers is so easy, the reason is that JavaScript isn't big on numerical types. You don't have to declare a number as being of type **int**, **double**, **byte**, **float**, etc. like you might have had to do in other languages.

In JavaScript, all numbers are converted into 64-bit floating point numbers.

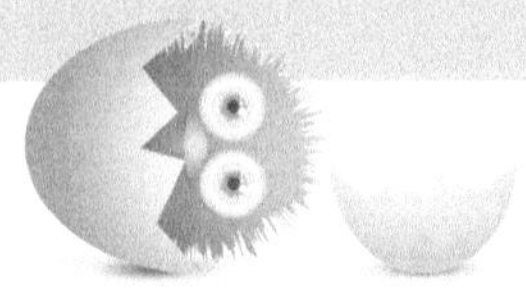

Operators

No introduction to numbers would be complete (...or started) without showing you how you can use mathematical operators in code to implement things you learned in first-grade Math class.

Let's look at the common operators in this section.

Doing Simple Math

In JavaScript, you can create simple mathematical expressions using the +, -, *, /, and % operators to add, subtract, multiply, divide, and find the remainder (modulus) of numbers respectively. If you can use a calculator, you can do simple math in JavaScript.

Here are some examples that put these operators to use:

```
var total = 4 + 26;
var average = total / 2;
var doublePi = 2 * 3.14159;
var removeItem = 50-25;
var remainder = total % 7;
var more = (1 + average * 10) / 5;
```

In the last line in the above example, notice that I am defining a particular order of operations by using parentheses around the expression I want to evaluate as a group. Again, all of this is just calculator stuff.

JavaScript evaluates expressions in the following order:

1. Parenthesis
2. Exponents
3. Multiply
4. Divide
5. Add
6. Subtract

There are various mnemonic devices out there to help you remember this. The one I grew up with since elementary school is "**P**lease **E**xcuse **M**y **D**ear **A**unt **S**ally."

Incrementing and Decrementing

A common thing you will do with numbers involves incrementing or decrementing a variable by a certain amount. Below is an example of me incrementing the variable `i` by 1:

```
var i = 4;
i = i + 1;
```

You don't have to increment or decrement by just 1. You can use any arbitrary number:

```
var i = 100;
i = i - 2;
```

All of this doesn't just have to just be addition or subtraction. You can perform other operations as well:

```
var i = 40;
i = i / 2;
```

You should start to see a pattern here. Regardless of what operator you are using, you'll notice that you are cumulatively modifying your `i` variable. Because of how frequently you will use this pattern, you have some operators that simplify this a bit (see Table 15.1).

TABLE 15.1 Operators

Expression	What It Does
`i++`	Increments i by 1 (i = i + 1)
`i--`	Decrements i by 1 (i = i – 1)
`i += n`	Increments i by n (i = i + n)
`i -= n`	Decrements i by n (i = i – n)
`i *= n`	Multiplies by n (i = i * n)
`i /= n`	Divides i by n (i = i / n)
`i %= n`	Finds the remainder of i when divided by n (i = i % n)

If I use these operators on the three examples you saw earlier, the code will look as follows:

```
i++;
i -= 2;
i /= 2;
```

Before we wrap this up, there is one quirk you should be aware of. It has to do with the -- and ++ operators for incrementing or decrementing a value by 1. Whether the ++ and -- operators appear before or after the variable they are incrementing matters.

Let's look at this example:

```
var i = 4;
var j = i++;
```

After executing these two lines, the value of `i` will be 5...just like you would expect. The value of `j` will be 4. Notice that in this example, the operator appears after the variable.

If we place the operator in front of the variable, the results are a bit different:

```
var i = 4;
var j = ++i;
```

The value of `i` will still be 5. Here is the kicker...the value of `j` will also be 5.

What changed between these two examples is the position of the operator. The position of the operator determines **whether the incremented value or the preincremented value will be returned**. Now, aren't you glad you learned that?

Special Values—Infinity and NaN

The last thing we will look at are two special/reserved keywords that you will encounter that aren't numerical values. These values are `Infinity` and `NaN`.

Infinity

You can use the `Infinity` and `-Infinity` values to define infinitely large or small numbers:

```
var reallyBigNumber = Infinity;
var reallySmallNumber = -Infinity;
```

The chances of you having to use `Infinity` are often very slim. Instead, you will probably see it returned as part of something else your code does. For example, you will see `Infinity` returned if you divide by 0.

NaN

The **NaN** keyword stands for "Not a Number", and it gets returned when you do some numerical operation that is invalid. For example, **NaN** gets returned in the following case:

```
var oops = Math.sqrt(-1);
```

The reason is that you cannot divide a number and a string. There are non-contrived cases where you will see this value returned. The **parseInt** function I described earlier will return a **NaN** if the string you are converting is invalid.

TRIVIA: NUMBERS IN JAVASCRIPT

Sometimes, you will have numbers that are buried inside Strings. To get the full scoop on that, read the **Going from a String to a Number** tutorial at the following location: **http://bit.ly/kirupaStrToNum**.

The Math Object

Numbers are used in a variety of mathematical expressions, and they often go beyond simple addition, subtraction, multiplication, and division. Your math classes back in the day would have been a whole lot easier if that's all there was to it. To help you more easily do complicated numerical things, you have the Math object. This object provides you with a lot of functions and constants that will come in handy, and we are going to very briefly look at some of the things this object does.

THIS IS BORING!

I am not going to lie to you. Looking at all the stuff the `Math` object provides is pretty boring. Unless you really want to know about all of this now, I would prefer you just very VERY quickly skim through the following sections and refer back as needed. The `Math` object isn't going anywhere (it has no friends), so it will be waiting for you at a later time.

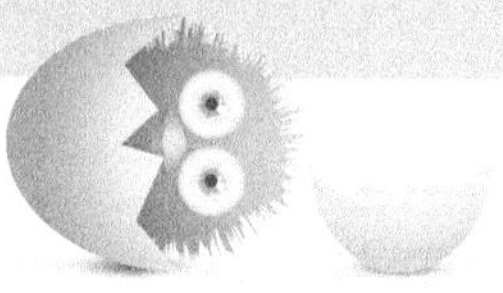

The Constants

To avoid you having to explicitly define mathematical constants like Pi, Euler's constant, LN10, and so on, the `Math` object defines many common constants for you:

Property	What It Stands for
`Math.E`	Euler's constant
`Math.LN2`	Natural logarithm of 2
`Math.LN10`	Natural logarithm of 10
`Math.LOG2E`	Base 2 logarithm of E
`Math.LOG10E`	Base 10 logarithm of E
`Math.PI`	3.14159 (that's all I remember, and I'm too lazy to look up the rest!)
`Math.SQRT1_2`	Square root of 1/2
`Math.SQRT2`	Square root of 2

Of all of these constants, the one I've used the most is `Math.PI`:

I just wanted an excuse to post this picture

You will use this in everything from drawing circles on your screen to specifying trigonometric expressions. In fact, I can't ever remember having used any of these other constants outside of `Math.PI`. Here is an example of a function that returns the circumference given the radius:

```
function getCircumference(radius) {
    return 2 * Math.PI * radius;
}

alert(getCircumference(2));
```

You would use `Math.PI` or any other constant just as you would any named variable.

Rounding Numbers

Your numbers will often end up containing a ridiculous amount of precision:

```
var position = getPositionFromCursor(); //159.3634493939
```

To help you round these numbers up to a reasonable integer value, you have the `Math.round()`, `Math.ceil()`, and `Math.floor()` functions that take a number as an argument:

Function	What It Does
`Math.round()`	Returns a number that is rounded to the nearest integer. You round up if your argument is greater than or equal to .5. You stay at your current integer, if your argument is less than .5.
`Math.ceil()`	Returns a number that is greater than or equal to your argument
`Math.floor()`	Returns a number that is less than or equal to your argument

The easiest way to make sense of the above table is to just see these three functions in action:

```
Math.floor(.5); // 0
Math.ceil(.5); // 1
Math.round(.5); // 1

Math.floor(3.14); // 3
Math.round(3.14); // 3
Math.ceil(3.14); // 4

Math.floor(5.9); // 5
Math.round(5.9); // 6
Math.ceil(5.9); // 6
```

These three functions always round you to an integer. If you want to round to a precise set of digits, check out the last half of the **Rounding Numbers in JavaScript** tutorial at the following location: **http://bit.ly/kirupaRounding**.

Trigonometric Functions

My favorite among all the functions, the `Math` object, gives you handy access to almost all of the trigonometric functions you will need.

Function	What It Does
`Math.cos()`	Gives you the cosine for a given argument
`Math.sin()`	Gives you the sine for a given argument
`Math.tan()`	Gives you the tan for a given argument
`Math.acos()`	Gives you the arccosine (isn't that such a cool name?) for a given argument
`Math.asin()`	Gives you the arcsine for a given argument
`Math.atan()`	Gives you the arctan for a given argument

To use any of these, just pass in a number as the argument:

```
Math.cos(0); // 1
Math.sin(0); // 0
Math.tan(Math.PI / 4); // 0.9999999999999999
Math.cos(Math.PI); // -1
Math.cos(4 * Math.PI); // 1
```

These trigonometric functions take arguments in the form of radian values. If your numbers are in the form of degrees, be sure to convert them to radians first.

Powers and Square Roots

Continuing down the path of defining the `Math` object functions, you have `Math.pow()`, `Math.exp()`, and `Math.sqrt()`:

Function	What It Does
`Math.pow()`	Raises a number to a specified power
`Math.exp()`	Raises the Euler's constant to a specified number
`Math.sqrt()`	Returns the square root of a giving argument

Let's look at some examples:

```
Math.pow(2, 4) //equivalent of 2^4 (or 2 * 2 * 2 * 2)
Math.exp(3) //equivalent of Math.E^3
Math.sqrt(16) //4
```

Note that `Math.pow()` takes two arguments. This might be the first built-in function we've looked at that takes two arguments. This little detail is somehow mildly exciting.

Getting the Absolute Value

If you want the absolute value of a number, simply use the `Math.abs()` function:

```
Math.abs(37) //37
Math.abs(-6) //6
```

The way this function works is pretty predictable if you looked at these in school. If you pass in a negative number, it returns the positive variant of it.

Random Numbers

To generate a somewhat random number between 0 and a smidgen less than 1, you have the `Math.random()` function. This function doesn't take any arguments, but you can simply use it as part of a mathematical expression:

```
var randomNumber = Math.random() * 100;
```

Each time your Math.random function is called, you will see a different number returned for `Math.random()`. To learn all about how to work with this function to generate random numbers, read the **Random Numbers in JS** tutorial here: **http://bit.ly/kirupaRandom**.

THE ABSOLUTE MINIMUM

That's all there is to it for this introductory chapter on numbers and the `Math` object in JavaScript. As you can see, it doesn't get much easier than this. JavaScript provides a very no-frills approach to working with them, and this chapter gave you a slight peek at the edges in case you needed to go there.

Some additional resources and examples that will help you to better understand how numbers in JavaScript can be used:

- **Going from a String to a Number: http://bit.ly/kirupaStrToNum**
- **Random Numbers in JS: http://bit.ly/kirupaRandom**
- **Advanced Random Numbers in JS: http://bit.ly/AdvRandom**
- **Why Don't My Numbers Add Up: http://bit.ly/kirupaFPG**
- **Random Colors in JS: http://bit.ly/kirupaRandomColors**

TIP Just a quick reminder for those of you reading these words in the print or e-book edition of this book: If you go to **www.quepublishing.com** and register this book, you can receive free access to an online Web Edition that not only contains the complete text of this book but also features a short, fun interactive quiz to test your understanding of the chapter you just read.

If you're reading these words in the Web Edition already and want to try your hand at the quiz, then you're in luck – all you need to do is scroll down!

IN THIS CHAPTER

- Understand at a deeper level how Objects work
- Learn to create custom objects
- Demystify the prototype property
- Do some inheriting

16

A DEEPER LOOK AT OBJECTS

In the *Introduction to Objects* ***schtuff*** in **Chapter 11, "Of Pizzas, Types, Primitives, and Objects,"** I provided a very high-level overview of what objects in JavaScript are and how to think about them. That was good enough to cover the basics and some of the built-in types, but we need to go a little deeper. In this chapter, we will make that earlier chapter seem like the tip of a ginormous iceberg:

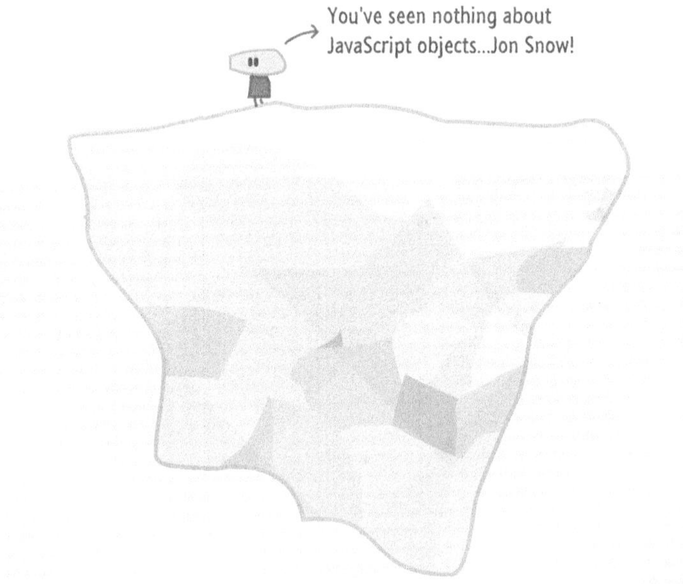

What we are going to do here is re-look at objects in greater detail and touch on the more advanced topics such as using the `Object` object, creating your own custom objects, inheritance, prototypes, and the `this` keyword. If all that I've listed so far makes no sense, it will after you've reached the end of this chapter…I hope.

Onwards!

Meet the Object

At the very bottom of the food chain, you have the `Object` type that lays the groundwork for both custom objects as well as built-in types like `Function,` `Array`, and `RegExp`. Pretty much everything except `null` and `undefined` is directly related to an `Object` or can become one as needed.

As you saw from the introduction to objects forever ago, the functionality that `Object` brings to the table is pretty minimal. It allows you to specify a bunch of named key and value pairs that we lovingly call **properties**. This isn't all that different from what you see in other languages with data structures like hashtables, associate arrays, and dictionaries.

Anyway, all of this is pretty boring. Let's get to some of the more exciting stuff!

Creating Objects

All the cool kids are creating objects these days by using the funny-looking (yet compact) **object literal** syntax:

```
var funnyGuy = {};
```

That's right. Instead of typing in `"new Object()"` like you may have seen in ***old-timey*** books, you can just initialize your object by saying `"{}"`. At the end of this line getting executed, you will have created an object called `funnyGuy` whose type is `Object`. If all of this makes sense so far, great!

This `funnyGuy` object isn't as simple as it looks. Let's dive a little bit deeper and visualize what exactly is going on. On the surface, you just have the `funnyGuy` object:

If you back up and look more broadly at the `funnyGuy` object, you'll realize that it isn't alone here. Because it is an object, is has a connection to the main `Object` type that it derives from:

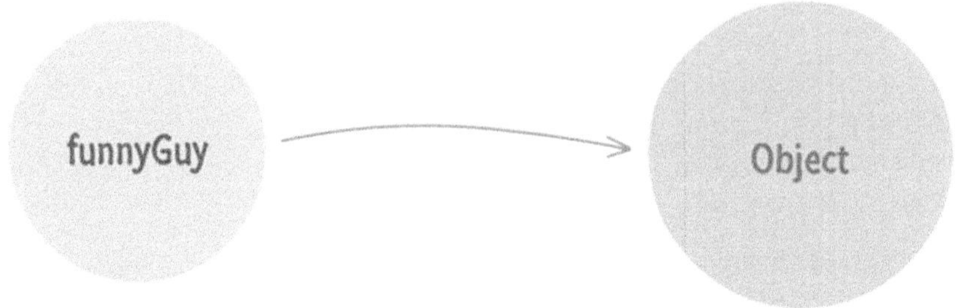

What this connection means is pretty significant. Let's add some more detail to what we have provided so far:

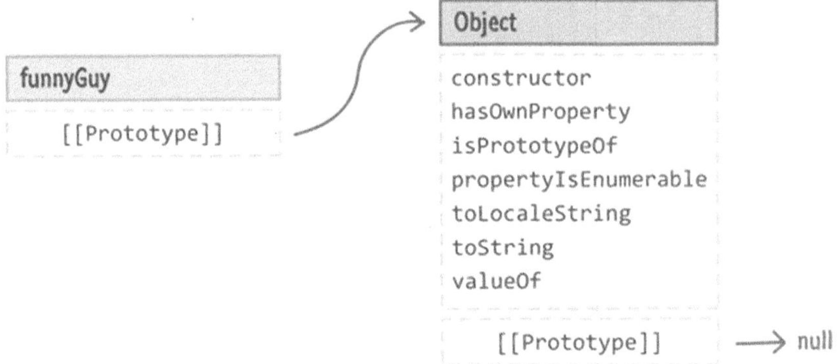

The `funnyGuy` object has no properties defined. That makes sense given what we specified in the code (and can see in the diagram above):

```
var funnyGuy = {};
```

Our `funnyGuy` is simply an empty object. While there may not be any properties *we defined* on it, there is a special internal property that exists called `__proto__` and often visualized as **[[Prototype]]** that points to the internally defined `Object`. If your mind just melted for a second, let me slow down and explain what is going on here.

What the `__proto__` property references is what is known as a `prototype` object:

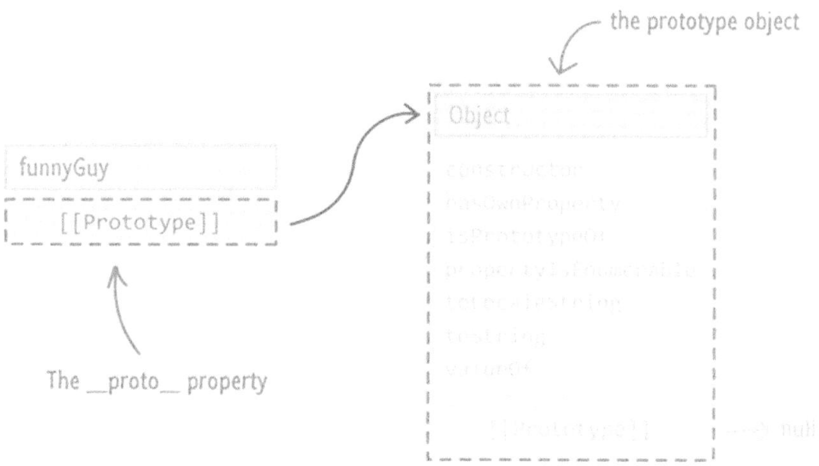

A prototype object is the source that another object is based on. In our case, the `funnyGuy` object is created in the likeness of our `Object` type. What this means is best highlighted by looking at an example. We know that `funnyGuy` contains no properties of its own. Because it is "derived" from our `Object` type, you can access any properties the `Object` contains through `funnyGuy` itself.

For example, I can do something like this:

```
var funnyGuy = {};
funnyGuy.toString();  // [object Object]
```

I am calling the `toString()` method on our `funnyGuy` object. Despite `funnyGuy` not having any property called `toString` on it, what gets returned isn't an error or `undefined`. You actually see the results of the `toString()` method having acted on our `funnyGuy` object.

Think about this in a different way. Your `funnyGuy` object is like a little kid. It doesn't have any money of its own to buy big and expensive things. What the `funnyGuy` object/kid does have is a parent with a credit card. Having access to this credit card allows the kid to go and buy things that he/she wouldn't otherwise be able to. The `funnyGuy/Object` relationship is very much like a child/parent relationship where if the child doesn't have something, he/she can check with a parent next.

ACTING THIS OUT

Getting back to our example and looking at it all one more time, what happened is this. Let's act this out:

Our JavaScript engine was like, ***Hey, funnyGuy! I'm going to call toString() on you.***

The funnyGuy object replied with a, ***Yo...dawg. I don't know what you are talking about.***

The JavaScript engine then said, ***Well, I'm going to check your prototype object and see if it contains a property called toString().***

A few milliseconds later, after finding the prototype object thanks to the `[[Prototype]]` property, our JavaScript engine says, ***Object, my old chum! Do you have a toString() property?***

The Object quickly replies with a **Yep.** and calls the `toString` method.

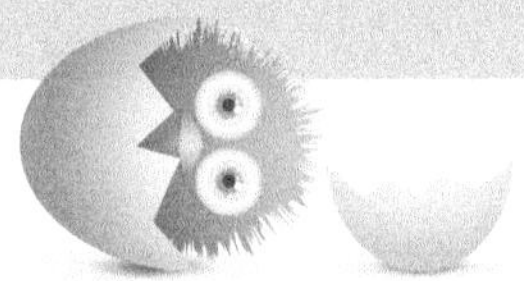

This entire (very dramatic) interaction is part of what is known as a **prototype chain**. If an object doesn't have what you are looking for, the JavaScript engine will navigate to the next object as determined by the `[[Prototype]]` property and keep going until it reaches the very end. The very end is when you try to access the `[[Prototype]]` property on the `Object` itself. You can't go any further beyond `Object`, since that is as basic a type as you can get. I highlight this in the diagrams by having your `Object`'s `[[Prototype]]` refer to **null**.

If you've ever heard of the term **inheritance** as it applies to programming before, what you've just seen is a simple example of it!

Specifying Properties

I bet you didn't imagine that a single line of JavaScript would result in that much explanation, did you? Well, the nice thing is, I front-loaded a lot of conceptual data on you. Hopefully, that makes everything else that you see from here on wards make a lot more sense.

Right now, we still just have an empty object:

```
var funnyGuy = {};
```

Let's specify some properties on it called `firstName` and `lastName`. As with all things in JavaScript, you have multiple ways of defining properties on an element. The method you've seen so far uses the dot notation:

```
var funnyGuy = {};
funnyGuy.firstName = "Conan";
funnyGuy.lastName = "O'Brien";
```

Another approach involves using the square bracket syntax:

```
var funnyGuy = {};
funnyGuy["firstName"] = "Conan";
funnyGuy["lastName"] = "O'Brien";
```

The final approach is by extending our object initializer syntax with the **literal notation** for declaring properties:

```
var funnyGuy = {
    firstName: "Conan",
    lastName: "O'Brien"
};
```

There is no right or wrong approach in how you want to specify properties, so be aware of all three variants and go with one that works best for the situation you find yourself in. In general, I use

1. The literal notation when I am specifying properties directly with a value.
2. The dot notation if I am specifying a property whose values are provided as part of an argument or expression.
3. The square bracket notation if the property name itself is something that is part of an argument or expression.

Regardless of which of the three approaches you used for specifying your properties, the end result is that your `funnyGuy` object will have these properties (and values) defined on itself:

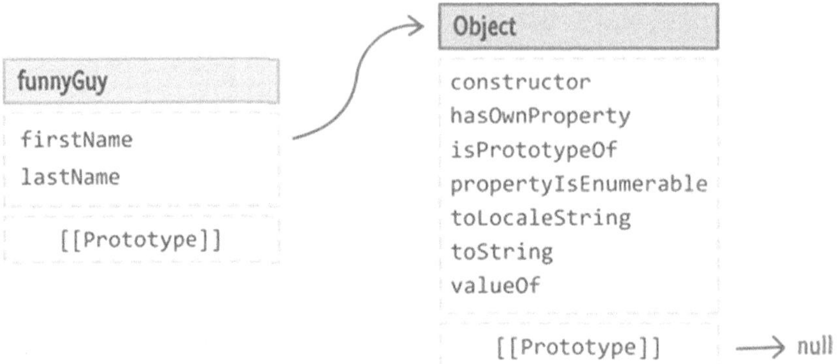

All of this should be straightforward. Let's just do one more thing before we move on to bigger and greener pastures. Let's create a method called **getName** on `funnyGuy` that will return the value of the `firstName` and `lastName` properties. I will just show what this looks like using the literal notation, for it is easy in the other approaches:

```
var funnyGuy = {
    firstName: "Conan",
    lastName: "O'Brien",

    getName: function() {
        return "Name is: " + this.firstName + " " + this.lastName;
    }
};
```

Our `getName` property's value is a function whose body simply returns a string that includes the value of our `firstName` and `lastName` properties. To call the `getName` property, ahem…method, this is all you have to do:

```
var funnyGuy = {
    firstName: "Conan",
    lastName: "O'Brien",
```

```
    getName: function() {
        return "Name is: " + this.firstName + " " + this.lastName;
    }
};

alert(funnyGuy.getName()); // Name is: Conan O'Brien
```

Yep, that's all there is to declaring an object and setting properties on it. Indirectly, you learned a whole lot about what goes on behind the scenes when a simple object is created. You'll need all of this fancy learnin' in the next section when we kick everything up a few notches.

Creating Custom Objects

Working with the generic `Object` and putting properties on it serves a useful purpose, but its awesomeness fades away really quickly when you are creating many objects that are basically the same thing:

```
var funnyGuy = {
    firstName: "Conan",
    lastName: "O'Brien",

    getName: function () {
        return "Name is: " + this.firstName + " " + this.lastName;
    }
};

var theDude = {
    firstName: "Jeffrey",
    lastName: "Lebowski",

    getName: function () {
        return "Name is: " + this.firstName + " " + this.lastName;
    }
};

var detective = {
    firstName: "Adrian",
    lastName: "Monk",
```

```
    getName: function () {
        return "Name is: " + this.firstName + " " + this.lastName;
    }
};
```

Currently, if we had to visualize what we have right now, this is what you will see:

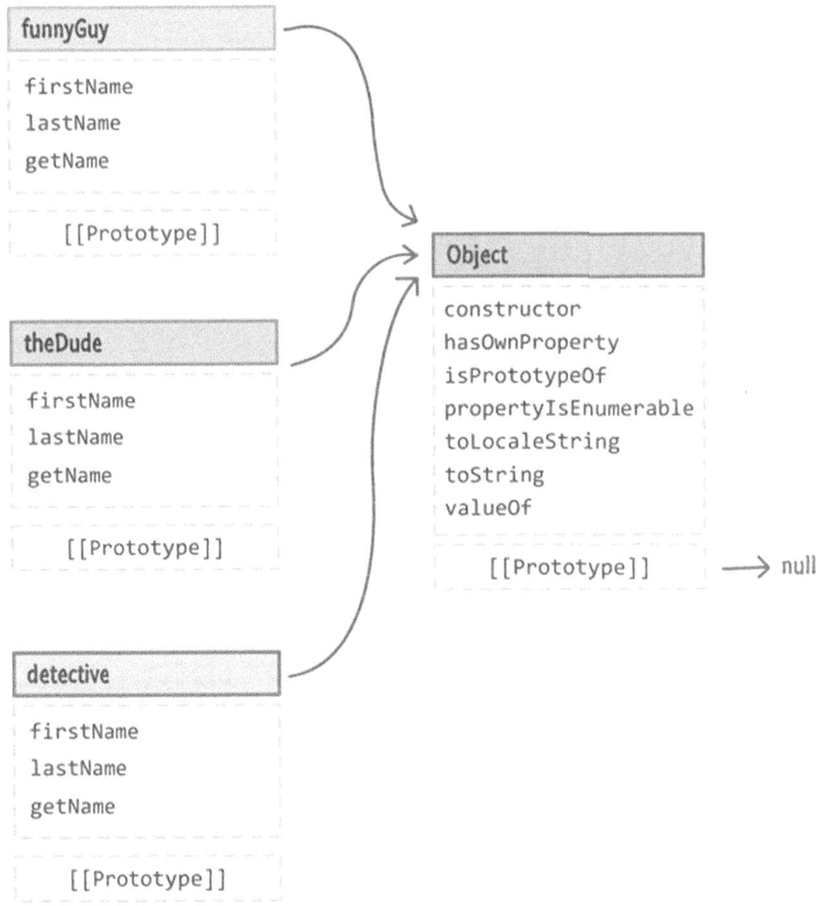

There is a lot of duplicated stuff here that is, frankly, unnecessary. Let's fix that using what we've learned about inheritance and the prototype chain.

What we want to do is create an intermediate **parent** object that contains the properties that are more generic and not necessary to be on the **child** object itself. From what we have here, the `firstName` and `lastName` properties are going to be unique for each object we create. Because of that, these two properties still belong on the `funnyGuy`, `theDude`, and `detective` objects.

Our `getName` property, though, does not have to be duplicated for each object. This is something we can parcel off into a parent object that the rest of the objects can inherit from. Let's call this object `person`:

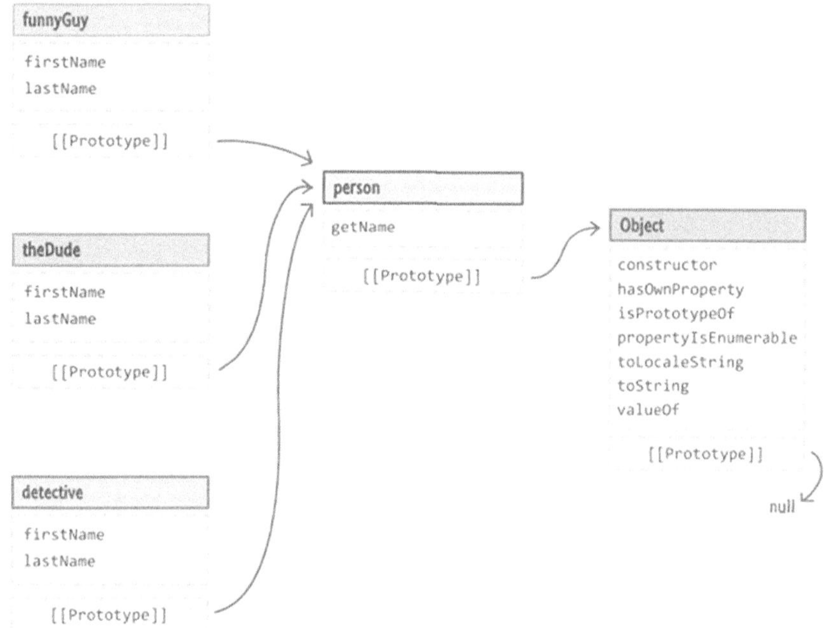

Visually, this makes sense. How do we end up creating something like this?

Well, thinking out loud, we need to create our `funnyGuy`, `theDude`, and `detective` objects and ensure the `firstName` and `lastName` properties are defined on them. That's easy. Of course, if this is all we did, this wouldn't be adequate. The prototype for these objects will be `Object`, and we don't want that. We want the `person` object with the `getName` property to be a part of our prototype chain as the immediate parent. The way we do that is by ensuring the `[[Prototype]]` property on `funnyGuy`, `theDude`, and `detective` references `person`.

In order to do this, we use the extremely awesome `Object.create` method. Let me quickly explain what it does before we see it in action. The `Object.create` method, as its name implies, creates a new object. As part of creating the object, it allows you to specify what your newly created object's prototype will be. Strange how what we want to do and what `Object.create` provides are identical! :P

Let's use `Object.create` and the rest of the code that brings the diagram and the explanation you've seen to life:

```
var person = {
    getName: function () {
        return "Name is " + this.firstName + " " + this.lastName;
    }
};

var funnyGuy = Object.create(person);
funnyGuy.firstName = "Conan";
funnyGuy.lastName = "O'Brien";

var theDude = Object.create(person);
theDude.firstName = "Jeffrey";
theDude.lastName = "Lebowski";

var detective = Object.create(person);
detective.firstName = "Adrian";
detective.lastName = "Monk";
```

Let's look at all of this code in greater detail. First, we have our **person** object:

```
var person = {
    getName: function () {
        return "Name is " + this.firstName + " " + this.lastName;
    }
};
```

There is nothing special going on here. We create a new **person** object whose type is `Object`. It's `[[Prototype]]` property will point you to the `Object` type. It contains a method called **getName** that returns some string involving **this.firstName** and **this.lastName**. We'll come back to the **this** keyword and how this works shortly, so keep that one under your hat for now.

After creating our person object, this is what our world looks like right now:

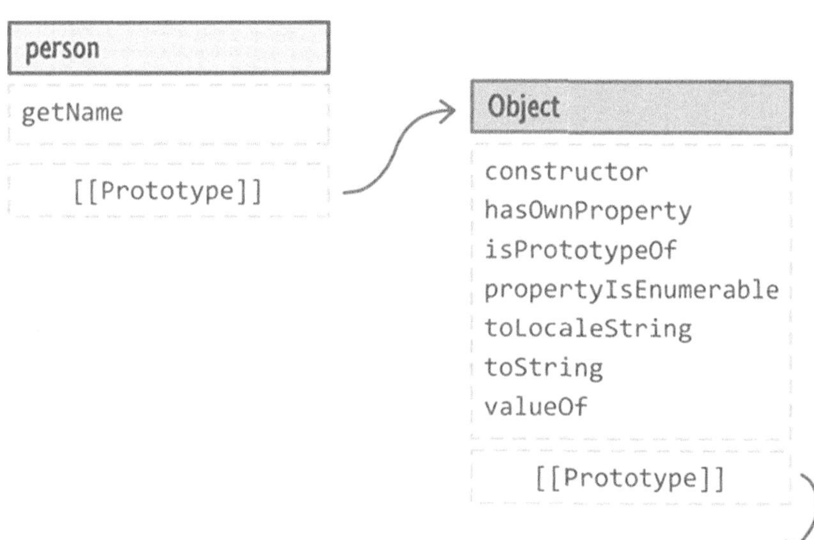

In the next line, we declare our funnyGuy variable and initialize it to the object that gets returned by Object.create:

```
var funnyGuy = Object.create(person);
```

Notice that I pass in the person object as an argument to Object.create. Like I mentioned earlier, what this means is you create a new object with the [[Prototype]] value pointing to our person object. This is how things look now:

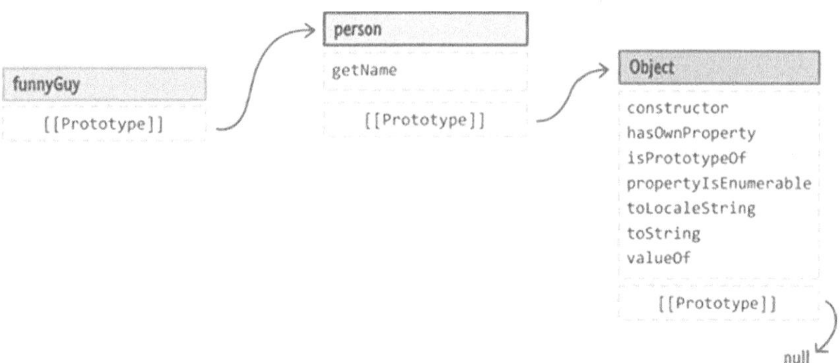

We created our **funnyGuy** object with the **person** object set as its prototype object. In the next two lines in our code, I define the **firstName** and **lastName** properties on the object:

```
var funnyGuy = Object.create(person);
funnyGuy.firstName = "Conan";
funnyGuy.lastName = "O'Brien";
```

This is your standard, run-of-the-mill property declaration on an object using a name and value. What happens should be of no surprise to you:

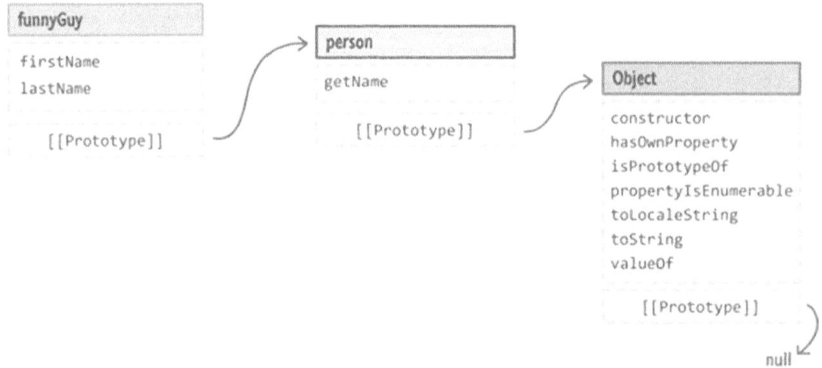

We just created our **funnyGuy** object and set the **firstName** and **lastName** properties on it. We just have our **theDude** and **detective** objects left, and the process for setting the **firstName** and **lastName** properties is the same, as you can see. Let's skip looking at them in further detail and move on to shinier and more awesome things instead :P

At this point, if you've been following along and understand what is going on, you should be quite impressed with yourself. Many people who work with JavaScript for a very long time have difficulty grasping how inheritance and prototypes tie in to object creation. Wrapping your head around all of this is quite an accomplishment.

However, we are not done yet. Before you pop the champagne bottle and start celebrating, there is one last thing we need to look at before we call it a day.

The this Keyword

Let's go back to our person object and, more specifically, the getName property:

```
var person = {
    getName: function () {
        return "The name is " + this.firstName + " " +
          this.lastName;
    }
};
```

When you call getName, depending on which object you called it from, you'll see the appropriate name returned. For example, let's say you do the following:

```
var funnyGuy = Object.create(person);
funnyGuy.firstName = "Conan";
funnyGuy.lastName = "O'Brien";

alert(funnyGuy.getName());
```

When you run this, you'll see a dialog box that looks as follows:

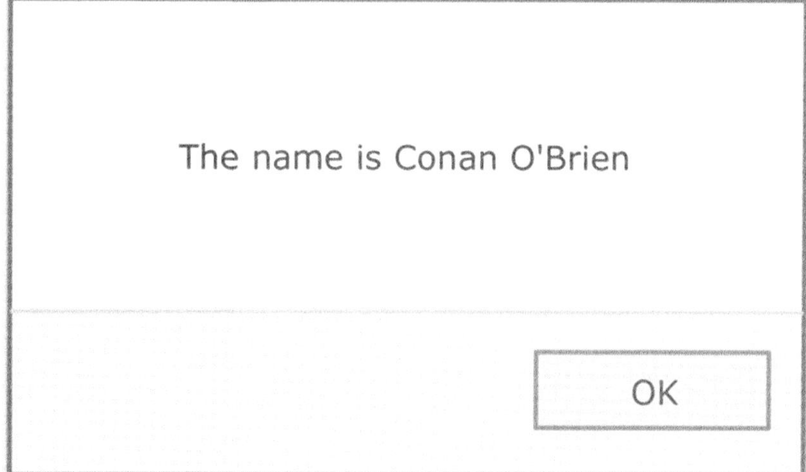

If you look at the `getName` method again, there is absolutely no sign of existence of the `firstName` or `lastName` properties on the `person` object. When a property doesn't exist, I mentioned that we walk down the prototype chain from parent to parent. In this case, that would be `Object`:

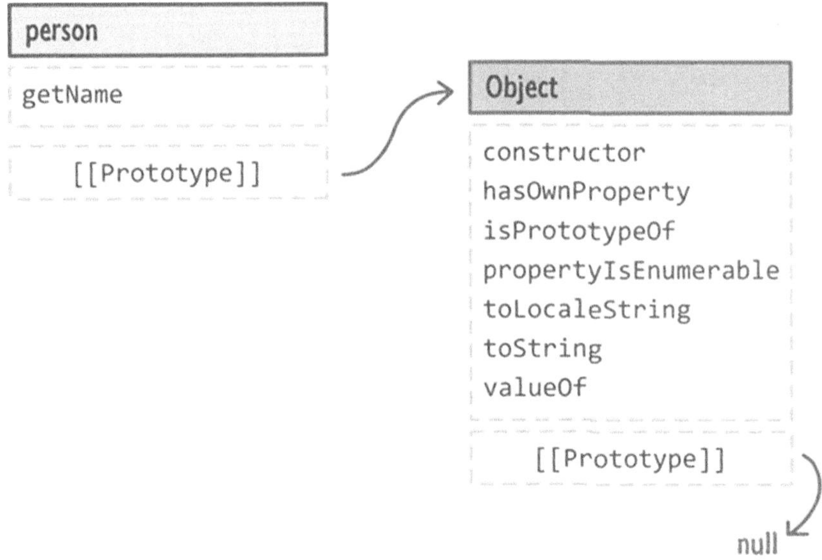

There is no sign of existence of the `firstName` or `lastName` properties on `Object` either. How is it that this `getName` method happens to work and return the right values?

The answer has to do with the `this` keyword that precedes `firstName` and `lastName`. The `this` keyword refers to the object that our `getName` method is pointing to. That object is, in this case, `funnyGuy`:

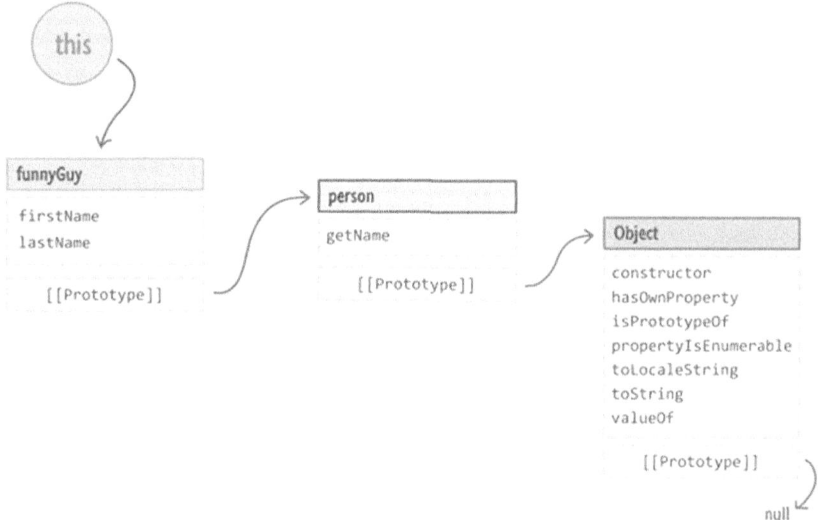

At the point where the `getName` method is evaluated and the `firstName` and `lastName` properties have to be resolved, the lookup starts at whatever the `this` keyword is pointing to. In our case, the `this` keyword is pointing to the `funnyGuy` object—an object that contains the `firstName` and `lastName` properties!

Knowing what the `this` keyword refers to is something we'll devote more time to later, but what you've seen until now will you get you pretty far.

THE ABSOLUTE MINIMUM

Because so much fuss is made about JavaScript's object orientedness, it is only natural that a topic that covers it would be as wide and deep as what you've seen here. A bulk of what you saw here dealt with inheritance directly or indirectly where objects are derived and based on other objects. Unlike other, more class-ical languages that use classes as templates for objects, JavaScript has no such concept of a class. JavaScript uses what is known as a **prototypical inheritance model**. You don't instantiate objects from a template. Instead, you create objects either from scratch or, more commonly, by copying/cloning another object.

In the bazillion pages here, I tried to reinforce JavaScript's new functionality for working with objects and extending them for your own needs. There is still more to cover, so take a break and we'll touch upon some more interesting topics in the near future that extend what you've seen in more powerful, expressive, and awesome ways.

Some additional resources and examples:

- **Understanding "Prototypes" in JS: http://bit.ly/kirupaJSPrototypes**
- **A Plain English Guide to JS Prototypes: http://bit.ly/kirupaPrototypesGuide**
- **How Does JavaScript ".prototype" Work?: http://bit.ly/kirupaPrototypeWork**

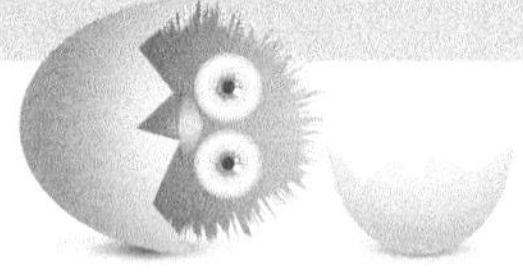

TIP Just a quick reminder for those of you reading these words in the print or e-book edition of this book: If you go to **www.quepublishing.com** and register this book, you can receive free access to an online Web Edition that not only contains the complete text of this book but also features a short, fun interactive quiz to test your understanding of the chapter you just read.

If you're reading these words in the Web Edition already and want to try your hand at the quiz, then you're in luck – all you need to do is scroll down!

IN THIS CHAPTER

- Extend your objects' functionality
- Learn more about the prototype chain

17

EXTENDING BUILT-IN OBJECTS

As you know very well by now, JavaScript comes from the factory with a good supply of built-in objects. These objects provide some of the core functionality for working with text, numbers, collections of data, dates, and a whole lot more. As you become more familiar with JavaScript and start doing ***interesting-er*** and ***cleverer*** things, you'll often find that you want to do more and go farther than what the built-in objects allow.

Let's take a look at an example of when something like this might occur. Below is an example of how you can shuffle the contents of an array:

```
function shuffle(input) {
    for (var i = input.length - 1; i >= 0; i--) {

        var randomIndex = Math.floor(Math.random() * (i + 1));
        var itemAtIndex = input[randomIndex];

        input[randomIndex] = input[i];
        input[i] = itemAtIndex;
    }
    return input;
}
```

The way you use this `shuffle` function is by simply calling it and passing in the array whose contents you want shuffled:

```
var tempArray = [1, 2, 3, 4, 5, 6, 7, 8, 9, 10];
shuffle(tempArray);

// and the result is...
alert(tempArray);
```

After this code has run, the end result is that the contents of your array are now rearranged. Now, this functionality is pretty useful. I would say this is sooo useful, the shuffling ability should be a part of the `Array` object and be as easily accessible as `push`, `pop`, `slice`, and other doo-dads the `Array` object has.

If the `shuffle` function were a part of the `Array` object, you could simply use it as follows:

```
var tempArray = [1, 2, 3, 4, 5, 6, 7, 8, 9, 10];
tempArray.shuffle();
```

This is an example of us extending a built-in object (the `Array`) with some functionality that we defined (the `shuffle`). In this chapter, we are going to look at how exactly to accomplish this, why it all works, and why extending built-in objects is pretty controversial.

Onwards!

Say Hello to Prototype...Again—Sort of!

Extending a built-in object with new functionality sounds complicated, but it is really simple once you understand what needs to be done. To help with this, we are going to look at a combination of sample code and diagrams all involving the very friendly `Array` object:

The Array, 1988

That is not what arrays look like! They are far less menacing.

Um...anyway, let's say that we have the following code:

```
var tempArray = [1, 2, 3, 4, 5, 6, 7, 8, 9, 10];
```

If we were to diagram the full hierarchy of the `tempArray` object, it would look as follows:

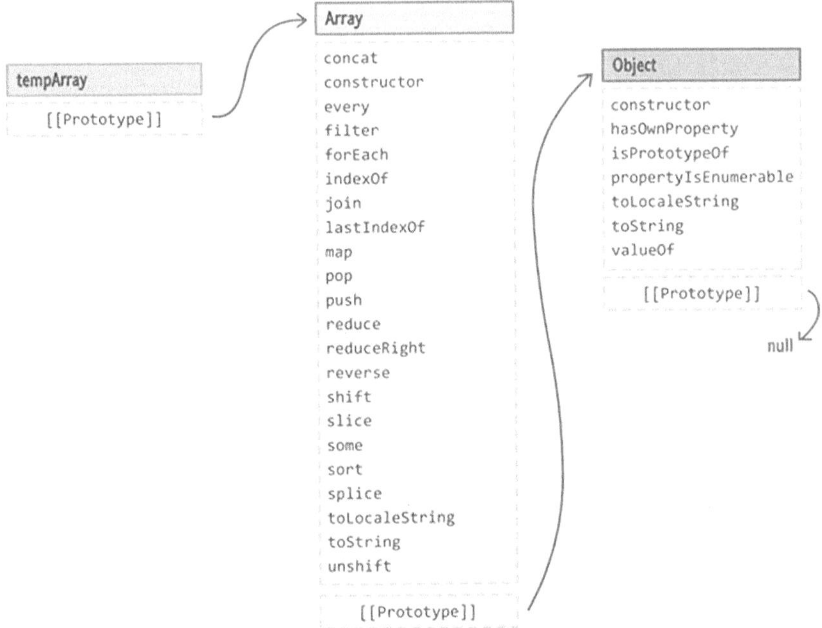

On the left, we have our `tempArray` object that is an instance of `Array`. The built-in `Array` object is derived from the basic `Object` type. Now, what we want to do is extend the `Array` object with our `shuffle` function. What this means is that we need to figure out a way to get our `shuffle` function inserted into our `Array` object itself:

Here is the part where the quirkiness of JavaScript shines through. We don't have access to the `Array` object source code. We can't find the function or object that makes up the `Array` and insert our shuffle function into it like we might for a custom object that we defined. Your built-in objects, such as the `Array`, are defined deep inside your browser's volcanic underbelly where no human being can go. We need to take another approach.

That *another approach* involves casually sneaking in and attaching your functionality by using the `Array` object's `prototype` property. That would look something like this:

```
Array.prototype.shuffle = function () {
    var input = this;

    for (var i = input.length - 1; i >= 0; i--) {

        var randomIndex = Math.floor(Math.random() * (i + 1));
        var itemAtIndex = input[randomIndex];

        input[randomIndex] = input[i];
        input[i] = itemAtIndex;
    }
    return input;
}
```

Notice that our `shuffle` function is declared on `Array.prototype`! As part of this attachment, we made a minor change to how the function works. The function no longer takes an argument for referencing the array you need shuffled:

```
function shuffle(input) {
        .
        .
        .
        .
        .
}
```

Instead, because this function is now a part of the `Array` object, the `this` keyword inside the function body points to the array that needs shuffling:

```
Array.prototype.shuffle = function () {
    var input = this;
        .
        .
        .
        .
}
```

Taking a step back, once you run this code, your `shuffle` function will find itself shoulder to shoulder with all of the other built-in methods the `Array` object provides:

If you wanted to access the `shuffle` property (err...method...I gotta stop doing that!), you can now do so using the approach we had initially desired:

```
var tempArray = [1, 2, 3, 4, 5, 6, 7, 8, 9, 10]
tempArray.shuffle();
```

This is because the `prototype` property provides you with direct access to your `Array` object's insides. Declaring the `shuffle` function on it gave us the result we wanted. Best of all, any new arrays you create will also have access to the shuffle functionality by default thanks to how prototype inheritance works.

Extending Built-in Objects Is Controversial

Given how easy it is to extend a built-in object's functionality by declaring methods and properties using the `prototype` object, it's easy to think that everybody loves the ability to do all of this. As it turns out, extending built-in objects is a bit controversial. The reasons for this controversy revolve around the fact that...

You Don't Control the Built-in Object's Future

There is nothing preventing a future implementation of JavaScript from including its own version of shuffle that applies to `Array` objects. At this point, you have a collision where your version of `shuffle` and the browser's version of `shuffle` are in conflict with each other - especially if their behavior or performance characteristics wildly differ. Rut ruh!

Some Functionality Should Not Be Extended or Overridden

Nothing prevents you from using what you've learned here to modify the behavior of existing methods and properties. For example, this is me changing how the `slice` behavior works:

```
Array.prototype.slice = function () {
    var input = this;
    input[0] = "This is an awesome example!";

    return input;
}

var tempArray = [1, 2, 3, 4, 5, 6, 7, 8, 9, 10];
tempArray.slice();

// and the result is...
alert(tempArray);
```

While this is a terrible example, this does show how easy it was for me to break existing functionality.

FURTHER READING

To see a more comprehensive discussion and further reading around this controversy, check out this StackOverflow thread: **http://stackoverflow.com/questions/8859828/**.

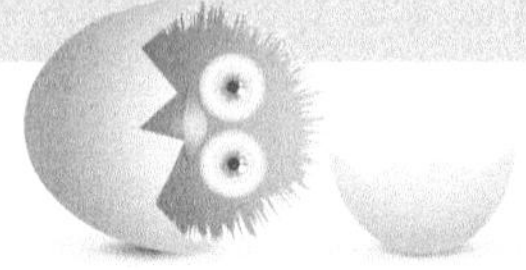

THE ABSOLUTE MINIMUM: WHAT SHOULD YOU DO?

My answer to what you need to do is simple: **Use your best judgment!** The two cases I outlined are only a few of the numerous issues that people raise when extending built-in objects is discussed. For the most part, all of the objections are valid. The question you need to ask is, "Are these objections valid for my particular scenario?" My guess is that they probably won't be.

From personal experience, I have never had any issues extending built-in objects with my own functionality. I wrote this shuffle function years ago, and no browser as of now has even hinted at implementing their own version of it. I am certainly not complaining! Second, for any functionality I do add, I test to make sure that it works well across the browsers I am currently targeting. As long as your testing is somewhat comprehensive (probably the latest one or two versions of the major browsers), you should be good to go.

If you are worried about future-proofing your app, name any properties or methods in such a way that only your app would use them. For example, the chances of `Array.prototype.kirupaShuffle` being introduced by any future browser release is pretty close to zero :P

Anyway, now that we've sufficiently covered some detailed topics around objects in this and the previous chapters, let's go back to looking at some of the other types you will run into before we move on to some really exciting stuff in a little bit.

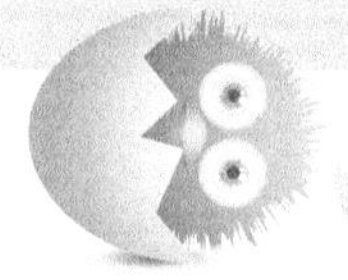

TIP Just a quick reminder for those of you reading these words in the print or e-book edition of this book: If you go to **www.quepublishing.com** and register this book, you can receive free access to an online Web Edition that not only contains the complete text of this book but also features a short, fun interactive quiz to test your understanding of the chapter you just read.

If you're reading these words in the Web Edition already and want to try your hand at the quiz, then you're in luck – all you need to do is scroll down!

IN THIS CHAPTER

- Learn more about what goes on behind *true* and *false*
- Understand what boolean objects and functions do
- Find out the difference between *simple* inequality operators and *strict* inequality operators

BOOLEANS AND THE STRICTER === AND !== OPERATORS

While it's polite to say that all types are interesting and fun to be around, you and I both know that is a lie. Some types are just boring. The boolean type is one such example. Here is the reason why. Whenever you initialize a variable using either **true** or **false**, you create a boolean:

```
var sunny = false;
var traffic = true;
```

Congratulations. If you know just this, you are 80% of the way there in fully understanding how booleans operate. Of course, 80% isn't really adequate when you think about it. It's like eating a hot dog without any condiments. It's like watching a live concert and leaving before the encore set. It's like leaving a sentence mid.

What I am going to expand upon a bit in this chapter is the other 20% made up of various boolean quirks; the `Boolean` object; the `Boolean` function; and the important === and `!==` operators.

The Boolean Object

Booleans are meant to be used as primitives. I'm going to be extra lazy and just reuse the example you saw a few moments earlier to show you an example of what a boolean primitive looks like:

```
var sunny = false;
var traffic = true;
```

Like you've seen so many times already, behind every primitive there is an Object-based representation lurking in the shadows. The way you create a new boolean Object is by using the `new` keyword, the `Boolean` constructor name, and an initial value:

```
var boolObject = new Boolean(false);
var anotherBool = new Boolean(true);
```

The initial values you can pass in to the Boolean constructor are commonly **true** and **false**, but you can pretty much pass anything in there that will result in the final evaluation being **true** or **false**. I will detail what kinds of values will predictably result in a **true** or **false** outcome in a little bit, but here is the obligatory warning from the Surgeon General about this approach: *Unless you really REALLY want a Boolean object, you should stick with primitives.*

The Boolean Function

There is one major advantage the `Boolean` constructor provides, and that advantage revolves around being able to pass in any arbitrary value or expression as part of creating your `Boolean` object:

```
var boolObject = new Boolean(arbitrary expression);
```

This is really advantageous because you may find yourself wanting to evaluate a boolean expression where the data you end up with isn't a clean **true** or a **false**. This is especially common when you are dealing with external data or code, and you have no control over which of the various ***falsey*** and ***truthy*** values you get. Here is a contrived example:

```
var isMovieAvailable = getMovieData[4];
```

The value for `isMovieAvailable` is probably a **true** or **false**. When it comes to processing data, you often have no guarantee that something at some point will break or change what gets returned. Just like in real life, simply hoping that things will work is never adequate without you taking some actionable steps. The Boolean function is one such step.

Now, creating your own function to deal with the ambiguity may be overkill, but the downside with the `Boolean` constructor is that you are obviously left with a boolean object—which isn't desirable. Fortunately, there is a way to get the flexibility of the `Boolean` constructor with the lightweightedness of a boolean primitive extremely easily. That way is led by the `Boolean` function:

```
var bool = Boolean(true);
```

The Boolean function allows you to pass in arbitrary values and expressions while still returning a **primitive boolean value of true or false**. The main difference in how you use it compared to the constructor approach is that you don't have the `new` keyword. W00t! Anyway, let's take a few moments and look at the variety of things you can pass in to the `Boolean` function, and note that all of this will also apply to what you can pass in to the `Boolean` constructor you saw in the previous section as well.

The values you can pass in to return **false** are `null`, `undefined`, empty/nothing, **0**, an empty string, **NaN**, and (of course) **false**.

```
var bool;

bool = Boolean(null);
bool = Boolean(undefined);
bool = Boolean();
bool = Boolean(0);
bool = Boolean("");
bool = Boolean(NaN);
bool = Boolean(false);
```

In all of these examples, the `bool` variable will return **false**. To return **true**, you can pass in a value of **true** or ANYTHING that results in something other than the various *false* values you saw earlier:

```
var bool;

bool = Boolean(true);
bool = Boolean("hello");
bool = Boolean("Liam Neesons" + "Bruce Willie");
bool = Boolean(new Boolean()); // Inception!!!
bool = Boolean("false"); // "false" is a string
```

In these examples, the `bool` variable will return a **true**. That may seem bizarre given some of the statements, so let's look at a few of the subtle things in play here. If what you are evaluating is an object, such as `new Boolean(new Boolean())` the evaluation will always be **true**. The reason is that the mere existence of an object will trigger the **true** switch, and calling `new Boolean()` results in a new object. Extending this logic a bit, it means the following if statement actually results in a **true** as well:

```
var boolObject = new Boolean(false);

if (boolObject) {
    alert("Bool, you so crazy!!!");
}
```

It doesn't matter that the object you are evaluating is secretly a **false** in disguise… or a `String` object or an `Array` and so on. The rules for primitives are more simple. If you are passing in a primitive (or something that evaluates to a primitive), anything other than `null`, `undefined`, **0**, an empty string, or **false** will result in a result of **true**.

Strict Equality and Inequality Operators

The last thing we are going to look at is going to combine what you know about types and booleans to add a twist to the various conditional operators you saw earlier. So, you know about == and != and have probably seen them in use a few times. These are the equality and inequality operators that let you know if two things are either equal or unequal. Here is the plot twist. There is a subtle and deviant behavior they exhibit that you may not be aware of.

Here is an example:

```
function theSolution(answer) {
    if (answer == 42) {
        alert("You have nothing more to learn!");
    }
}

theSolution("42"); //42 is passed in as a string
```

In this example, the expression `answer == 42` will evaluate to **true**. This works despite the 42 you are passing in being a string and the 42 you are checking against being a number. What is going on here? In what kind of a world is a string and a number equal? With the == and != operators, this is expected behavior. The value for the two things you are comparing is 42. To make this work, JavaScript forces the two different yet similar values to be the same under the hood. This is formally known as **type coercion**.

The problem is that this behavior can be undesirable—especially when this is happening without you knowing about it. To avoid situations like this, you have stricter versions of the equality and inequality operators, and they are === and !== respectively. What these operators do is that they check for **both value and type** and do not perform any type coercion. They basically force you to write code where the burden on ensuring true equality or inequality falls squarely on you. That is a good thing™.

Let's fix our earlier example by replacing the == operator with the === operator:

```
function theSolution(answer) {
    if (answer === 42) {
        alert("You have nothing more to learn!");
    }
}

theSolution("42"); // 42 is passed in as a string
```

This time around, the conditional expression will evaluate to **false**. In this stricter world, a string and number are of different types despite the values being similar. Because no type coercion takes place, the final result is **false**.

The general word on the street is *to always use the stricter forms of the equality and inequality operators.* If anything, using them will help you to spot errors in your code—errors that might otherwise turn out very difficult to identify.

CAUTION If you are comparing two different objects, the strict equality operator (and the not-so-strict equality operator) won't work as you might expect. For example `new String("A") == new String("A")` will be **false**. Keep that in mind when comparing the equality or inequality of two individual objects.

THE ABSOLUTE MINIMUM

Booleans make up one of the most frequently used types in your code. They play a key role in allowing your code to branch out into different directions despite the simplicity they exhibit on the surface. While I can count on one hand the number of times I had to use the `Boolean` function, there aren't enough hands with fingers for me to count the number of times I've encountered these strange things in the wild.

TIP Just a quick reminder for those of you reading these words in the print or e-book edition of this book: If you go to **www.quepublishing.com** and register this book, you can receive free access to an online Web Edition that not only contains the complete text of this book but also features a short, fun interactive quiz to test your understanding of the chapter you just read.

If you're reading these words in the Web Edition already and want to try your hand at the quiz, then you're in luck – all you need to do is scroll down!

IN THIS CHAPTER

- Learn about when values don't exist
- Understand what to do with *null* and *undefined*

19

NULL AND UNDEFINED

One of the great mysteries of the world revolves around making sense of `null` and `undefined`. Most code you see is littered with them, and you've probably run into them yourself a few times. As mysteries go, making sense of `null` and `undefined` isn't particularly bizarre. It is just dreadfully boring...like the most boring (yet important) thing about JavaScript you'll ever have to learn.

Onward!

Null

Let's start with `null`. The `null` keyword is also sort of a primitive that fills a special role in the world of JavaScript. It is an explicit definition that stands for **no value**. If you've ever browsed through code others have written, you'll probably see `null` appear quite a number of times. It is quite popular, for the advantage of `null` lies in its definitiveness. Instead of having variables contain stale values or mystery `undefined` values, setting it to `null` is a clear indication that you *want the value to not exist.*

This advantage is important when you are writing code and want to initialize or clear a variable to something that represents nothing.

Here is an example:

```
var test = null;

if (test === null) {
    test = "Peter Griffin";
} else {
    test = null;
}
```

The `null` primitive isn't a naturally occurring resource. It is something you consciously assign, so you will often see it used as part of variable declarations or passed in as arguments to function calls. Using `null` is easy. Checking for the value of `null` is pretty easy as well:

```
if (test === null) {
    // do something interesting...or not
}
```

The only thing to note is that you should use the === operator instead of the lowly == one. While the world won't end if you use ==, it's good practice.

IS NULL A PRIMITIVE OR AN OBJECT?

The **null** primitive is similar to your string and boolean built-in types in that it also has an object representation. There is one quirk you need to note, though. Despite what I just said, doing `typeof null` at any given time will show it as being an object. That isn't how a primitive behaves, and the reason for this behavior has to do with a longstanding bug in the JavaScript language. The word on the street is that this bug may get fixed in the future, so...yeah! Go team.

Undefined

Here is where things get a little interesting. To represent something that isn't defined, you have the `undefined` primitive. You see `undefined` in a few cases, the most common ones being when you try to access a variable that hasn't been initialized or when accessing the value of a function that doesn't actually return anything.

Here is a code snippet that points out `undefined` in a few of its natural habitats:

```
var myVariable;
alert(myVariable); // undefined

function doNothing() {
    // watch paint dry
    return;
}

var weekendPlans = doNothing();
alert(weekendPlans); // undefined
```

In your code, you probably won't be assigning `undefined` to anything. Instead, you will spend time checking to see if the value of something is `undefined`. You have several ways to perform this check. The first is a naive way that usually almost always works:

```
if (myVariable == undefined) {
    // do something
}
```

The downside of this approach is that you could potentially overwrite `undefined` to something like **true**, and that would break your code. The safest way to perform a check for `undefined` involves `typeof` and the === operator:

```
var myVariable;

if (typeof myVariable === "undefined") {
    alert("Define me!!!");
}
```

This ensures that you will perform a check for undefined and always return the correct answer.

NULL == UNDEFINED, BUT NULL !== UNDEFINED

Continuing the == and === weirdness, if you ever check for `null == undefined`, the answer will be a **true**. If you use === and have null === `undefined`, the answer in this case will be **false**.

The reason is that == does type coercion where it arm-twists types to conform to what JavaScript thinks the value should be. Using ===, you check for both type and value. This is a more comprehensive check that detects that `undefined` and `null` are indeed two different things.

A hat tip to senocular[1] (aka Trevor McCauley) for pointing this out!

1. **https://twitter.com/senocular**

THE ABSOLUTE MINIMUM

There is a reason why I saved these built-in types for last. `Null` and `undefined` are the least exciting of the bunch, but they are also often the ones that are the most misunderstood. Knowing how to use `null` and detecting for it and `undefined` is a very important skill to get right. Not getting it right will lead to very subtle errors that are going to be hard to pinpoint.

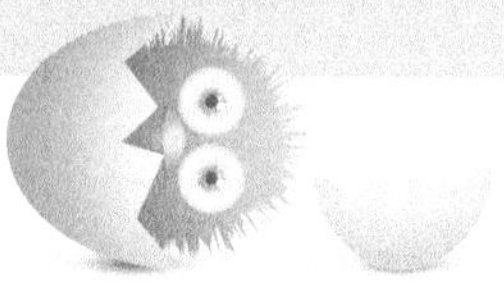

TIP Just a quick reminder for those of you reading these words in the print or e-book edition of this book: If you go to **www.quepublishing.com** and register this book, you can receive free access to an online Web Edition that not only contains the complete text of this book but also features a short, fun interactive quiz to test your understanding of the chapter you just read.

If you're reading these words in the Web Edition already and want to try your hand at the quiz, then you're in luck – all you need to do is scroll down!

IN THIS CHAPTER

- Understand anonymous functions
- Learn how to invoke a block of code immediately
- Take our knowledge of scope further by creating data that is private

20

IMMEDIATELY INVOKED FUNCTION EXPRESSIONS

We are going to take a slight detour from our coverage of objects to focus on something important that can only properly make sense at this point. You'll see why in a few moments when we walk through some examples. Anyway, by now, you probably know enough functions in JavaScript to be dangerously productive. Functions allow you to group statements together. If you give your function a name, you can re-use those grouped statements a whole bunch of times, as in the example that follows:

```
function areYouLucky() {
    // Pick a random number between 0 and 100
    var foo = Math.floor(Math.random() * 100);

    if (foo > 50) {
        alert("You are lucky!");
    } else {
        alert("You are not lucky!");
    }
}

// calling this function!
areYouLucky();
```

If you don't give your functions a name, that is totally cool as well. They are known as anonymous functions, and they look as follows:

```
// anonymous function #1
var isLucky = function () {
    var foo = Math.round(Math.random() * 100);

    if (foo > 50) {
        return "You are lucky!";
    } else {
        return "You are not lucky!";
    }
};
var me = isLucky();
alert(me);
// anonymous function #2
window.setTimeout(function () {
    alert("Everything is awesome!!!");
}, 2000);
```

These anonymous functions can only be called if they are associated with a variable as shown in the first example. They can also be called if they are provided as part of another function (such as `setTimeOut`) that knows what to do with them.

In this chapter, we are going to look at another function variation known as an **Immediately Invoked Function Expression**. Friends like us just call it IIFE (pronounced "iffy"). At first, what it does might seem a bit boring and unnecessary. As we get more familiar with it, I will describe some of its use cases and why you may find yourself both seeing and using these IIFEs a whole lot. By the end, IIFEs will probably still be very boring, but at least they will seem quite useful and necessary...hopefully!

Onwards!

Writing a Simple IIFE

To be very blunt, an IIFE is nothing more than a function (surrounded by a whole bunch of parentheses) that executes immediately. Before we do anything else, let's just write an IIFE and prove to ourselves that it actually does whatever it is supposed to do. Below is a simple IIFE:

```
(function() {
    var shout = "I AM ALIVE!!!";
    alert(shout);
})();
```

Go ahead and add these few lines of code and preview it in your browser. If everything worked properly, you will see *I AM ALIVE!!!* displayed. If things didn't work properly and you don't see that, make sure your many parentheses are in the correct locations. The most common illness that afflicts IIFEs are mismatched or misplaced parentheses! Anyway, now that you have created a working IIFE, let's peel back the layers and look at what exactly is going on.

First, you have your function with the code you want to execute:

```
function() {
    var shout = "I AM ALIVE!!!";
    alert(shout);
}
```

This is just a simple anonymous function that displays some obnoxious all-caps text. As this function stands, though, JavaScript has no idea what to do with it. This function is invalid syntax. To make it more valid, add the `()` after the function body:

```
function() {
    var shout = "I AM ALIVE!!!";
    alert(shout);
}()
```

Adding the `()` generally means you intend for whatever preceded the `()` to execute immediately. When you do this, JavaScript will still complain because this is also not valid syntax. The reason is that you need to tell JavaScript that this function you want to execute is actually an expression. The easiest way to do that is to *wrap your function inside another pair of parentheses*:

```
(function() {
    var shout = "I AM ALIVE!!!";
    alert(shout);
})();
```

Your entire function is now treated as an expression. Following this with the `()` you saw a few moments ago allows your function expression to be executed. You could say that this *function expression* gets executed (aka *invoked*) *immediately* once JavaScript encounters it.

Writing an IIFE That Takes Arguments

At first, the most difficult thing to grasp about IIFEs is that they are nothing more than simple functions. These simple functions just happen to wear all sorts of crazy parentheses to help them execute immediately. Despite that, there are some minor differences in how you work with IIFEs. Once major difference is how you deal with passing in arguments.

The general structure for creating an IIFE that takes arguments looks as follows:

```
(function (a, b) {
    /* code */
})(arg1, arg2);
```

Just like with any function call, the order of the arguments you pass in maps to the order of the arguments your function will take.

Here is a slightly fuller example:

```
(function (first, last) {
    alert("My name is " + last + ", " + first + " " + last + ".");
})("James", "Bond");
```

If you run this in your browser (or run it in your mind), what gets displayed is *My name is Bond, James Bond.* And with this, you have learned the basics of how to write an IIFE. This is the easy part. The more interesting (and difficult) part is figuring out the cases when to use an IIFE.

QUICK REVIEW OF SCOPING AND FUNCTIONS

To help make the next few sections digestible, let's review one important detail. From the Variable Scope chapter, you learned that JavaScript doesn't have the concept of block scoping. It only has **lexical scope**. This means that variables declared using `var` inside a block such as an `if` statement or loop will actually be accessible to the entire enclosing function:

```
function scopeDemo() {
    if (true) {
        var foo = "I know what you did last summer!";
    }

    alert(foo); // totally exists!
}
scopeDemo();
```

As you can see in this example, the `foo` variable, despite being stuck inside the `if` statement, is accessible outside of it because your `if` is not a scope-able block. This ability to have your "supposedly inner" variables promoted and accessible to the entire enclosing function is known as *variable hoisting*!

When to Use an IIFE

At this point, the value IIFEs bring to the table seems a little odd. After all, what is so different about an IIFE compared to a function you declare and call immediately like you have always done? *The main difference is that an IIFE leaves behind no evidence of its existence after it has run.* This is largely because IIFEs are typically anonymous functions that are nameless. This means you can't track them by examining variables. Because the code you put inside an IIFE is actually inside a function, any variables you declare are local to that function. *Putting all of this together, an IIFE provides you with a very simple way of running code fully inside its own bubble and then disappearing without a trace.*

Now that you know what makes IIFEs unique (and extremely confusing), let's look at when you will need to use them.

Avoiding Code Collisions

One of the biggest advantages of IIFEs is their ability to insulate any code from outside interference. This is important if you are writing code that will be used widely in someone else's application. You want to ensure that any existing (or new) code doesn't accidentally clobber your variables or override functions and methods. The way to ensure that such accidents don't happen is to wrap all of your code inside an IIFE.

For example, here is some code for a **content slider** I created wrapped into an IIFE:

```
(function() {
    // just querying the DOM...like a boss!
    var links = document.querySelectorAll(".itemLinks");
    var wrapper = document.querySelector("#wrapper");

    // the activeLink provides a pointer to the currently displayed
      item
    var activeLink = 0;

    // setup the event listeners
    for (var i = 0; i < links.length; i++) {
        var link = links[i];
        link.addEventListener('click', setClickedItem, false);

        // identify the item for the activeLink
        link.itemID = i;
    }

    // set first item as active
    links[activeLink].classList.add("active");

    function setClickedItem(e) {
        removeActiveLinks();
```

```
        var clickedLink = e.target;
        activeLink = clickedLink.itemID;

        changePosition(clickedLink);
    }

    function removeActiveLinks() {
        for (var i = 0; i < links.length; i++) {
            links[i].classList.remove("active");
        }
    }

    // Handle changing the slider position as well as ensure
    // the correct link is highlighted as being active
    function changePosition(link) {
        var position = link.getAttribute("data-pos");
        wrapper.style.left = position;

        link.classList.add("active");
    }
})();
```

As highlighted in this example, just add the first and last line that wraps everything you are doing into a function that gets immediately executed. You don't have to make any additional modifications. Because all of the code inside the IIFE runs in its own scope, you don't have to worry about someone else creating their own copies of things found in *your* code and breaking *your* functionality.

Closures and Locking in State

There is an important detail about closures that I didn't highlight in the Closures in JavaScript article: closures store their outer values by referencing them. They don't directly store the actual values. I am fairly certain that line didn't make much sense, so let's take a look at an example.

Let's say we have a function called `quotatious`:

```
function quotatious(names) {
    var quotes = [];
```

```
        for (var i = 0; i < names.length; i++) {

            var theFunction = function() {
                return "My name is " + names[i] + "!";
            }

            quotes.push(theFunction);
        }
        return quotes;
    }
```

What this function does should seem pretty simple. It takes an **array** (for now, just think of it as a collection of values separated by a comma) of names and returns an array of functions that print out the name when called. To use this function, add the following lines of code:

```
// our list of names
var people = ["Tony Stark", "John Rambo", "James Bond", "Rick
 James"];

// getting an array of functions
var peopleFunctions = quotatious(people);

// get the first function
var person = peopleFunctions[0];

// execute the first function
alert(person());
```

When the last line with the `alert` statement is executed, what would you expect to see? Because our person variable is getting the first item from the array of functions returned by `peopleFunctions`, it would seem reasonable to expect *My name is Tony Stark!* to appear.

What you will actually see is the following:

You will see **undefined** appearing instead of any person's name from the `people` array...much less the supposedly correct value of **Tony Stark**. What is going on here?

What is going on is very subtle and highlighted in the following two lines of code:

```
function quotatious(names) {
    var quotes = [];

    for (var i = 0; i < names.length; i++) {

        var theFunction = function() {
            return "My name is " + names[i] + "!";
        }

        quotes.push(theFunction);
    }
    return quotes;
}
```

Your `theFunction` function relies on the value of `names[i]`. The value of `i` is defined by the `for` loop (in the scope of the parent function), and the `for` loop is outside of the `theFunction`'s scope. What you have is basically a closure with the `theFunction` function and the variable `i` being an outer variable. Figure 20.1 presents a visualization of what this situation looks like.

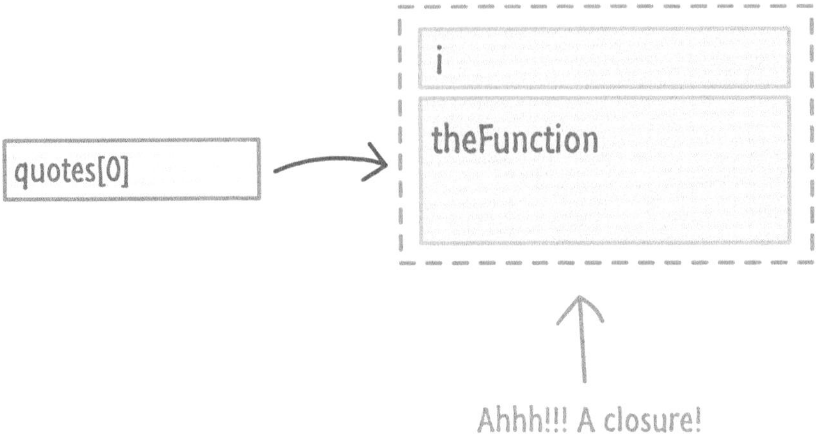

FIGURE 20.1

Closures. Can't live with them. Can't live without them.

Here is where the important detail I mentioned about closures comes into play. The value of `i` is never locked into the `theFunction` or the closure. Its value is simply **referenced**. What you have is something similar to what you see in Figure 20.2.

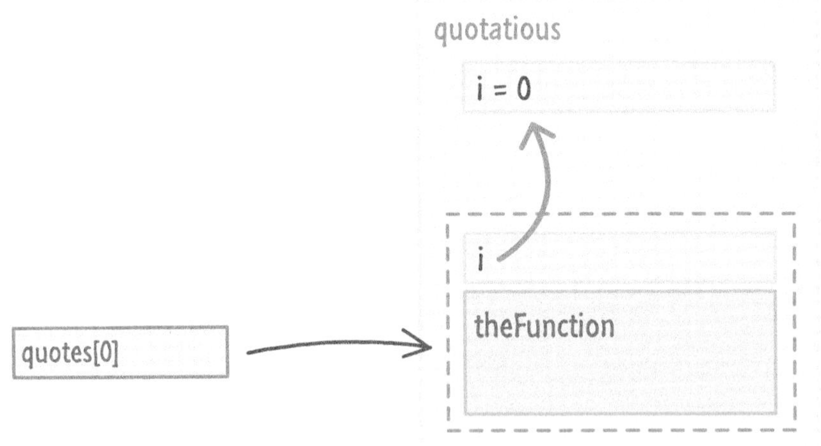

FIGURE 20.2

When values are referenced, that complicates what actually gets stored inside the closure.

Because the value of the `i` variable is actually referenced, the value of `i` that your closures reference is increased by one with each iteration of your `for` loop. That isn't the behavior we want. We want each function in the `quotes` array to store the value of `i` that it had when the function was first created. By the time our loop has fully run to completion, the value of `i` is **4**.

Figure 20.3 helps you visualize what is going on.

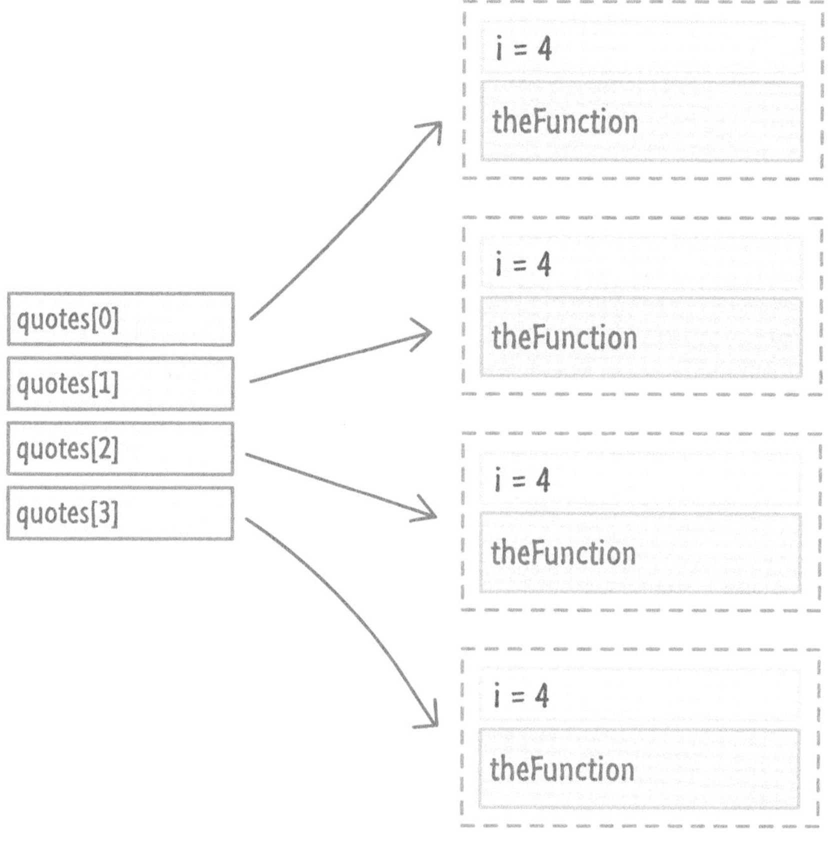

FIGURE 20.3

Why our code isn't running exactly as we had hoped.

Because `i` is **4** and greater than the number of items in the `names` array input, you get **undefined** when the following line executes with `names[4]`:

```
function quotatious(names) {
    var quotes = [];

    for (var i = 0; i < names.length; i++) {

        var theFunction = function() {
```

```
            return "My name is " + names[i] + "!";
        }

        quotes.push(theFunction);
    }
    return quotes;
}
```

At this point, we understand what the code does and why it doesn't work as it is currently written. The solution is to lock in the value of our outer variable, the troublesome i, inside the closure. This will involve, as you might have guessed, the assistance of an IIFE.

Below is the modified version of the **`quotatious`** function that does what we want it to do:

```
function quotatious(names) {
    var quotes = [];

    for (var i = 0; i < names.length; i++) {
        (function(index) {
            var theFunction = function() {
                return "My name is " + names[index] + "!";
            }
            quotes.push(theFunction);
        })(i);
    }
    return quotes;
}
```

Notice that the `i` variable is passed in as an argument to our IIFE. This argument, now referenced inside the IIFE by the **`index`** variable, *is local to whatever the function does.* The state of what used to be an outer variable is now locked in! This change ensures that the function inside the quotes array has its own copy of the array index it needs so that the right person is being referenced. You no longer have references to outer variables that change and cause your code to break. W00t!

SOMETIMES REFERENCING OUTER VARIABLES IS WHAT YOU WANT!

I am most certainly not suggesting that you should always use an IIFE when an outer variable changes after a closure has been created. There may be times where you want your closure to work with the updated value of an outer variable, so in those cases, don't use an IIFE to lock-in the value.

Making Things Private

In JavaScript, you don't have an easy, built-in way to limit the visibility of variables and properties you end up creating. This means it is difficult to have parts of your app hidden from other parts of your app. That's why we spent a fair amount of time in the previous sections looking into this. For good measure, let us cover this topic one more time :P

Take a look at the following example that highlights this problem:

```
var weakSauce = {
    secretCode: "Zorb!",

    checkCode: function (code) {
        if (this.secretCode == code) {
            alert("You are awesome!");
        } else {
            alert("Try again!");
        }
    }
};
```

You have this object called **weakSauce** that has these two properties called **secretCode** and **checkCode**. This is a very naive password checker. When you pass in a code value to the **checkCode** function, it will check if what you entered matches the value of **secretCode**. If it matches, *you are awesome* will get displayed. If it doesn't, you will see *Try again!* appear instead.

Now, here is where some privacy in your code may help. Nothing prevents me, you, or someone who uses this code from checking the value of **secretCode** directly:

```
var bar = Object.create(weakSauce);
alert(bar.secretCode); // sigh :(
```

This is probably not what you intended when creating the **secretCode** property. The reason isn't because **secretCode** is named with the word *secret* in it. It is part of an implementation detail that you may want to change at any time. The **checkCode** function is what you would intend people to use. Any other variable or property is fair game for you to change whenever you want. If other pieces of code take a dependency on implementation details, their code may break whenever you make a change. That's why keeping some items private is important. That is why the **secretCode** property should be hidden to everything except the internals of the **weakSauce** object. In other languages, you could add an access modifier like **private** to **secretCode**, and that would be the end of this entire conversation. JavaScript isn't like other languages. You have to jump through hoops to solve your problem, and one such awesome hoop to jump through is our friendly IIFE.

By taking advantage of the local scope IIFEs create, you can selectively choose what to expose or what not to expose. Here is a version of the same example that works as we would want it to:

```
var awesomeSauce = (function () {
    var secretCode = "Zorb!";

    function privateCheckCode(code) {
        if (secretCode == code) {
            alert("You are awesome!");
        } else {
            alert("Try again!");
        }
    }

    // the public method we want to return
    return {
        checkCode: privateCheckCode
```

```
    };
})();
```

Let's repeat what we tried earlier with `awesomeSauce`:

```
var foo = Object.create(awesomeSauce);
alert(foo.secretCode); // undefined
```

This time around, you won't be able to access `secretCode`. The reason is that the contents of `secretCode` are buried inside the IIFE and not accessible publicly. In fact, the only thing that is publicly exposed is what you have here:

```
var awesomeSauce = (function () {
    var secretCode = "Zorb!";

    function privateCheckCode(code) {
        if (secretCode == code) {
            alert("You are awesome!");
        } else {
            alert("Try again!");
        }
    }

    // the public method we want to return
    return {
        checkCode: privateCheckCode
    };
})();
```

By only returning an object that contains the `checkCode` property—that internally references the `privateCheckCode` function (which is a closure), you get all the functionality you originally had.

There is a more formal name for what I've just shown you here. It's known as the **Revealing Module Pattern**, and there is a ton of good stuff on the net about it. My favorite is the following concise take of this pattern by Addy Osmani: **http://bit.ly/kirupaRMP**.

REMEMBER, YOUR JAVASCRIPT CODE IS AN OPEN BOOK!

While you may have just learned about a way to keep the internals of your code private, it is only private to the typical code you write. Unlike other languages, JavaScript's source is always fully accessible. Even with obfuscation and other techniques, if your browser can see your code, then anybody else with a few extra seconds to spare can as well.

For example, using the Chrome Developer Tools, I can easily inspect the closure stored by `checkCode` and clearly see the value of the `secretCode` variable.

```
        var foo = Object.create(awesomeSauce);
        alert(foo.secretCode);

        Object
        ▼ __proto__: Object
          ▼ checkCode: function privateCheckCode(cod…
              arguments: null
              caller: null
              length: 1
              name: "privateCheckCode"
            ▶ prototype: privateCheckCode
            ▶ __proto__: function Empty() {}
            ▼ <function scope>
              ▼ Closure
                  secretCode: "Zorb!"
              ▶ Global: Window
          ▶ __proto__: Object

    </scri
</body>

</html>
```

Essentially, what I'm trying to say is this: don't rely on client-side JavaScript for dealing with things you truly want to keep private. Instead, do what everyone else does and use some server-side service that provides you with a private environment where top-secret things get done. The server then only returns the things you want exposed publicly back to JavaScript.

THE ABSOLUTE MINIMUM

An **IIFE** (short for **Immediately Invoked Function Expression**) is one of those bizarre things in JavaScript that turns out to play a very useful role once you give it a chance. The main reason you will need to learn about IIFEs is because JavaScript lacks privacy. This problem becomes more annoying when you are working on increasingly larger and more complex JavaScript apps (which usually have increasingly larger and more complex closures), so the local scope created by an IIFE is the ultimate blunt instrument for solving all of your problems. As with all blunt instruments, do be careful when using them.

TIP Just a quick reminder for those of you reading these words in the print or e-book edition of this book: If you go to **www.quepublishing.com** and register this book, you can receive free access to an online Web Edition that not only contains the complete text of this book but also features a short, fun interactive quiz to test your understanding of the chapter you just read.

If you're reading these words in the Web Edition already and want to try your hand at the quiz, then you're in luck – all you need to do is scroll down!

IN THIS CHAPTER

- Learn how JavaScript and the rest of your page interact
- Understand what the fuss about the Document Object Model (DOM) is all about
- Figure out the fuzzy boundaries between HTML, CSS, and JavaScript

21

JS, THE BROWSER, AND THE DOM

So far, we've looked at JavaScript in isolation. We learned a lot about its basic functionality, but we did so with little to no connection with how it ties to the real world—a world that is represented by your browser and swimming with little HTML tags and CSS styles. This chapter will serve as an introduction to this world, and subsequent chapters will dive in much deeper.

In the following sections, you will learn about the mysterious data structure and programming interface known as the **Document Object Model (DOM)**. You'll learn what it is, why it is useful, and how it ties in to everything that you'll be doing in the future.

Onwards!

What HTML, CSS, and JavaScript Do

Before we dive in and start answering the meaning of life…err, the DOM, let's quickly look at some things you probably already know. For starters, the stuff you put into your HTML documents revolves around HTML, CSS, and JavaScript. We treat these three things as equal partners in building up what you see in your browser:

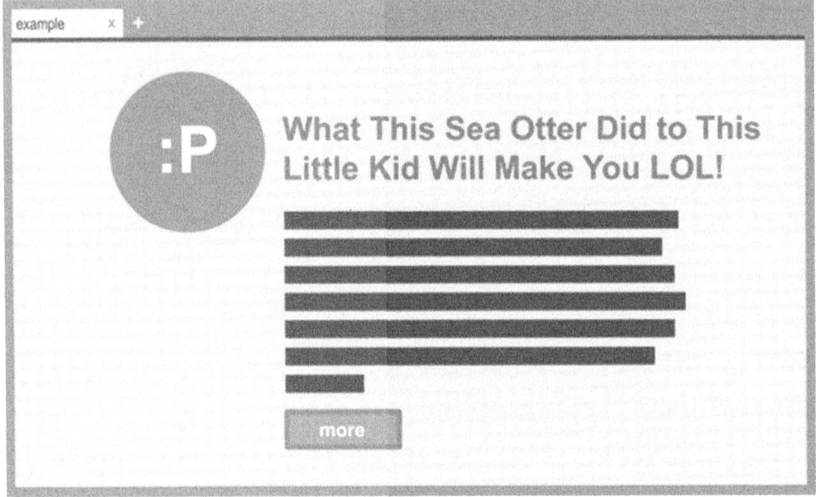

Each partner has an important role to play, and the role each one plays is very different.

HTML Defines the Structure

Your HTML defines the structure of your page and typically contains the content that you see:

```
<!DOCTYPE html>
<html>
```

```
<head>
    <meta content="sea otter, kid, stuff" name="keywords">
    <meta content="Sometimes, sea otters are awesome!"
      name="description">
    <title>Example</title>

    <link href="foo.css" rel="stylesheet" />
</head>

<body>
    <div id="container">
        <img src="seaOtter.png" />

        <h1>What This Sea Otter Did to This Little
          Kid Will Make You LOL!</h1>

        <p class="bodyText">
            Nulla tristique, justo eget semper viverra,
            massa arcu congue tortor, ut vehicula urna mi
            in lorem. Quisque aliquam molestie dui, at tempor
            turpis porttitor nec. Aenean id interdum urna.
            Curabitur mi ligula, hendrerit at semper sed,
            feugiat a nisi.
        <p>

        <div class="submitButton">
            more
        </div>
    </div>
    <script src="stuff.js"></script>
</body>
</html>
```

HTML by itself, kinda like Meg Griffin in Family Guy, is pretty boring. If you don't know who Meg is and are too lazy to Google her, Figure 21.1 is an approximation of what she looks like.

FIGURE 21.1

An artistic interpretation of Meg Griffin.

Anyway, you don't want your HTML documents to be boring. To transform your content from something plain and drab to something appealing, you have CSS.

Prettify My World, CSS!

CSS is your primary styling language that allows you to give your HTML elements some much-needed aesthetic and layout appeal:

```
body {
    font-family: "Arial";
    background-color: #CCCFFF;
}
#container {
    margin-left: 30%;
}
#container img {
    padding: 20px;
}
```

```
#container h1 {
    font-size: 56px;
    font-weight: 500;
}
#container p.bodyText {
    font-size: 16px;
    line-height: 24px;
}
.submitButton {
    display: inline-block;
    border: 5px solid #669900;
    background-color: #7BB700;
    padding: 10px;
    width: 150px;
    font-weight: 800;
}
```

For the longest time, between HTML and CSS, you had everything you needed to create an awesome-looking and functioning page. You had structure and layout. You had navigation. You even had simple interactions such as mouseovers. Life was good.

It's JavaScript Time!

For all the great things HTML and CSS had going for them, they were both limited in how much interactivity they provided. People wanted to do more on a web document than just passively sit back and observe what is going on. They wanted their web documents to do more. They wanted their documents to help them play with media; remember where they left off; do things with their mouse clicks, keyboard taps, and finger presses; use fancy navigation menus; see spiffy (yes, I used the word spiffy) programmatic animations; interact with their webcams/ microphones; not require a page reload/navigation for any kind of action; and a whole lot more:

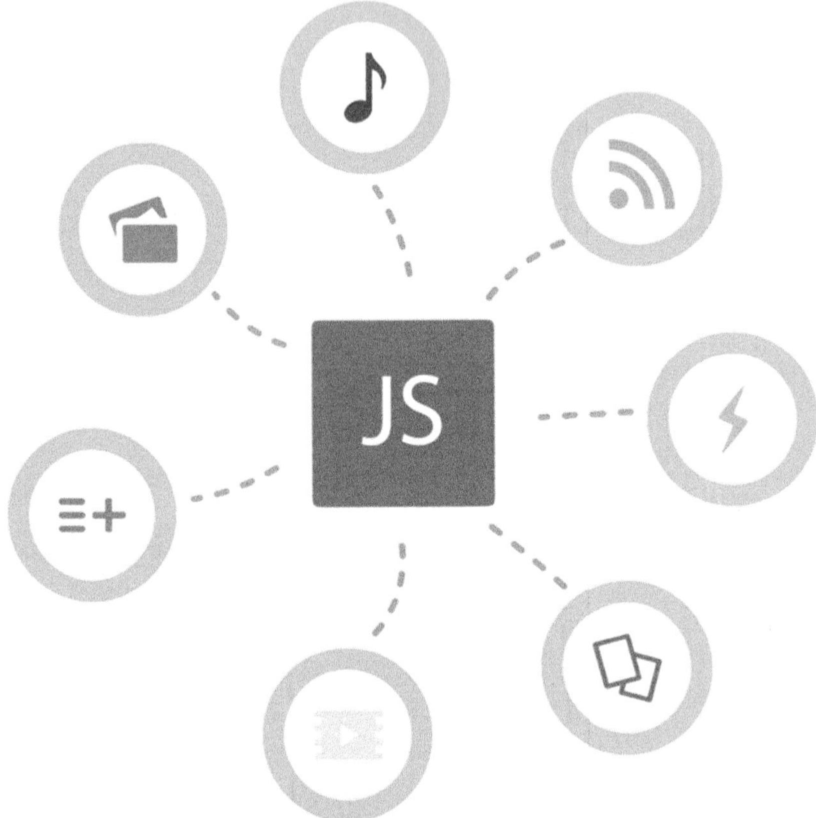

It certainly helped that web developers and designers (aka you and me) were itching for a way to help create these kinds of things as well.

To fill in this gap between what HTML and CSS provided and what people wanted, you had third-party components like Java and Flash that thrived for many years. It wasn't until recently that this trend changed. There were many technical and political reasons for this shift, but one reason was that JavaScript for many years just wasn't ready. It didn't have what it took either in the core language or in what browsers supported to be effective.

That's no longer the case today. JavaScript is now a perfectly capable language that allows you to add the kinds of interactive things that people are looking for. All of these capabilities are accessed by the real star of all this, the DOM.

Meet the Document Object Model

What your browser displays is a web document. More specifically, to summarize the entirety of the previous sections, what you see is a collision of HTML, CSS, and JavaScript working together to create what gets shown. Digging one step deeper, under the covers, there is a hierarchical structure that your browser uses to make sense of everything going on.

This structure is known (again) as the Document Object Model. Friends just call it the DOM. Figure 21.2 shows a very simplified view of what the DOM for our earlier example would look like:

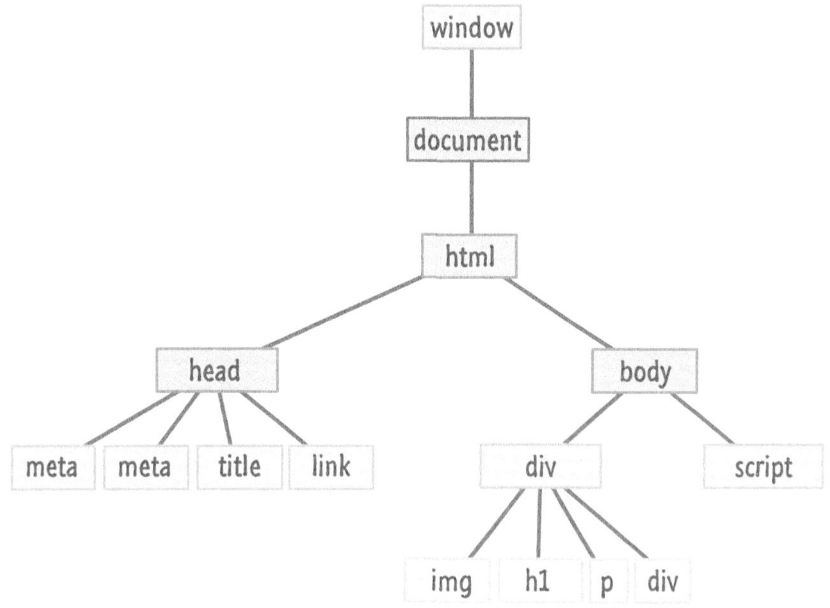

FIGURE 21.2

Our DOM for all the HTML you saw earlier looks sorta like this!

Despite the simplicity, there are several things to drill in on that apply to all DOM structures in general. Your DOM is actually made up many kinds of things beyond just HTML elements. All of those things that make up your DOM are more generically known as **nodes**.

These nodes can be elements (which shouldn't surprise you), attributes, text content, comments, document-related stuff, and various other things you simply never think about. That detail is important to someone, but that "someone" shouldn't be you and me. Almost always, the only kind of node we will care about is the element kind because that is what we will be dealing with 99% of the time. At the boring/technical level, nodes still play a role in our element-centric view.

Every HTML element you want to access has a particular type associated with it, and all of these types extend from the **Node** base that make up all nodes:

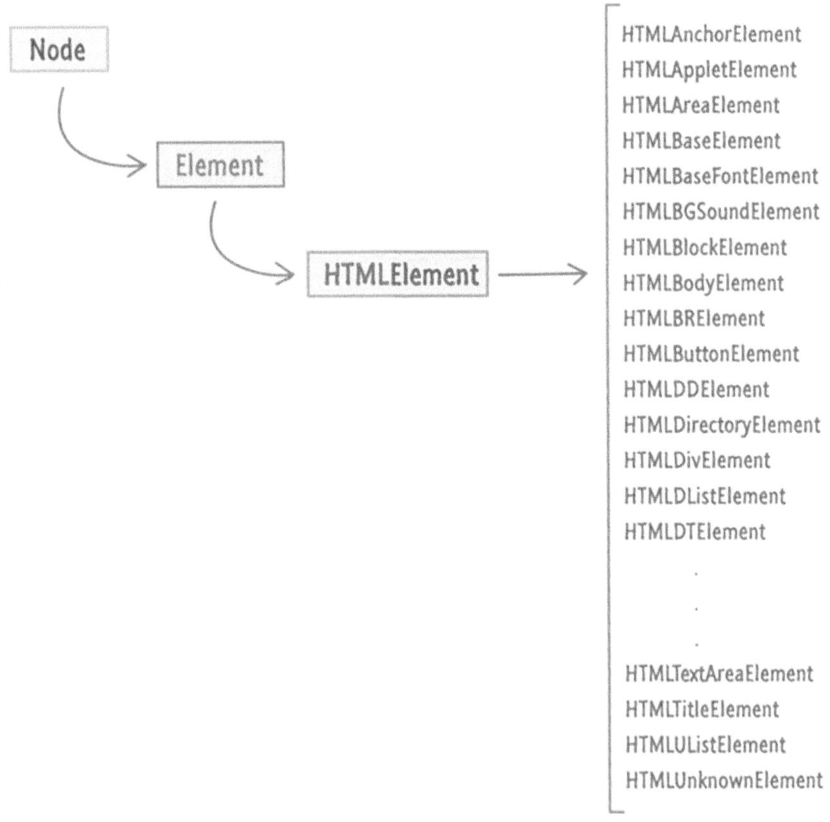

Your HTML elements are at the end of a chain that starts with Node and continues with Element and `HTMLElement` before ending with a type (ie: `HTMLDivElement`, `HTMLHeadingElement`, and so on.) that matches the HTML element itself. The properties and methods you will see for manipulating HTML elements are introduced at some part of this chain.

Now, before we run toward using the DOM to modify HTML elements, let's first talk about two special objects that get in the way before the road clears up for what we want to do.

The Window Object

In the browser, the root of your hierarchy is the `window` object that contains many properties and methods that help you work with your browser:

the `window` object deals with your browser window

Some of the things you can do with the help of the `window` object include accessing the current URL, getting information about any frames in the page, using local storage, seeing information about your screen, fiddling with the scrollbar, setting the statusbar text, and all sorts of things that are applicable to the container your web page is displayed in.

The Document Object

Now, we get to the document object. Here is where things get interesting, and it is also where you and I will be focusing a lot of our time on:

the document object deals with EVERYTHING that lives in your document

The document object is the gateway to all the HTML elements that make up what gets shown. The thing to keep in mind (and one that makes more sense as we look at future chapters) is that the document object does not simply represent a read-only version of the HTML document. It is a two-way street where you can read as well as manipulate your document at will.

Any change you make to the DOM via JavaScript is reflected in what gets shown in the browser. This means you can dynamically add elements, remove them, move them around, modify attributes on them, set inline CSS styles, and perform all sorts of other shenanigans. Outside of the very basic HTML needed via a script tag to get some JavaScript to run in an HTML document, you can construct a fully functioning page using nothing but JavaScript if you felt like it. Used properly, this is a pretty powerful feature.

Another import aspect of the document object has to do with events. I will go into more detail on this shortly, but if you want to react to a mouse click/hover, checking a check box, detecting when a key was pressed, and so on, you will be relying on functionality the document object provides for listening to and reacting to events.

There are a few more big buckets of functionality the DOM provides, but I'll highlight them as we get to them.

THE ABSOLUTE MINIMUM

The DOM is the single most important piece of functionality you have for working with your HTML documents. It provides the missing link that ties your HTML and CSS with JavaScript. It also provides access one level up to your browser.

Now, knowing about the DOM is just part of the fun. Actually using its functionality to interact with your web document is the much larger and ***funner*** other part. When you are ready, turn (or flip) on over to the next chapter where we will go further.

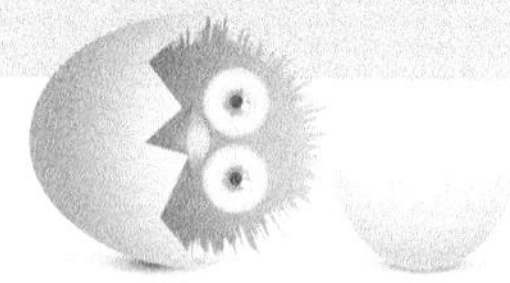

TIP Just a quick reminder for those of you reading these words in the print or e-book edition of this book: If you go to **www.quepublishing.com** and register this book, you can receive free access to an online Web Edition that not only contains the complete text of this book but also features a short, fun interactive quiz to test your understanding of the chapter you just read.

If you're reading these words in the Web Edition already and want to try your hand at the quiz, then you're in luck – all you need to do is scroll down!

IN THIS CHAPTER

- Learn how to find elements in the DOM
- Use the CSS selector syntax for cleverer element discovery

22

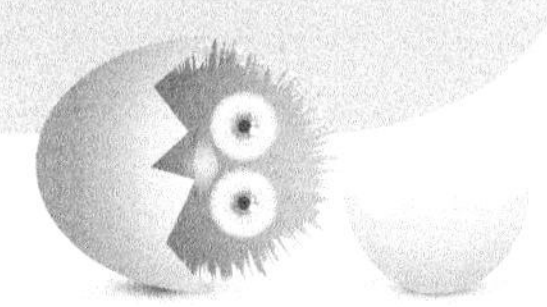

FINDING ELEMENTS IN THE DOM

As you saw in previous chapter, your DOM is nothing more than a tree-like structure made up of all the elements that exist in your HTML document:

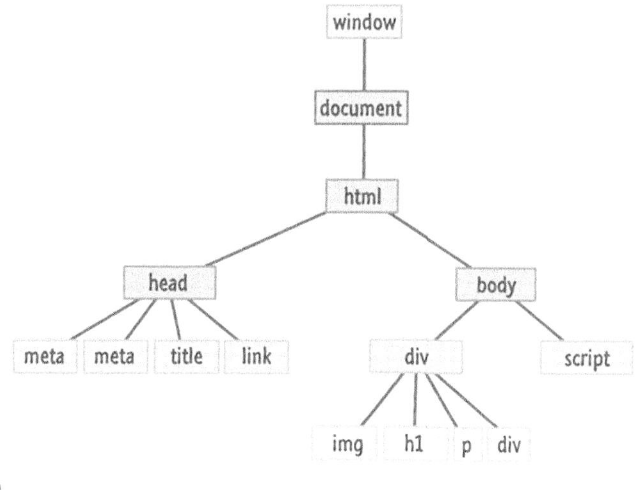

Yes, I know...you've seen this diagram a bunch of times!

That detail is only sort of important. What is important is that you have all of these HTML elements floating around that you want to access and read data from or modify. There are many ways to find these HTML elements. After all, these elements are arranged in a tree-like structure, and if there is one thing computer scientists like to do, it is figuring out crazy ways to run up and down a tree to find something.

I won't subject you to that torture...just yet. In this chapter, you are going to learn how to use two built-in functions called **`querySelector`** and **`querySelectorAll`** to solve a good chunk of all your DOM searching needs.

Onwards!

Meet the `querySelector` Family

To help explain the awesomeness that **`querySelector`** and **`querySelectorAll`** bring to the table, take a look at the following HTML:

```
<div id="main">
    <div class="pictureContainer">
        <img class="theImage" src="smiley.png" height="300"
         width="150" />
    </div>
    <div class="pictureContainer">
        <img class="theImage" src="tongue.png" height="300"
         width="150" />
    </div>
    <div class="pictureContainer">
        <img class="theImage" src="meh.png" height="300"
         width="150" />
    </div>
    <div class="pictureContainer">
        <img class="theImage" src="sad.png" height="300"
         width="150" />
    </div>
</div>
```

In this example, you have one `div` with an `id` of **main**, and then you have four `div` and `img` elements each with a class value of **pictureContainer** and **theImage** respectively. In the next few sections, we'll set the `querySelector` and `querySelectorAll` functions loose on this HTML and see what happens.

querySelector

The `querySelector` function basically works as follows:

```
var element = document.querySelector("CSS selector");
```

The `querySelector` function takes an argument, and this argument is a CSS selector for the element you wish to find. What gets returned by `querySelector` is the first element it finds—even if other elements exist—that could get targeted by the selector. This function is pretty stubborn like that.

Taking the HTML from our earlier example, if we wanted to access the `div` whose `id` is **main**, you would write the following:

```
var element = document.querySelector("#main");
```

Because **main** is the `id`, the selector syntax for targeting it would be `#main`. Similarly, let's specify the selector for the **pictureContainer** class:

```
var element = document.querySelector(".pictureContainer");
```

What gets returned is the first `div` whose class value is **pictureContainer**. The other `div` elements with the class value of **pictureContainer** will simply be ignored.

The selector syntax is not modified or made special because you are in JavaScript. The exact syntax you would use for selectors in your stylesheet or style region can be used!

querySelectorAll

The `querySelectorAll` function returns all elements it finds that match whatever selector you provide:

```
var element = document.querySelectorAll("CSS selector");
```

With the exception of the number of elements returned, everything I described about `querySelector` above applies to `querySelectorAll` as well. That important detail changes how you end up actually using the `querySelectorAll` function. What gets returned is not a single element. Instead, what gets returned is an array-like container of elements!

Continuing to use the HTML from earlier, here is what our JavaScript would look like if we wanted to use `querySelectorAll` to help us display the `src` attribute of all the `img` elements that contain the class value **theimage**:

```
var images = document.querySelectorAll(".theImage");

for (var i = 0; i < images.length; i++) {
    var image = images[i];
    alert(image.getAttribute("src"));
}
```

See? This is pretty straightforward. The only thing you need to do is remember how to work with Arrays (**Chapter 13, "When Primitives Behave Like Objects"**). The one weird thing is the mysterious `getAttribute` function. If you aren't familiar with `getAttribute` and how to read values from elements, that's totally okay. We'll look at all that really soon.

It Really Is the CSS Selector Syntax

The thing that surprised me when I first used `querySelector` and `querySelectorAll` is that it actually takes the full range of CSS selector syntax variations as its argument. You don't have to keep it simple like I've shown you so far.

If you wanted to target all of the `img` elements without having to specify the class value, here is what our `querySelectorAll` call could look like:

```
var images = document.querySelectorAll("img");
```

If you wanted to target only the image whose `src` attribute is set to **meh.png**, you can do the following:

```
var images = document.querySelectorAll("img[src='meh.png']");
```

Note that I just specified an **attribute selector**[1] as my argument to `querySelectorAll`. Pretty much any complex expression you can specify for a selector in your CSS document is fair game for specifying as an argument to either `querySelector` or `querySelectorAll`.

There are some caveats that you should be aware of:

- Not all pseudo-class selectors are allowed. A selector made up of `:visited` or `:link` is ignored and no elements are found.

1. http://bit.ly/kirupaAttribute

- How crazy you can get with the selectors you provide depends on the browser's CSS support. Internet Explorer 8 supports `querySelector` and `querySelectorAll`. It doesn't support CSS3. Given that situation, using anything more recent than the selectors defined in CSS 2 will not work when used with `querySelector` and `querySelectorAll` on IE8. Chances are, this doesn't apply to you because you are probably supporting more recent versions of browsers where this IE8 issue isn't even on the radar.
- The selector you specify only applies to the descendants of the starting element you are beginning your search from. The starting element itself is not included. Not all `querySelector` and `querySelectorAll` calls need to be made from a `document`.

THE ABSOLUTE MINIMUM

The `querySelector` and `querySelectorAll` functions are extremely useful in complex documents where targeting a particular element is often not straightforward. By relying on the well-established CSS selector syntax, we can cast as small or as wide a net over the elements that we want. If I want all image elements, I can just say `querySelectorAll("img")`. If I only want the immediate `img` element contained inside its parent `div`, I can say `querySelector("div + img")`. Now, that's pretty awesome.

Before we wrap up, there is one more thing I'd like to chat with you about. Missing in all of this element-finding excitement were the `getElementById`, `getElementsByTagName`, and `getElementsByClassName` functions. Back in the day, these were the functions you would have used to find elements in your DOM. The `querySelector` and `querySelectorAll` functions are the present and future solutions for finding elements, so don't worry about the `getElement*` functions anymore. As of right now, the only slight against the `querySelector` and `querySelectorAll` functions is performance. The `getElementById` function is still pretty fast, and you can see the comparison for yourself here: **http://jsperf.com/getelementbyid-vs-queryselector**.

Like a wise person once said, life is too short to spend time learning about old JavaScript functions...even if they are a bit faster!

TIP Just a quick reminder for those of you reading these words in the print or e-book edition of this book: If you go to **www.quepublishing.com** and register this book, you can receive free access to an online Web Edition that not only contains the complete text of this book but also features a short, fun interactive quiz to test your understanding of the chapter you just read.

If you're reading these words in the Web Edition already and want to try your hand at the quiz, then you're in luck – all you need to do is scroll down!

IN THIS CHAPTER

- Understand how JavaScript can be used to modify the DOM
- Meet the HTML Element
- Learn how to modify attributes

23

MODIFYING DOM ELEMENTS

At this point, you kinda sorta know what the DOM is. You also saw how to find elements using `querySelector` and `querySelectorAll`. What's next is for us to learn how to modify the DOM elements you found. After all, what's the fun in having a giant lump of clay (or cookie dough) if you can't put your hands on it and make a giant mess?

1. Get a vague overview of the DOM
2. Learn to find elements
3. Modify elements
4. ???
5. Profit!!!

You are here!

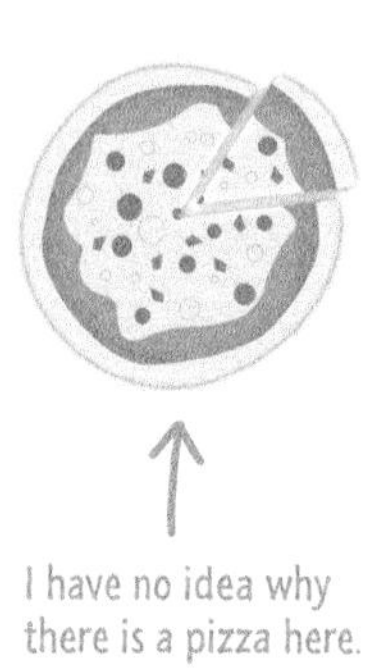

I have no idea why there is a pizza here.

Anyway, besides it being fun and all, you will find yourself modifying the DOM all the time. Whether you are using JavaScript to change some element's text, swap out an image with a different one, move an element from one part of your document to another, set an inline style, or perform any of the bazillion other changes you will want to do, *you will be modifying the DOM*. This chapter will teach you the basics of how to go about doing that.

Onwards!

DOM Elements Are Objects—Sort of!

Your ability to use JavaScript to modify what gets shown by the browser is made possible because of one major detail. That detail is that every HTML tag, style rule, and other things that go into your page have some sort of a representation in the DOM.

To visualize what I just said, let's say you have an image element defined in markup:

```
<img src="images/lol_panda.png" alt="Sneezing Panda!" width="250"
  height="100" />
```

When your browser parses the document and hits this image element, it creates a node in the DOM that represents it as illustrated in Figure 23.1.

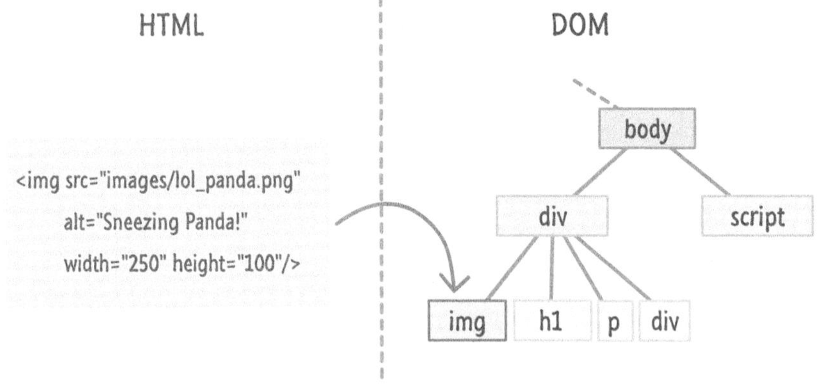

FIGURE 23.1

Your DOM stores an entry for the image element at the appropriate location.

This DOM representation provides you with the ability to do everything you could have done in markup. As it turns out, this DOM representation actually ends up allowing *you to do more with your HTML elements* than you could have done using just plain old markup itself. This is something you'll see a little bit of here and a whole lot of in the future. The reason why your HTML elements are so versatile when viewed via the DOM is because they share a lot of similarities with JavaScript `Objects`. Your DOM elements contain properties that allow you to get/set values and call methods. They have a form of inheritance that you read a little bit about earlier where the functionality each DOM element provides is spread out across the `Node`, `Element`, and `HTMLElement` base types.

This hierarchy (which you've seen earlier) is illustrated again in Figure 23.2.

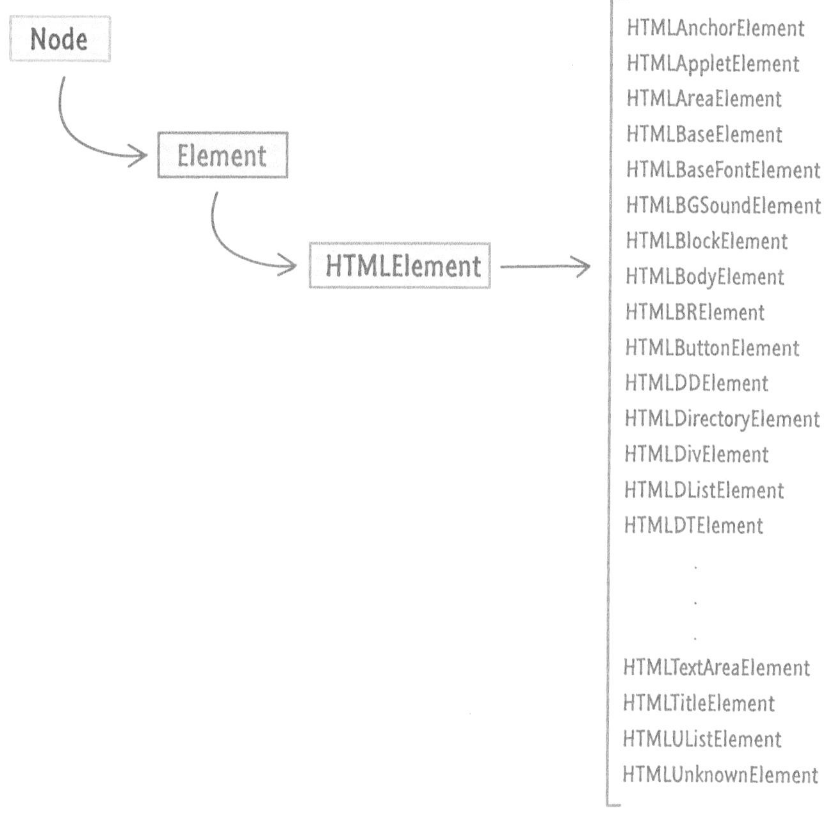

FIGURE 23.2

JavaScript is big on hierarchies...even when representing the DOM!

DOM elements probably even smell like an `Object` when they run inside the house after rolling around in the rain for a bit.

Despite all of the similarities, for legal and...possibly health reasons, I need to provide the following disclaimer: *the DOM was never designed to mimic the way Objects work*. Many of the things you can do with objects you can certainly do with the DOM, but that is because the browser vendors help ensure that.

The W3C specification doesn't state that your DOM should behave identically to how you may expect things to behave with plain old Objects. While I wouldn't lose any sleep worrying about this, if you ever decide to extend DOM elements or perform more advanced object-related gymnastics, be sure to test across all browsers just to make sure everything works the way you intended.

Now that we got this awkward conversation out of the way, let's start to actually modify the DOM.

Let's Actually Modify DOM Elements

While you can certainly lean back and passively learn all there is about how to modify elements in the DOM, this is one of those cases where you may have more fun following along with a simple example. If you are interested in following along, we'll be using the following HTML as a sandbox for the techniques you will be learning:

```
<!DOCTYPE html>
<html>

<head>

  <title>Hello...</title>

  <style>
    .highlight {
      font-family: "Arial";
      padding: 30px;
    }

    .summer {
      font-size: 64px;
      color: #0099FF;
    }
  </style>

</head>

<body>

  <h1 id="theTitle" class="highlight summer">What's happening?</h1>
```

```
    <script>
    </script>
  </body>

  </html>
```

Just put all of that code into an HTML document and follow along. If you preview this HTML in the browser, you will see some text appear that looks as follows:

What's happening?

There isn't really a whole lot going on here. The main piece of content is the `h1` tag that displays the *What's happening?* text:

```
<h1 id="theTitle" class="highlight summer">What's happening?</h1>
```

Now, switching over to the DOM side of things, Figure 23.3 shows what this example looks like with all of the HTML elements (and `document` and `window`) mapped:

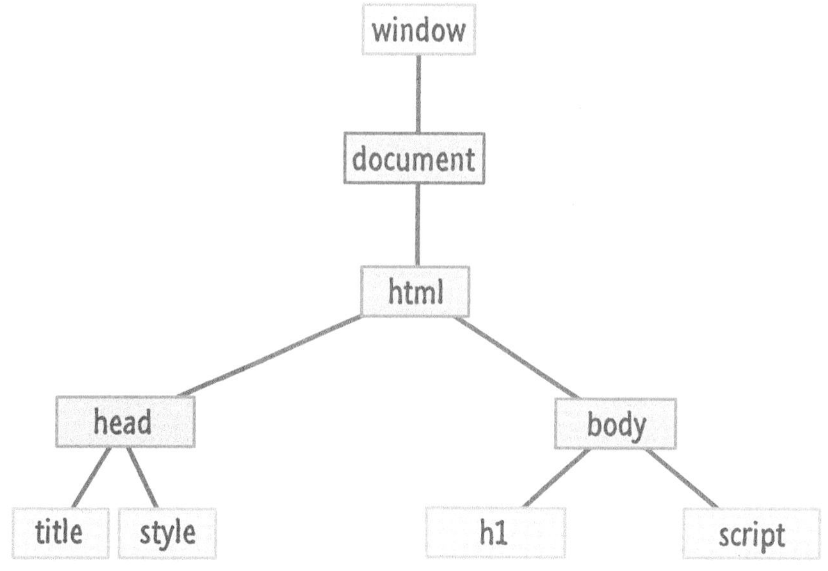

FIGURE 23.3

What our DOM looks like for the markup that we are working with.

In the following sections, we'll look at some of the common things you can do in terms of modifying a DOM element.

Changing an Element's Text Value

Let's start off with an easy one. Many HTML elements have the ability to display some text. Examples of such elements are your headings, paragraphs, sections, inputs, buttons, and many more. There is one thing they all have in common. The way you modify the text value is by setting the **textContent** property.

Let's say we want to change the text that appears in the h1 element from our example. The following snippet shows what that would look like:

```
<body>
    <h1 id="theTitle" class="highlight summer">What's happening?</h1>

    <script>
        var title = document.querySelector("#theTitle");
        title.textContent = "Oppa Gangnam Style!";
    </script>
</body>
```

If you make this change and preview it in a browser, you will see the words *Oppa Gangnam Style!* show up.

Let's look at what exactly we did to cause this change. The first step to modifying any HTML element in JavaScript is to first get a reference to it:

```
var title = document.querySelector("#theTitle");
```

Here is where our old friends **querySelector** and **querySelectorAll** come in. As you will see later, you also have indirect ways of referencing an element. The direct approach shown here, though, is what you will use when you have a very specific idea of what element or elements you wish to target.

Once you have the reference to the element, just set the **textContent** property on it:

```
title.textContent = "Oppa Gangnam Style!";
```

The **textContent** property can be read like any variable to show the current value. You can also set the property to change it to whatever you want. In this example, we are setting our **textContent** property to say *Oppa Gangnam Style!* After this line has run, your markup's original value of *What's happening?* will have been replaced!

Attribute Values

One of the primary ways your HTML elements distinguish themselves is through their attributes and the values these attributes store. For example, the **src** and **alt** attributes are what distinguish the following three **img** elements:

```
<img src="images/lol_panda.png" alt="Sneezing Panda!"/>
<img src="images/cat_cardboard.png" alt="Cat sliding into box!"/>
<img src="images/dog_tail.png" alt="Dog chasing its tail!"/>
```

Every HTML attribute (including custom `data-*` ones) can be accessed via JavaScript. To help you deal with attributes, your elements expose the somewhat self-explanatory `getAttribute` and `setAttribute` methods.

The `getAttribute` method allows you to specify the name of an attribute on the element it is living on. If the attribute is found, this method will then return the value associated with that attribute. What follows is an example:

```
<body>
    <h1 id="theTitle" class="highlight summer">What's happening?</h1>

    <script>
        var title = document.querySelector("h1");
        alert(title.getAttribute("id"));
    </script>
</body>
```

In this snippet, notice that we are getting the value of the `id` attribute on our `h1` element. If you specify an attribute name that doesn't exist, you will get a nice value of **null**. The opposite of getting the value of an attribute is to actually set the value. To set the value, you would use the appropriately named `setAttribute` method. You use this method by calling `setAttribute` on the element that you want to affect and specifying both the attribute name as well as the value that attribute will store.

Here is an example of `setAttribute` at work:

```
<body>
    <h1 id="theTitle" class="highlight summer">What's happening?</h1>

    <script>
        document.body.setAttribute("class", "bar foo");
    </script>
</body>
```

We are setting the `class` attribute on the `body` element to **bar foo**. The `setAttribute` function doesn't do any validation to ensure that the attribute you are setting is valid for the element you are setting it on. Nothing prevents you from doing something silly as follows:

```
<body>
    <h1 id="theTitle" class="highlight summer">What's happening?</h1>

    <script>
        document.body.setAttribute("src", "http://www.kirupa.com");
    </script>
</body>
```

The **body** element doesn't contain the **src** attribute, but you can get away with specifying it. When your code runs, your **body** element will sport the **src** attribute...probably very uncomfortably.

There is something I need to clarify before we move on. In the examples for how to use **setAttribute** and **getAttribute**, I picked on **id** and **class**. For these two attributes, you do have another way of setting them. Because of how common setting **id** and **class** attributes are, your HTML elements expose the **id** and **className** properties directly:

```
<body>
    <h1 id="theTitle" class="highlight summer">What's happening?</h1>

    <script>
        var title = document.querySelector("h1");
        alert(title.id);

        document.body.className = "bar foo";
    </script>
</body>
```

In this example, notice that I switched from using **getAttribute** and **setAttribute** to use the **id** and **className** properties instead in lines 6 and 8. The end result is identical. The only difference is that you had a direct way of setting these attributes values without having to use **getAttribute** or **setAttribute**.

TIP There is a much better way of setting class values besides using `className`. That way is via the much more awesome `classList` property that you will learn all about in the next chapter.

THE ABSOLUTE MINIMUM

It may seem a bit odd to end our discussion around modifying DOM elements at this point. While changing an element's text and attribute values is very popular, they are by no means the only major kinds of modifications you will perform. The reason for ending at this cliffhanger is because manipulating the DOM and using an element's properties and methods to accomplish our task is central to everything we are going to be seeing. In subsequent chapters, you are going to see a whole lot more of what you've seen here.

Your main takeaway from this chapter is that the DOM changes you perform will almost always take one of the following two forms:

- Setting a property
- Calling a method

The `textContent`, `setAttribute`, and `getAttribute` methods you saw here cover both of those approaches, and you'll see a lot more of them and their friends shortly.

TIP Just a quick reminder for those of you reading these words in the print or e-book edition of this book: If you go to **www.quepublishing.com** and register this book, you can receive free access to an online Web Edition that not only contains the complete text of this book but also features a short, fun interactive quiz to test your understanding of the chapter you just read.

If you're reading these words in the Web Edition already and want to try your hand at the quiz, then you're in luck – all you need to do is scroll down!

IN THIS CHAPTER:

- Learn how to change CSS using JavaScript
- Understand the pros and cons of setting styles directly as opposed to adjusting class values
- Use classList to make fiddling with element class values a breeze

24

STYLING YOUR CONTENT

In the previous chapter, we looked at how to modify your DOM's content using JavaScript. The other part of what makes our HTML elements stand out is their appearance, their styling. When it comes to styling stuff, the most common way is by creating a style rule and have its selector target an element or elements. A style rule would look as follows:

```
.batman {
    width: 100px;
    height: 100px;
    background-color: #333;
}
```

An element that would be affected by this style rule could look like this:

```
<div class="batman"></div>
```

On any given web page, you'll see anything from just a few to many MANY style rules each beautifully stepping over each other to style everything that you see. This isn't the only approach you can use to style content using CSS, though. It wouldn't be HTML if there weren't multiple ways to accomplish the same task!

Ignoring inline styles, the other approach that you can use to introduce elements to the goodness that is CSS that revolves around the DOM and JavaScript. Basically, you can use JavaScript to *directly style an element*, and you can also use JavaScript to *add or remove class values on elements* which will alter which style rules get applied. In this chapter, you're going to learn about both of these approaches.

Onwards!

Why Would You Set Styles Using JavaScript?

Before we go further, it is probably useful to explain why you would ever want to use JavaScript to affect the style of an element in the first place. In the common cases where you use style rules or inline styles to affect how an element looks, the styling kicks in when the page is loaded. That's awesome, and that's probably what you want most of the time.

There are many cases, especially as your content gets more interactive, where you want styles to dynamically kick in based on user input, some code having run in the background, and more. In these sorts of scenarios, the CSS model involving style rules or inline styles won't help you. While pseudoselectors like hover provide some support, you are still greatly limited in what you can do.

The solution you will need to employ for all of them is one that involves JavaScript. JavaScript not only lets you style the element you are interacting with, but more importantly, it allows you to style elements all over the page. This freedom is very powerful and goes well beyond CSS's limited ability to style content inside (or very close to) itself.

A Tale of Two Styling Approaches

Like I mentioned in the introduction, you have two ways to alter the style of an element using JavaScript. One way is by setting a CSS property directly on the element. The other way is by adding or removing class values from an element which may result in certain style rules getting applied or ignored. Let's look at both of these cases in greater detail.

Setting the Style Directly

Every HTML element that you access via JavaScript has a `style` object. This object allows you to specify a CSS property and set its value. For example, this is what setting the background color of an HTML element whose `id` value is *superman* looks like:

```
var myElement = document.querySelector("#superman");
myElement.style.backgroundColor = "#D93600";
```

To affect many elements, you can do something as follows:

```
var myElements = document.querySelectorAll(".bar");


for (var i = 0; i < myElements.length; i++) {
    myElements[i].style.opacity = 0;
}
```

In a nutshell, to style elements directly using JavaScript, the first step is to access the element. I am using the `querySelector` function to make that happen. The second step is just to find the CSS property you care about and give it a value. Remember, many values in CSS are actually strings. Also remember that many values require a unit of measurement like **px** or **em** or something like that to actually get recognized.

SPECIAL-CASING SOME NAMES OF CSS PROPERTIES

JavaScript is very picky about what makes up a valid property name. Most names in CSS would get JavaScript's seal of approval, so you can just use them straight-up from the carton. There are a few things to keep in mind, though.

To specify a CSS property in JavaScript that contains a dash, simply remove the dash and capitalize the first letter of the second word. For example, `background-color` becomes `backgroundColor`, the `border-radius` property transforms into `borderRadius`, and so on.

Also, certain words in JavaScript are reserved and can't be used directly. One example of a CSS property that falls into this special category is **float**. In CSS it is a layout property. In JavaScript, it stands for something else. To use a property whose name is entirely reserved, prefix the property with css where **float** becomes **cssFloat**.

Adding and Removing Classes Using classList

A common way to style elements is by adding and removing class values on their **class** attribute. Let's say we have the following **div** element:

```
<div id="myDiv" class="bar foo zorb"> ... </div>
```

From looking at the markup, we can see that this element has a **class** attribute with the **bar**, **foo**, and **zorb** values set. What we are going to do in this section is see how easy it is to manipulate these class values using the **classList** API. This API is great because it is simple and provides the following methods to manipulate class values:

- add
- remove
- toggle
- contains

What these four methods do may be pretty self-explanatory from their names, but let's look at them in further detail anyway. Gotta get the page count up somehow, right?

Adding Class Values

To add a class value to an element, call the **add** method on **classList**:

```
var divElement = document.querySelector("#myDiv");
divElement.classList.add("baz");


alert(divElement.classList);
```

After this code runs, our `div` element will have the following class values: **bar**, **foo**, **zorb**, **baz**. The `classList` API takes care of ensuring that spaces are added between class values and all the other sort of stuff that CSS expects from your HTML content.

If you specify an invalid class value, the `classList` API will throw an exception and not add it. If you tell the `add` method to add a class that already exists on the element, your code will run without exception (ha!) but the duplicate class value will not get added.

Removing Class Values

To remove a class value, just call the `remove` method on `classList`:

```
var divElement = document.querySelector("#myDiv");
divElement.classList.remove("foo");

alert(divElement.classList);
```

After this code executes, the **foo** class value will be removed. What you will be left with is just **bar** and **zorb**. Pretty simple, right?

Toggling Class Values

For many styling scenarios, there is one very common workflow. First, you check if a class value on an element exists. If the value exists, you remove it from the element. If the value does not exist, you add that class value to the element. To simplify this very common toggling pattern, the `classList` API provides you with the `toggle` method:

```
var divElement = document.querySelector("#myDiv");
divElement.classList.toggle("foo"); // remove foo
divElement.classList.toggle("foo"); // add foo
divElement.classList.toggle("foo"); // remove foo

alert(divElement.classList);
```

The `toggle` method, as its name implies, adds or removes the specified class value on the element each time it is called. In our case, the **foo** class is removed the first time the toggle method is called. The second time, the **foo** class is added. The third time, the **foo** class is removed. You get the picture.

Checking Whether a Class Value Exists

The last thing we are going to look at is the `contains` method:

```
var divElement = document.querySelector("#myDiv");

if (divElement.classList.contains("bar") == true) {
    // do something
}
```

This method checks to see if the specified class value exists on the element. If the value exists, you get **true**. If the value doesn't exist, you get **false**.

Going Further

As you can see, the `classList` API provides you with almost everything you need to add, remove, or inspect class values on an element very easily. The emphasis being on the word almost. For the few things the API doesn't provide by default, you can go online and read my full article on everything that you can do with `classList`: **http://bit.ly/kClassList**.

THE ABSOLUTE MINIMUM

So, there you have it—two perfectly fine JavaScript-based approaches you can use for styling your elements. Of these two choices, if you have the ability to modify your CSS, I would prefer that you style elements by adding and removing classes using the `classList` approach. The simple reason is that this approach is far more maintainable. It is much easier to add and remove style properties from a style rule in CSS as opposed to adding and removing lines of JavaScript.

TIP Just a quick reminder for those of you reading these words in the print or e-book edition of this book: If you go to **www.quepublishing.com** and register this book, you can receive free access to an online Web Edition that not only contains the complete text of this book but also features a short, fun interactive quiz to test your understanding of the chapter you just read.

If you're reading these words in the Web Edition already and want to try your hand at the quiz, then you're in luck – all you need to do is scroll down!

IN THIS CHAPTER

- Learn how to navigate the DOM tree
- Use the various APIs you have for moving and re-parenting elements
- Find an element's sibling, parent, children, and more

25

TRAVERSING THE DOM

As you may have realized by now, your DOM looks like a giant tree—a giant tree with elements dangerously hanging on to branches and trying to avoid the pointy things that litter the place. To get a little more technical, elements in your DOM are arranged in a hierarchy that defines what you eventually see in the browser:

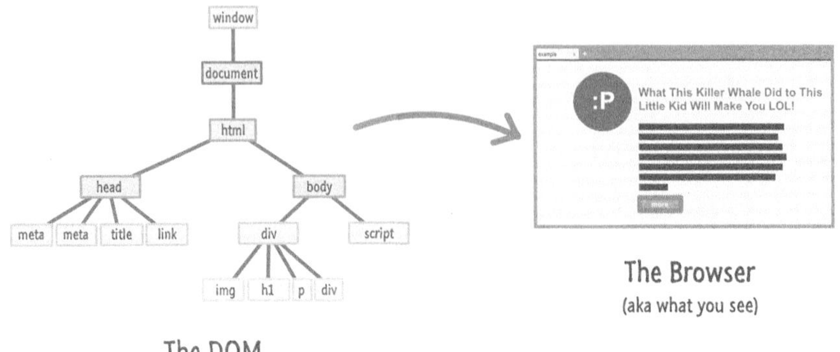

The DOM

The Browser
(aka what you see)

This hierarchy is used to help organize your HTML elements. It is also used to help your CSS style rules make sense of what styles to apply on which things. From the JavaScript angle, this hierarchy does add a bit of complexity. That's where this chapter comes in. To help you understand how to easily navigate from branch to branch (basically, like a monkey), the DOM provides you with a handful of properties that you can combine with techniques you already know. This chapter will give you an overview of all that and more.

Onwards!

Finding Your Way Around

Before you can find elements and do awesome things with them, you need to first get to where the elements are. The easiest way to tackle this topic is to just start from the top and slide all the way down. That's exactly what we are going to do.

The view from the top of your DOM is made up of your `window`, `document`, and `html` elements:

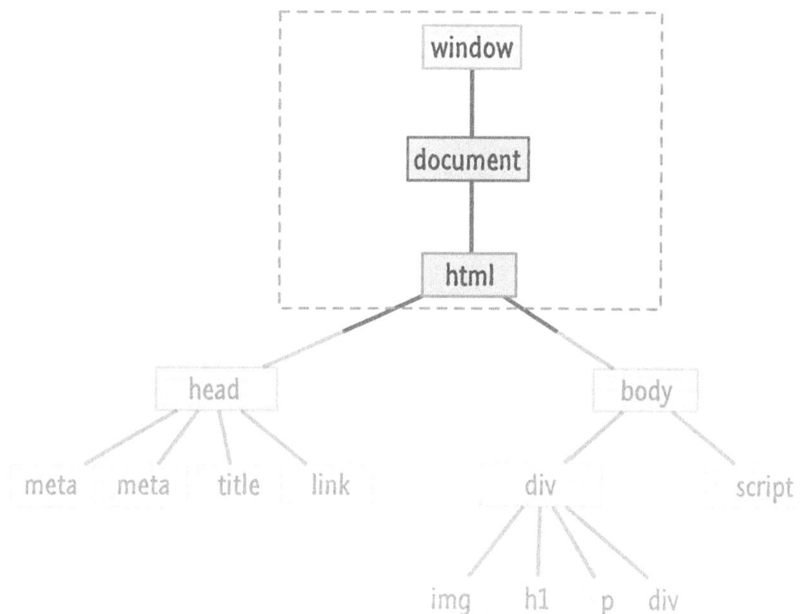

You've already seen a blurb about them a few chapters ago, so I'll make this quick. Because of how important these three things are, the DOM provides you with easy access to them via `window`, `document`, and `document.documentElement`:

```
var windowObject = window; // um....
var documentObject = document;  // this is probably unnecessary
var htmlElement = document.documentElement;
```

One thing to note is that both `window` and `document` are global properties. You don't have to explicitly declare them like I did. Just shake and use them straight out of the container.

Once you go below the HTML element level, your DOM will start to branch out and get more interesting. At this point, you have several ways of navigating around. One way that you've seen plenty of (mostly in the previous chapter) is by using `querySelector` and `querySelectorAll` to precisely get at the elements you are interested in. For many practical cases, these two methods are too limiting.

Sometimes, you don't know where you want to go. The `querySelector` and `querySelectorAll` methods won't help you here. You just want to get in the car and drive...and hope you find what you are looking for. When it comes to navigating the DOM, you'll find yourself in this position all the time. That's where the various built-in properties the DOM provides for will help you out, and we are going to look at those properties next.

The thing that will help you out is knowing that all of our elements in the DOM have at least one combination of parents, siblings, and children to rely on. To visualize this, take a look at the row containing the `div` and `script` elements in Figure 25.1.

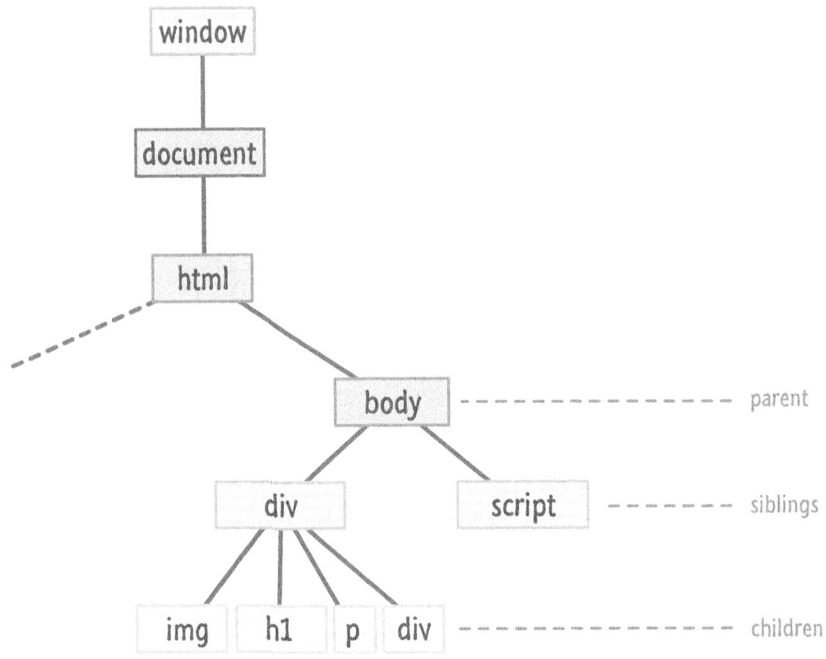

FIGURE 25.1

Your DOM elements are part of some parent/sibling/child arrangement.

Both the `div` and `script` elements are siblings. The reason they are siblings is because they share the body element as their parent. The `script` element has no children, but the `div` element does. The `img`, `h1`, `p`, and `div` are children of the `div` element, and all children of the same parent are siblings as well. Just like in real life, the parent, child, and sibling relationship is based on where in the tree you are focusing on. Almost every element, depending on the angle with which you look at them under, can play multiple familial roles.

To help you through all of this, you have a handful of properties that you will rely on. These properties are `firstChild`, `lastChild`, `parentNode`, `children`, `previousSibling`, and `nextSibling`. From just looking at their names, you should be able to infer what role these properties play. The guy in red with the pointed pitchfork is in the details, so we'll look at this in greater detail next.

Dealing with Siblings and Parents

Of these properties, the easiest ones to deal with are the parents and siblings. The relevant properties for this are `parentNode`, `previousSibling`, and `nextSibling`. The diagram in Figure 25.2 gives you an idea of how these three properties work:

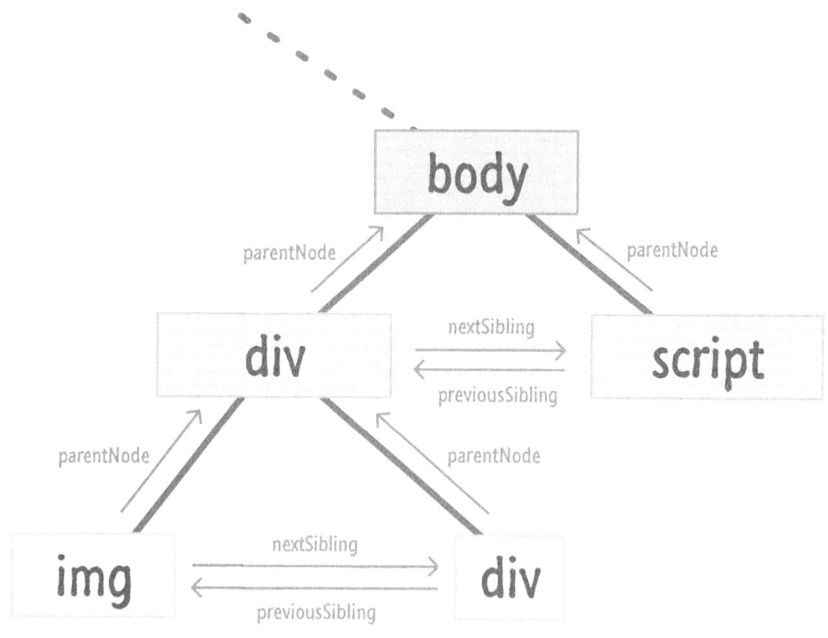

FIGURE 25.2

All in the family!

This diagram is a little busy, but if you squint really hard you can sort of make out what is going on here. The parentNode property points you to the element's parent. The `previousSibling` and `nextSibling` properties allow an element to find its previous or next sibling. You can see this visualized in the diagram by just moving in the direction of the arrow. In the last line, our `img`'s `nextSibling` is the `div`. Our `div`'s `previousSibling` is the `img`. Accessing `parentNode` on either of these elements will take you to the parent `div` in the second row. It's all pretty straightforward.

Let's Have Some Kids!

What is a little less straightforward is how the children fit into all of this, so let's take a look at the `firstChild`, `lastChild`, and `children` properties in the diagram in Figure 25.3.

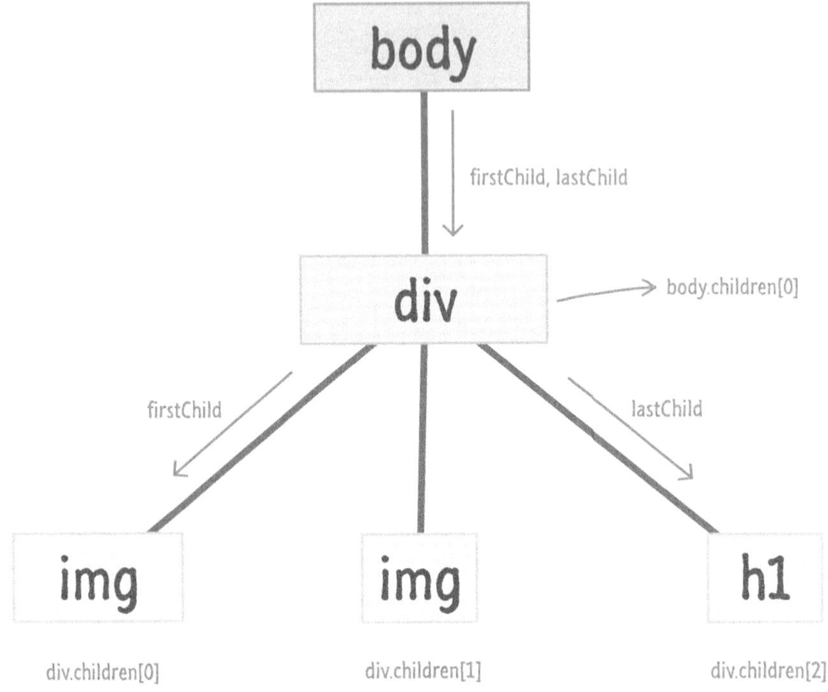

FIGURE 25.3

Navigating via children is another way of getting around.

The `firstChild` and `lastChild` properties refer to a parent's first and last child elements. If the parent only has one child, as is the case with the `body` element in our example, then both `firstChild` and `lastChild` point to the same thing. If an element has no children, then these properties return a **null**.

The tricky one compared to the other properties we've looked at is the `children` property. When you access the `children` property on a parent, you basically get a collection of the child elements the parent has. This collection is not an `Array`, but it does have some `Array`-like powers. Just like with an `Array`, you can iterate through this collection or access the children individually kind of like what you see in the diagram. This collection also has a `length` property that tells you the count of how many children the parent is dealing with. If your head is spinning from all of this, don't worry. The snippets in the next section will help clarify the vagueness.

Putting It All Together

Now that you have a good idea of all the important properties you have for traversing the DOM, let's look at some code snippets that tie in all the diagrams and words into some sweet lines of JavaScript.

Checking Whether a Child Exists

To check if an element has a child, you can do something like the following:

```
var bodyElement = document.body;

if (bodyElement.firstChild) {
    // do something interesting
}
```

This chunk of code will return **null** if there are no children. You could also have used `bodyElement.lastChild` or `bodyElement.children.length` if you enjoy typing, but I prefer to just keep things simple.

Accessing All the Child Elements

If you want to access all of a parent's children, you can always rely on good old uncle `for` loop:

```
var bodyElement = document.body;

for (var i = 0; i < bodyElement.children.length; i++) {
    var childElement = bodyElement.children[i];

    document.writeln(childElement.tagName);
}
```

Notice that I am using the `children` and `length` properties property just like I would an `Array`. The thing to remember is that this collection is actually not an `Array`. Almost all of the `Array` methods that you may want to use will not be available in this collection returned by the `children` property.

Walking the DOM

The last snippet touches upon a little bit of everything you've seen so far. This snippet recursively walks the DOM and awkwardly runs into every HTML element it can find:

```
function theDOMElementWalker(node) {
    if (node.nodeType == 1) {

        // do something with the node

        node = node.firstChild;

        while (node) {
            theDOMElementWalker(node);
            node = node.nextSibling;
        }
    }
}
```

To see this function in action, simply call it by passing in a node that you want to start your walk from:

```
var texasRanger = document.querySelector("#texas");
theDOMElementWalker(texasRanger);
```

In this example, we are calling `theDOMElementWalker` function on an element referenced by the `texasRanger` variable. If you want to run some code on the element that this script found, replace my commented out line with whatever you want to do.

THE ABSOLUTE MINIMUM

Finding your way around the DOM is one of those skills that every JavaScript developer should be familiar with. This chapter provided you an overview of what is technically possible. The onus of applying this in more practical ways falls entirely on you....or a cool friend who helps you out with these things. With that said, in subsequent chapters, we will expand upon what you've seen here as part of continuing our deep dive into everything you can do with the DOM. *Doesn't that sound exciting?*

TIP Just a quick reminder for those of you reading these words in the print or e-book edition of this book: If you go to **www.quepublishing.com** and register this book, you can receive free access to an online Web Edition that not only contains the complete text of this book but also features a short, fun interactive quiz to test your understanding of the chapter you just read.

If you're reading these words in the Web Edition already and want to try your hand at the quiz, then you're in luck – all you need to do is scroll down!

IN THIS CHAPTER

- Understand how easy it is to use JavaScript to create DOM elements from nothing
- Learn how to clone existing DOM elements as well as remove DOM elements you no longer want

26

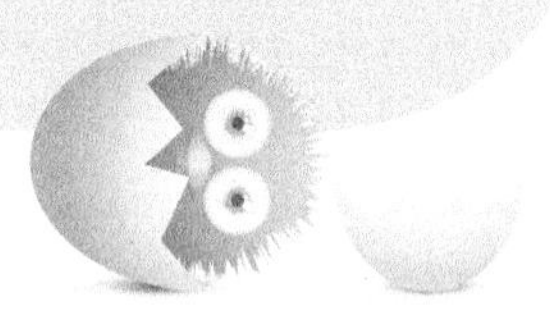

CREATING AND REMOVING DOM ELEMENTS

This part may blow you away. For the following sentences, I suggest you hold on to something sturdy:

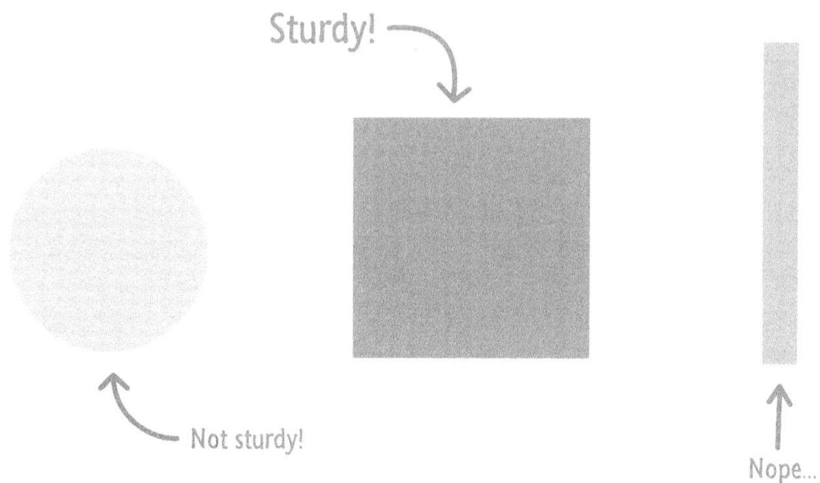

Despite what my earlier chapters may have led you to believe, your DOM does not have to be made up of HTML elements that exist in markup. You have the ability to create HTML elements out of thin air and add them to your DOM using just a few lines of JavaScript. You also have the ability to move elements around, remove them, and do all sorts of God-like things. Let's pause for a bit while we let all of that sink in. This is pretty big.

Besides the initial coolness of all this, the ability to dynamically create and modify elements in your DOM is an important detail that makes a lot of your favorite websites and applications tick. When you think about this, this makes sense. Having everything predefined in your HTML is very limiting. You want your content to change and adapt when new data is pulled in, when you interact with the page, when you scroll further, or when you do a billion other things.

In this chapter, we are going to cover the basics of what makes all of this work. We are going to look at how to create elements, remove elements, re-parent elements, and clone elements. This is also the last of our chapters looking directly at DOM-related shenanigans, so get your friends and the balloons ready!

Onwards!

Creating Elements

Like I mentioned in the introduction, it is very common for interactive sites and apps to dynamically create HTML elements and have them live in the DOM. If this is the first time you are hearing about something like this being possible, you are going to love this section!

The way to create elements is by using the `createElement` method. The way `createElement` works is pretty simple. You call it via your `document` object and pass in the tag name of the element you wish to create. In the following snippet, you are creating a paragraph element represented by the letter `p`:

```
var el = document.createElement("p");
```

If you run this line of code as part of your app, it will execute and a `p` element will get created. If you assign the `createElement` call to a variable (`el` in our case), then the variable will store a reference to this newly created element. Now, creating an element is the simple part. Actually raising it to be a fun and responsible member of the DOM is where you need some extra effort. You need to actually place this element somewhere in the DOM, for your dynamically created `p` element is just floating around aimlessly right now:

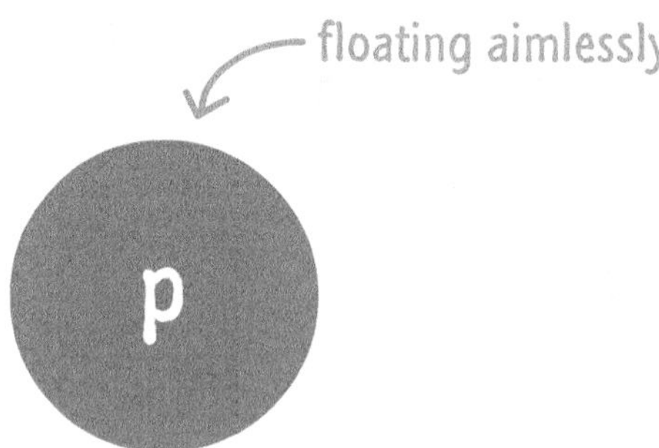

The reason for this aimlessness is because your DOM has no real knowledge that this element exists. In order for an element to be a part of the DOM, there are two things we need to do:

1. Find an element that will act as the parent
2. Use `appendChild` and add the element you want into that parent element

The following highlighted line shows both of these steps in action:

```
<body>
    <h1 id="theTitle" class="highlight summer">What's happening?
      </h1>

    <script>
        var newElement = document.createElement("p");
        newElement.textContent = "I exist entirely in your
          imagination.";

        document.body.appendChild(newElement);
    </script>
</body>
```

Our parent is going to be the **body** element, which I access via `document.body`. On the **body** element, we call `appendChild` and pass in an argument to our newly created element, to which I hold a reference with the `newElement` variable.

After these lines of code have run, your newly created p element will not only exist but also be a card-carrying member of the DOM.

The following is a visualization of what the DOM for our simple example looks like (assume we also have a **head**, **title**, and **style** element in the markup defined):

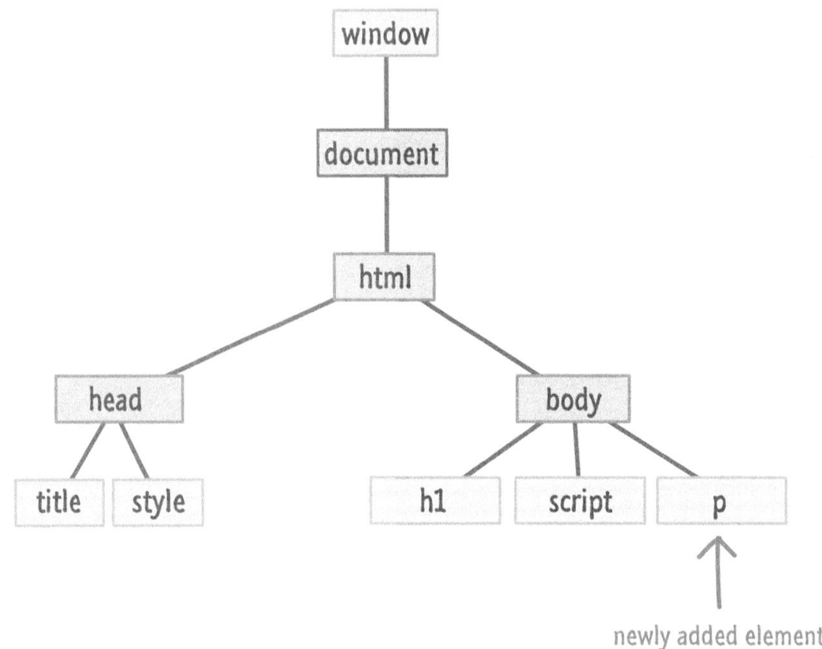

Now, one thing to note about the **appendChild** function is that it always adds the element to the end of whatever children a parent may have. In our case, our **body** element already has the h1 and **script** elements as its children. The p element gets appended after them as the youngest child. With that said, you do have control over the exact order where a particular element will live under a parent.

If you want to insert **newElement** directly after your h1 tag, you can do so by calling the insertBefore function on the parent. The insertBefore function takes two arguments. The first argument is the element you want to insert. The second argument is a reference to the sibling (aka child of a parent) you want to precede. Here is our example modified to have our **newElement** live after your h1 element (and before your script element):

```
<body>
    <h1 id="theTitle" class="highlight summer">What's happening?</h1>
```

```
    <script>
        var newElement = document.createElement("p");
        newElement.textContent = "I exist entirely in your
          imagination.";

        var scriptElement = document.querySelector("script");
        document.body.insertBefore(newElement, scriptElement);
    </script>
</body>
```

Notice that I call `insertBefore` on the `body` element and specify that `newElement` should be inserted before our `script` element. Our DOM in this case would look as follows:

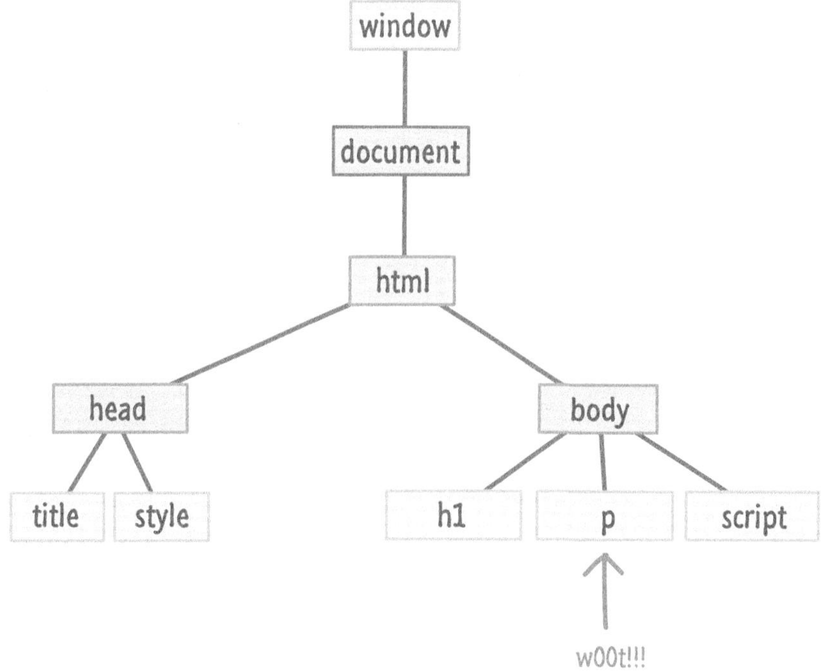

You might think that if there is an `insertBefore` method, there must be an `insertAfter` method as well. As it turns out, that isn't the case. There isn't a widely supported built-in way of inserting an element AFTER an element instead of before it. What you can do is trick the `insertBefore` function by telling it to insert an element *an extra element ahead*. That probably makes no sense, so let me show you the code first and explain later:

```
<body>
    <h1 id="theTitle" class="highlight summer">What's happening?</h1>

    <script>
        var newElement = document.createElement("p");
        newElement.textContent = "I exist entirely in your
          imagination.";

        var h1Element = document.querySelector("h1");
        document.body.insertBefore(newElement, h1Element.
          nextSibling);
    </script>
</body>
```

Pay attention to the highlighted lines, and then take a look at the following diagram, which illustrates what is happening:

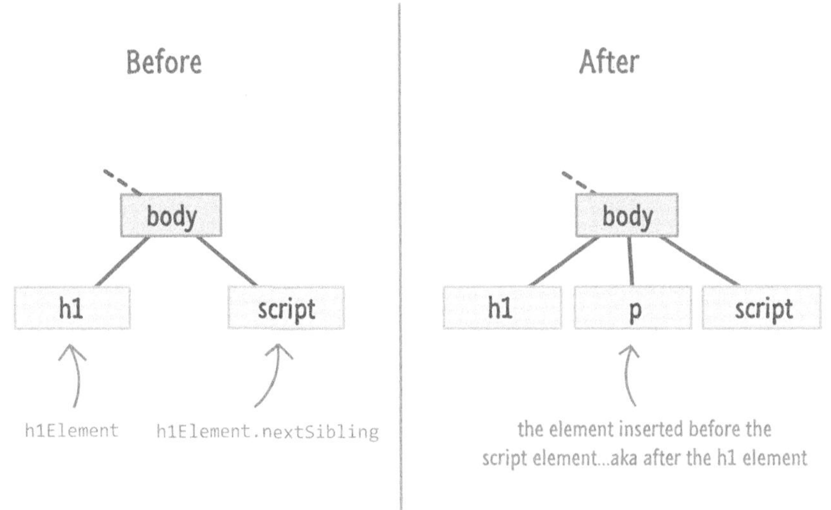

The **h1Element.nextSibling** property references the **script** element. Inserting your **newElement** before your script element accomplishes your goal of inserting your element after your **h1** element. What if there is no sibling element to target? Well, the **insertBefore** function in that case is pretty clever and just appends the element you want to the end automatically.

HANDY DANDY FUNCTION

If for some reason you find yourself wanting to insert elements after another sibling all the time, then you may want to use this function to simplify your life a bit:

```
function insertAfter(target, newElement) {
    target.parentNode.insertBefore(newElement, target.nextSibling);
}
```

Yes, I do realize this is a roundabout way of doing this, but it works...really well. You can even go all out and extend `HTMLElement` with this function to provide this functionality more conveniently to all your HTML elements. **Chapter 17**, which you probably already read and told everyone about, covers how to do something like that in greater detail. Note that extending your DOM is frowned upon by some people, so make sure to have some witty banter on the ready to lighten the mood if you ever are accosted by these "some people".

Removing Elements

I think somebody smart (probably Drake?) once said the following: *That which has the ability to create, also has the ability to remove*. In the previous section, we saw how you can use the `createElement` method to create an element. In this section, we are going to look at `removeChild` which, given its slightly unsavory name, is all about removing elements.

Take a look at the following example:

```
<body>
    <h1 id="theTitle" class="highlight summer">What's happening?</h1>

    <script>
        var newElement = document.createElement("p");
```

```
        newElement.textContent = "I exist entirely in your
          imagination.";

        document.body.appendChild(newElement);

        document.body.removeChild(newElement);
    </script>
</body>
```

The p element stored by **newElement** is being added to our **body** element by the **appendChild** method. You saw that earlier. To remove this element, we call **removeChild** on the **body** element and pass in a pointer to the element we wish to remove. That element is, of course, **newElement**. Once **removeChild** has run, it will be as if your DOM never knew that **newElement** existed.

The main thing you should note is that you need to call **removeChild** from the parent of the child you wish to remove. This method isn't going to traverse up and down your DOM trying to find the element you want to remove. Now, let's say that you don't have direct access to an element's parent and don't want to waste time finding it. You can still remove that element very easily by using the **parentNode** property as follows:

```
<body>
    <h1 id="theTitle" class="highlight summer">What's happening?</h1>

    <script>
        var newElement = document.createElement("p");
        newElement.textContent = "I exist entirely in your
          imagination.";

        document.body.appendChild(newElement);

        newElement.parentNode.removeChild(newElement);
    </script>
</body>
```

In this variation, I remove **newElement** by calling **removeChild** on its parent by specifying **newElement.parentNode**. This looks like a roundabout method, but it gets the job done.

Besides these minor quirks, the `removeChild` function is quite merciless in its efficiency. It has the ability to remove any DOM element—including ones that were originally created in markup. You aren't limited to removing DOM elements you dynamically added. If the DOM element you are removing has many levels of children and grandchildren, all of them will be removed as well.

Cloning Elements

This chapter just keeps taking a turn for the ***weirderer*** the further we go into it, but fortunately we are at the last section. The one remaining DOM manipulation technique you need to be aware of is one that revolves around cloning elements where you start with one element and create identical replicas of it:

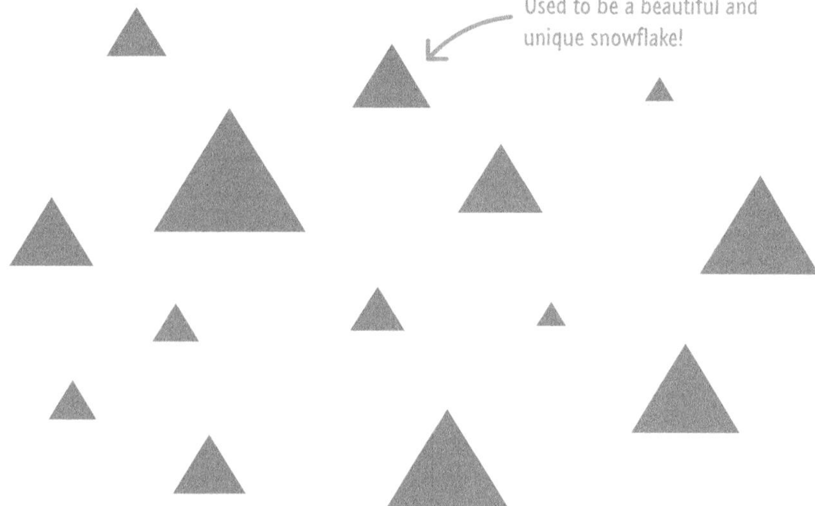

The way you clone an element is by calling the `cloneNode` function on the element you wish to clone along with providing a **true** or **false** argument to specify whether you want to clone just the element or the element and all of its children.

Here is an example that makes sense of the previous sentence with the relevant lines highlighted:

```
<!DOCTYPE HTML>
<html>
<body>
    <div id="outerContainer">
        <div>
```

```
            <h1>This one thing will change your life!!!</h1>
        </div>
    </div>
    <div id="footer">
        <div class="share">
            <p>Something</p>
            <img alt="#" src="blah.png"/>
        </div>
    </div>

    <script>
        var share = document.querySelector(".share");
        var shareClone = share.cloneNode(false);

        document.querySelector("#footer").appendChild(shareClone);
    </script>
</body>
</html>
```

Take a moment to understand what is going on here. The **share** variable gets a reference to the **div** whose **class** value is *share*. In the next line, we clone this **div** by using the **cloneNode** function:

```
var shareClone = share.cloneNode(false);
```

The **shareClone** variable now contains a reference to the cloned version of the **div** stored in the **share** variable. Note that we are calling **cloneNode** with an argument of **false**. This means that only the **div** referenced by **share** is cloned.

The postoperative steps after calling **cloneNode** are identical to what you would do with **createElement**. In the next line, we are simply appending our cloned element to the **footer div** element so that it actually finds mention in the DOM. The DOM for all of this after our code has run looks as follows:

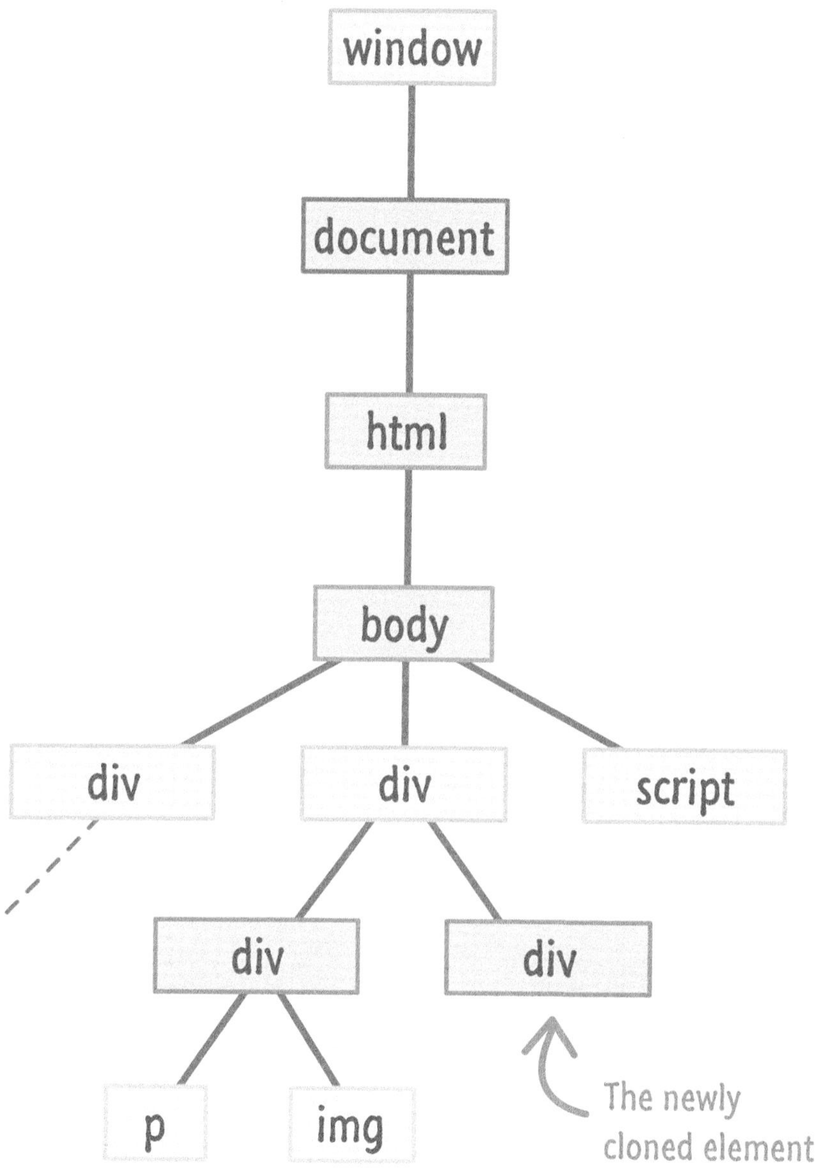

Notice that our cloned element now appears as a peer of the existing `div` element. The thing to also notice is that this cloned element contains all of the attributes that the original/source element had. For example, this `div` will also have a `class` value of **share**. Keep that in mind when you are cloning elements that contain `id` values set on them. Because `id` values need to be unique in the DOM, you may need to do some extra cleanup work to ensure the uniqueness is maintained.

We are almost done here. The last thing to look at is what happens when we call `cloneNode` and specify that the children get cloned as well. Let's change our earlier behavior by passing in a **true** instead of a **false** in our `cloneNode` call:

```
var shareClone = share.cloneNode(true);
```

When the code runs now, the end result of this minor change is that our DOM will now have a few more people in it because the children of the **.share** `div` will also be brought along:

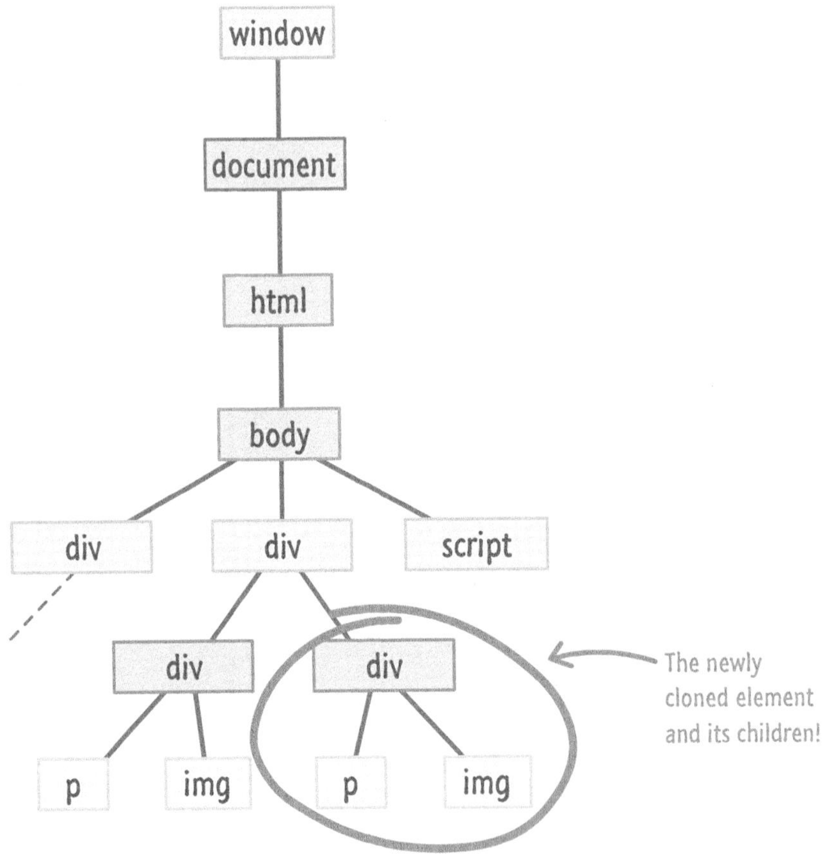

See, told you!!! The `p` and `img` elements have also been cloned and dragged along with the parent **.share** `div`. Once your cloned elements have been added to the DOM, you can then use all the tricks you've learned to modify them.

THE ABSOLUTE MINIMUM

If there is anything you walk away from after reading all this, I hope you walk away with the knowledge that your DOM is something you can touch and extensively modify. We sort of talked about how everything in the DOM can be altered earlier, but it is here where we saw first-hand the depth and breadth of the alterations you can easily make using methods like **createElement**, **removeChild**, and **cloneNode**.

With everything you've learned here, there is nothing preventing you from starting off with a completely empty page and using just a few lines of JavaScript to populate everything inside it:

```
<!DOCTYPE html>
<html>
<head>
    <title>Look what I did, ma!</title>
</head>
<body>
    <script>
        var bodyElement = document.querySelector("body");

        // create an h1 element
        var h1Element = document.createElement("h1");
        h1Element.textContent = "Do they speak English in 'What'?";

        bodyElement.appendChild(h1Element);

        var pElement = document.createElement("p");
        pElement.textContent = "I am adding some text here...like a
          boss!";

        bodyElement.appendChild(pElement);
    </script>
</body>
</html>
```

Just because you can do something like this doesn't mean you always should. The main problem with dynamically creating content is that search engines, screen readers, and other accessibility tools (even with ARIA attributes defined) probably won't know what to do if they don't have JavaScript enabled. They are more familiar with content specified in markup than they are with things created using JavaScript. Just be aware of that limitation if you ever decide to get overenthusiastic with dynamically modifying your DOM.

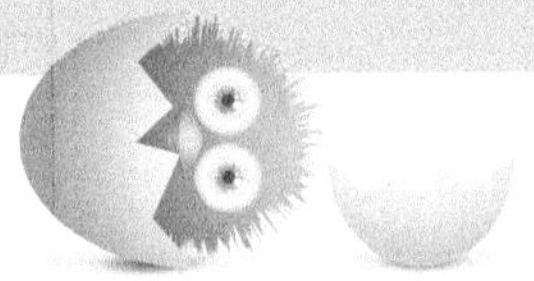

TIP Just a quick reminder for those of you reading these words in the print or e-book edition of this book: If you go to **www.quepublishing.com** and register this book, you can receive free access to an online Web Edition that not only contains the complete text of this book but also features a short, fun interactive quiz to test your understanding of the chapter you just read.

If you're reading these words in the Web Edition already and want to try your hand at the quiz, then you're in luck – all you need to do is scroll down!

IN THIS CHAPTER

- Learn how browser developer tools can save you a lot of time
- Familiarize yourself with what Chrome's Developer Tools offer

27

IN-BROWSER DEVELOPER TOOLS

All of the major browsers—Google Chrome, Apple Safari, Mozilla Firefox, and Microsoft Edge (formerly Internet Explorer)—do more than just display web pages. For developers, they provide access to a lot of cool functionality for figuring out what is actually going on with the web page that is displayed. They do all of this via what I'll generically just call the **Developer Tools**. These are tools that are built in to the browser, and they give you the ability to fiddle with your HTML, CSS, and JavaScript in a lot of neat and interesting ways.

In this chapter, let's look at these Developer Tools and learn how we can use them to make our lives easier.

Onwards!

I'LL BE USING GOOGLE CHROME

For all of the examples you are about to see, I'll be using Google's Chrome browser. While each browser provides similar functionality for what I'll be describing, the exact UI and steps to get there will vary. Just be aware of that, and also note that the version of Chrome you may be using might be more recent than the one that is used in this chapter.

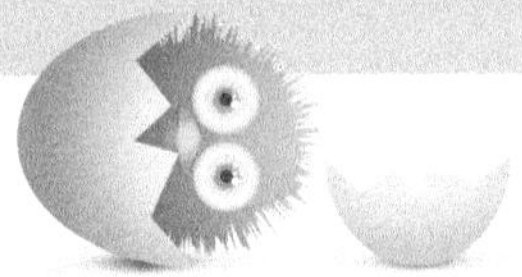

Meet the Developer Tools

Let's start at the very beginning. When you navigate to a web page, your browser will load whatever document it was told to load:

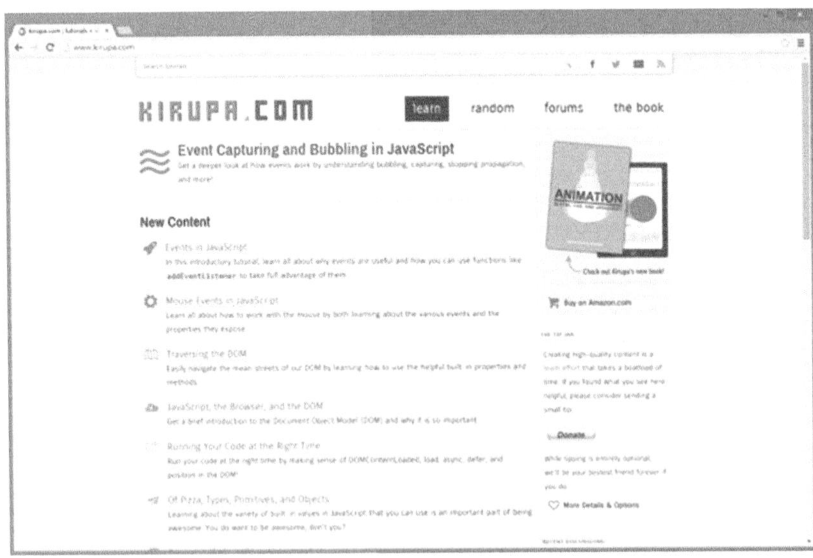

This should all be very familiar for you, as this part of the browser functionality really hasn't changed much since the very first browser that was released in the 1800s...or therabouts. While using Chrome, *press (Cmd-Opt-I) on the Mac or the F12 key [or Ctrl+Shift+I] in Windows.*

Once you've pressed those key or keys, notice what happens. While you may not hear heavenly music followed by the earth rumbling and laser beams shooting across the sky, you will see your browser's layout change to show something mysterious (usually) toward the bottom or right of the screen as shown in Figure 27.1.

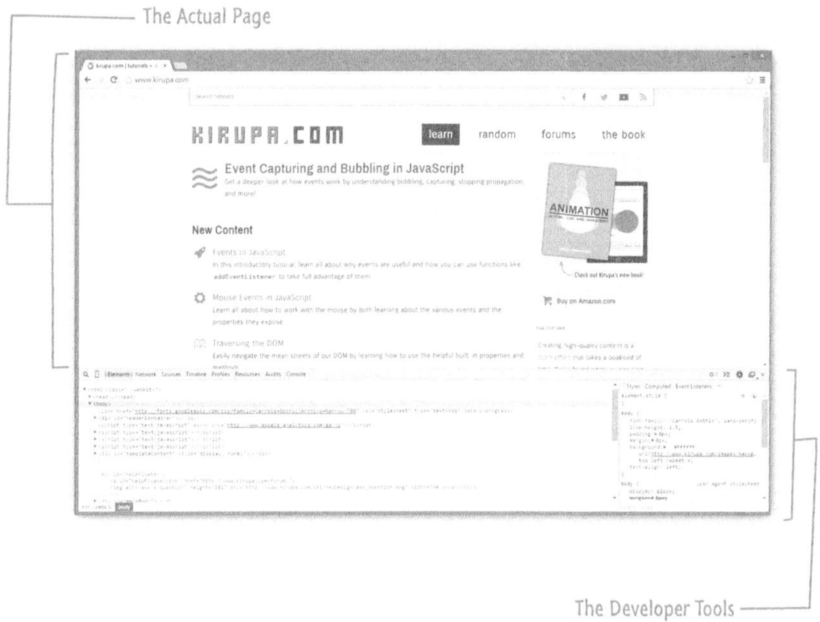

FIGURE 27.1

Your browser with its developer tools displayed right below it.

Your browser will split into two parts. One part is where your browser deals with displaying your web pages. We like this guy and have known him for quite some time. The other part, the new guy whom we eye suspiciously from a distance, provides you with access to information about the currently displayed page that only a developer such as yourself would appreciate. This guy is better known as the Developer Tools.

The Developer Tools provide you with the ability to:

- Inspect the DOM
- Debug JavaScript
- Inspect objects and view messages via the console
- Figure out performance and memory issues
- See the network traffic
- ...and a whole lot more!

In the interest of time (**Game of Thrones** is about to start soon, and this is the episode where I believe Ned Stark comes back to life as a dire wolf), what I'm going to do is focus on the first three items that are directly related to what you are learning about in this book.

Inspecting the DOM

The first Developer Tool feature we will look at is how you can inspect and even manipulate the contents of your DOM. With Chrome launched, navigate to **http://bit.ly/kirupaDevTool**.

NO BROWSER? NO PROBLEM!

Now, if you don't have a browser handy or simply can't access that link, don't worry. I'll explain what is going on at each step of the way so that you aren't left out of all the fun.

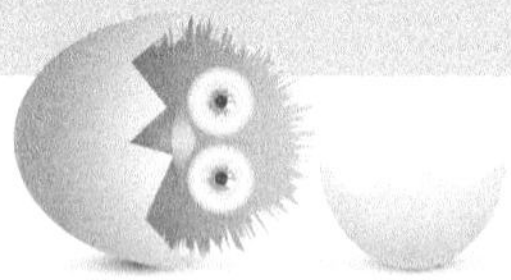

When you load this page, you will see a colorful background with some text displayed:

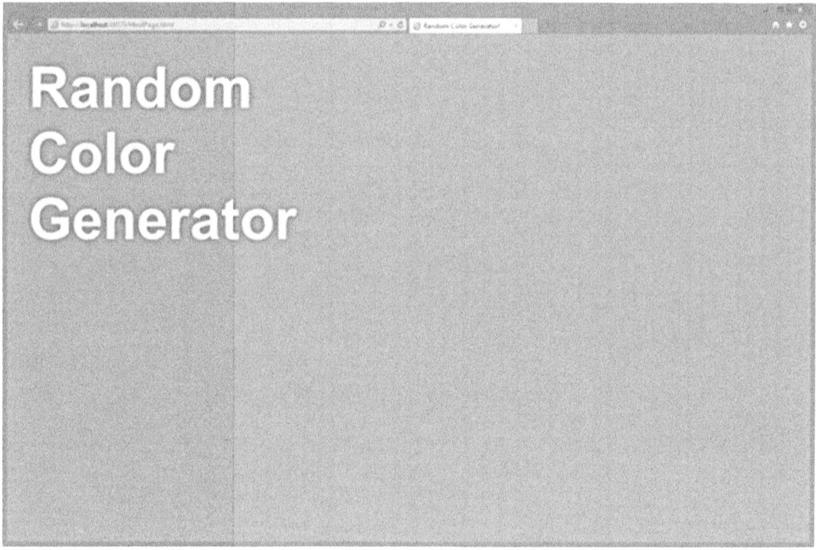

If you reload this page, you'll see this page showing up with a different background color. As you can guess, each page reload will result in a different background color getting generated:

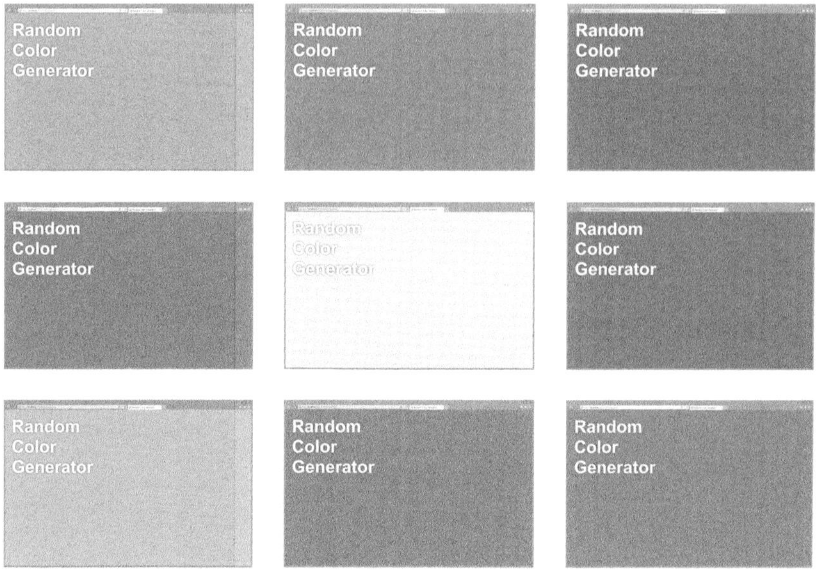

The first thing we'll do with this example is examine the DOM to see what is going on. Make sure your Developer Tools are visible, and ensure the Elements tab is selected:

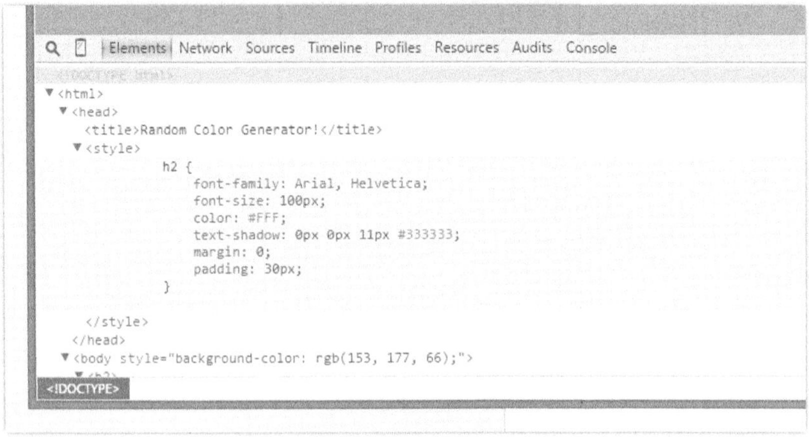

What you will see is a view of your ***live*** markup from the page that is currently shown. To be more specific, this is a **view of your DOM**. The importance of this distinction is that this view provides you with a live version of what your page looks like. Any shenanigans JavaScript or your browser may have pulled on the DOM will be shown in this view.

Using our example as an…um…example, using **View Source** will result in something that looks as follows:

```
<!DOCTYPE html>
<html>


<head>
  <title>Random Color Generator!</title>
  <style>
    h2 {
      font-family: Arial, Helvetica;
      font-size: 100px;
      color: #FFF;
      text-shadow: 0px 0px 11px #333333;
      margin: 0;
      padding: 30px;
    }
```

```
  </style>
</head>

<body>
  <h2>Random
    <br />Color
    <br />Generator</h2>
  <script src="js/randomColor.js"></script>
  <script>
    var bodyElement = document.querySelector("body");
    bodyElement.style.backgroundColor = getRandomColor();
  </script>
</body>

</html>
```

The View Source command simply gives you a view of the markup as stored in the HTML page. Another way of saying this is that View Source gives you a (stale) version of the markup as it lives is on the server and not a version of the DOM.

If you use the Developer Tool's DOM view, you will see a *DOM-based representation* of your document based on the *live version of the page*:

```
<!DOCTYPE html>
<html>

<head>
  <title>Random Color Generator!</title>
  <style>
    h2 {
      font-family: Arial, Helvetica;
      font-size: 100px;
      color: #FFF;
      text-shadow: 0px 0px 11px #333333;
      margin: 0;
      padding: 30px;
    }
  </style>
```

```
<body style="background-color: rgb(75, 63, 101);">
  <h2>Random
    <br>Color
    <br>Generator</h2>
  <script src="js/randomColor.js"></script>
  <script>
    var bodyElement = document.querySelector("body");
    bodyElement.style.backgroundColor = getRandomColor();
  </script>

</body>

</html>
```

If you pay close attention, you'll notice some subtle differences in how some elements look. The biggest difference is the highlighted inline `background-color` style on the `body` element that only exists in the DOM view but not in the traditional View Source view. The reason is that we have some JavaScript that dynamically sets an inline style on the `body` element. The following note expands on why this happens!

THE DIFFERENCE BETWEEN THE DOM VIEW AND VIEW SOURCE

The reason for the discrepancy between the two code views goes back to what the DOM represents. To repeat this one more time, your DOM is the result of your browser and JavaScript having run to completion. It provides you with a fresh-from-the-oven look that mimics what your browser sees.

View Source is just a static representation of your document as it was on the server (or your computer). It doesn't contain any of the liveliness of your running page that the DOM view highlights. If you look at our JavaScript, you'll see that I specified that our `body` element get its `backgroundColor` set dynamically:

```
var bodyElement = document.querySelector("body");
bodyElement.style.backgroundColor = getRandomColor();
```

When this code runs, it modifies the DOM to set the `backgroundColor` property on the `body` element. You would never see this using View Source. Ever. That's why the DOM view the Developer Tools provide is your bestest friend in the whole wide world.

As examples highlighting the differences between the source and DOM go, our example was quite simple. To see the real benefit of the DOM view, you should experiment with some element reparentings, creations, and deletions to really see the divergence between viewing the source and examining the DOM. Some of the examples you saw in the previous chapters around DOM manipulation would be good things to inspect as well.

Debugging JavaScript

Moving along, the other big thing that the Developer Tools bring to the table is **debuggability**. I don't know if that is a really word or not, but the Developer Tools allow you to poke and prod at your code to figure out what is going wrong (or not wrong). The general catch-all phrase for all this is known as **debugging**.

In your Developer tools, click on the **Sources** tab:

Elements Network Sources Timeline Profiles Resources Audits Console

Sources Content scripts Snippets | randomColorGenerator.htm ×

www.kirupa.com
html5/examples
js
randomColorGenerator.htm

```
<!DOCTYPE html>
<html>
<head>
    <title>Random Color Generator!</title>
    <style>
        h2 {
            font-family: Arial, Helvetica;
            font-size: 100px;
            color: #FFF;
            text-shadow: 0px 0px 11px #333333;
            margin: 0;
            padding: 30px;
        }
    </style>
</head>
<body>
```

{} Line 1, Column 1

The Sources tab gives you access to all the files that are currently being used by your document. As the name implies, you are looking at the raw contents of these files—not the DOM-generated version from earlier that is your ***bestest*** friend.

From the tree view on the left, ensure the **randomColorGenerator.htm** file is selected. This will ensure that the contents of this file are displayed for you to examine on the right. In the displayed file, scroll all the way down until you see the `script` tag with the two lines of code that you saw earlier. Based on the line counts shown in the left gutter, our lines of JavaScript should be lines 20 and 21.

What we want to do is examine what happens when the code in Line 21 is about to execute. To do this, we need to tell the browser to stop when Line 21 is about to get executed. The way you do that is by setting what is known as a **breakpoint**. To set a breakpoint, click directly on the 21 label on the left gutter.

Once you've done that, you'll see the **21** getting highlighted:

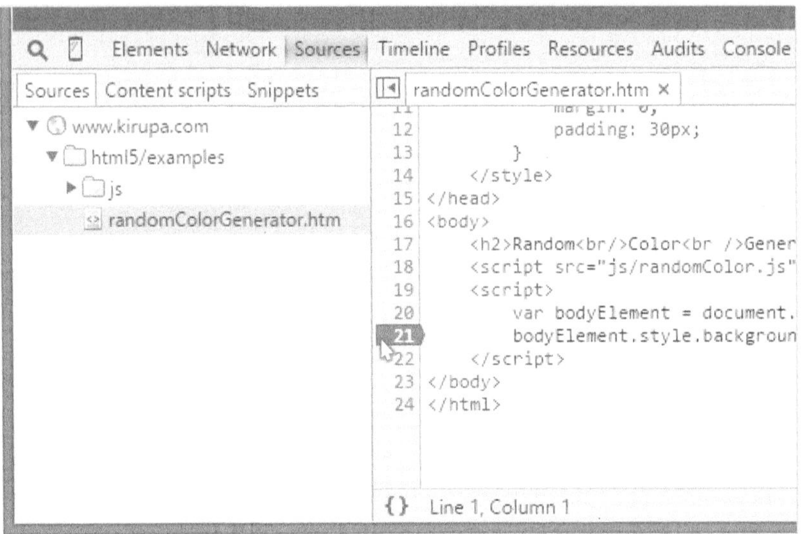

At this point, a breakpoint has been set. The next step is to actually have your browser run into this breakpoint. This is more peacefully known as "hitting the breakpoint." The way a breakpoint is hit is by ensuring your code runs into it. In our case, all we need to do is just hit F5 to refresh the page, as Line 21 will just execute as part your page loading and executing everything inside the `script` tags.

If everything worked as expected, you'll see your page load and suddenly pause with line 21 getting highlighted:

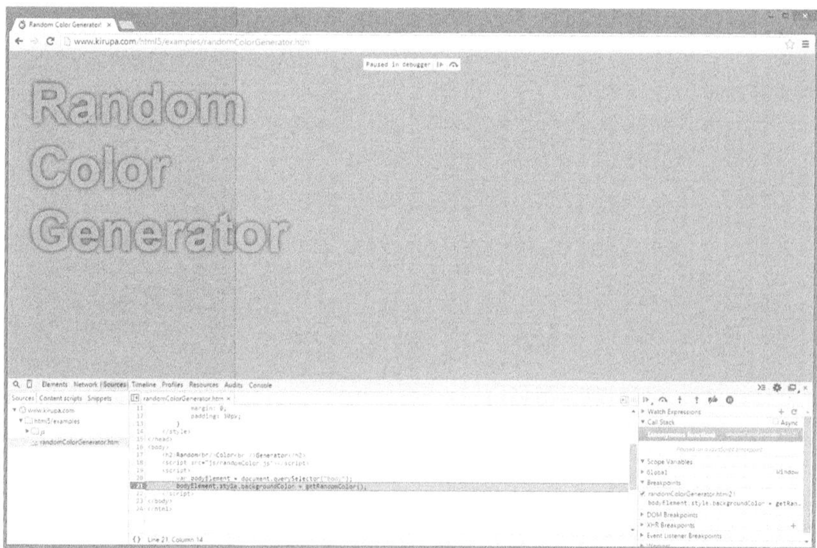

You are currently in **debugging mode**. The breakpoint you set on Line 21 has been hit. This means your entire page ground to a screeching halt the moment the browser hit it. At this point, with your browser being in suspended animation, you have the ability to fiddle with everything going on in your page. Think of this as time having stopped with only you having the ability to move around, inspect, and alter the surroundings. If a movie hasn't been made about this, somebody should get on it!

While in this mode, go back to Line 21, and hover over the `bodyElement` variable. When you hover over it, you'll see a tooltip indicating the various properties and values that this particular object contains:

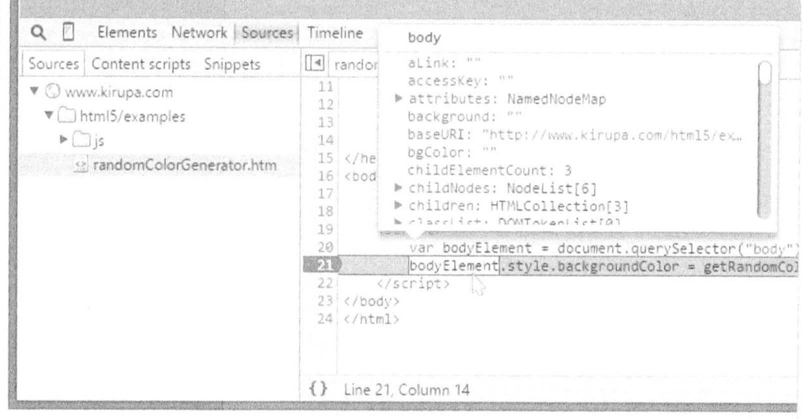

You can then interact with the tooltip, scroll through all the objects, and even dig deeper into complex objects that have more objects inside them. Because `bodyElement` is basically the JavaScript/DOM representation of the `body` element, you'll see a lot of properties that you encountered indirectly from our look at `HTMLElement` a few chapters ago.

On the right side of your source view, you have more angles through which you can inspect your code:

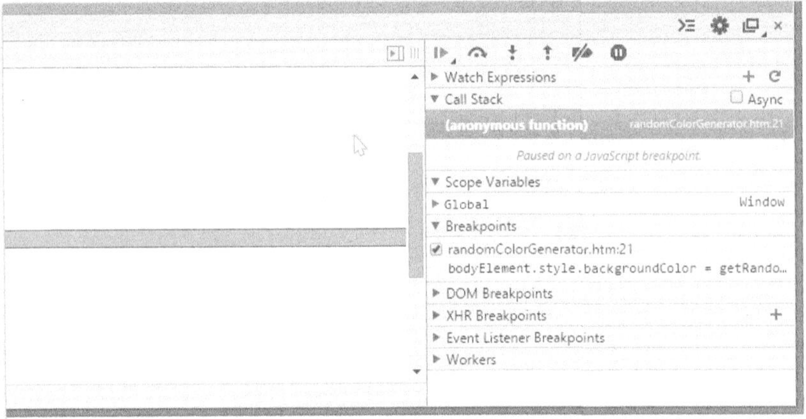

I won't be explaining what all of those categories do, but I am pointing that area out just so you know that you have the ability to examine the current state of all your JavaScript variables and objects in much greater detail if you so wanted to.

The other big advantage a breakpoint provides is the ability for you to step through your code just like your browser would. Right now, we are stuck on Line 21. To step through the code, click on the "Step into function call" button found on the right-hand side:

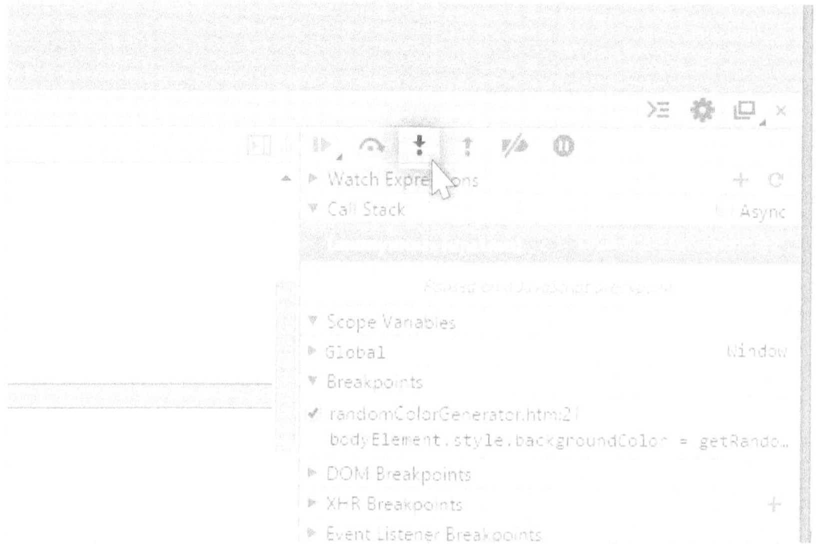

Remember, this is the line of code you are currently broken at:

```
bodyElement.style.backgroundColor = getRandomColor();
```

Once you've clicked that button, notice what happens. You will find yourself inside **randomColor.js** where the `getRandomColor` function has been defined. Keep clicking on the "Step into function call" to continue stepping into your code and going through each line of the `getRandomColor` function. Notice that you now get to see how the objects in your browser's memory update as you go line-by-line and execute the code sequentially. If you are tired of doing that, you can **Step back** by clicking on the **Step out of current function** button (found to the right of your **Step into** button) that exits you out of this function. In our case, that is back to Line 21 in randomColorGenerator.htm.

If you just want to execute your app without stepping through any more of the code, click on the **Play** button found a few pixels to the left of **Step into**:

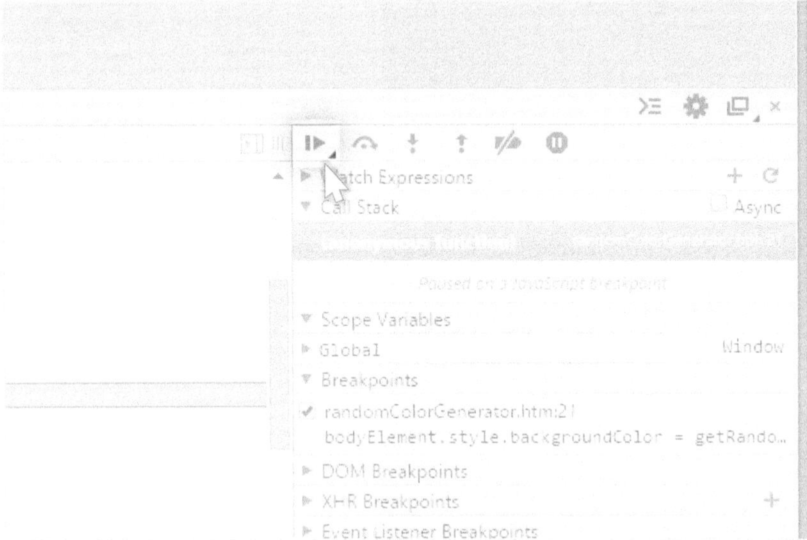

When you hit Play, your code will execute. If you happen to have another breakpoint set somewhere in your code's path, that breakpoint will also get hit. When stopped at any breakpoint, you can choose to Step into, Step out, or just resume execution with Play. Because we only set one breakpoint, hitting Play will just run the code to completion and have your random color appear as the background for your body element:

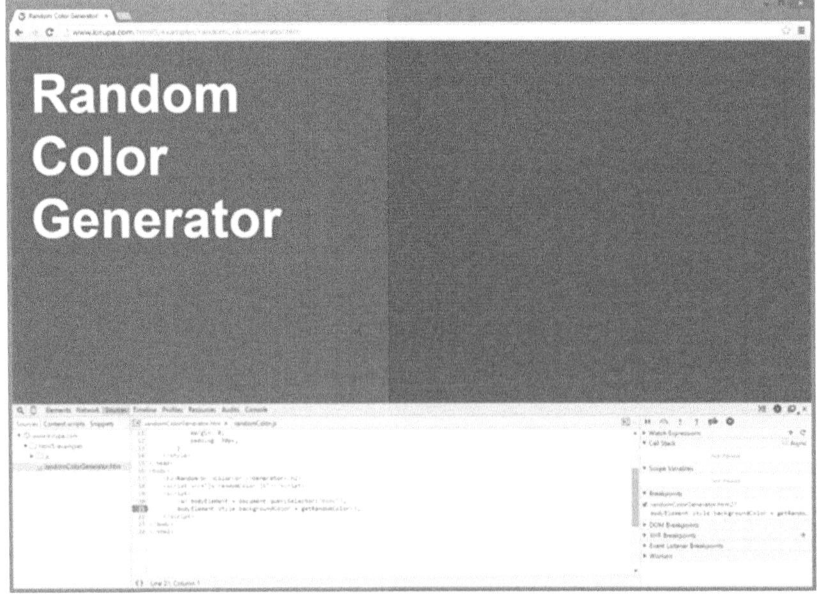

To remove a breakpoint, just click on the line number that you set the breakpoint on. If you click on the Line 21 label again, the breakpoint will toggle itself off and you can just run your application without getting into debugging mode.

So, there you have it. A whirlwind tour of how to use some of the debugging functionality you have at your disposal. To reiterate something I mentioned at the beginning of this chapter, I am only scratching the surface of what is possible. The resources I provide toward the end should help you out further.

Meet the Console

The other OTHER big Debugging Tool functionality we will look at is using what is known as the **Console**. The console provides you with the ability to do several things. It allows you to see messages logged by your code. It also allows you to pass commands and inspect any object that is currently in scope.

To show the Console, navigate to the Console tab by clicking (or tapping) on it:

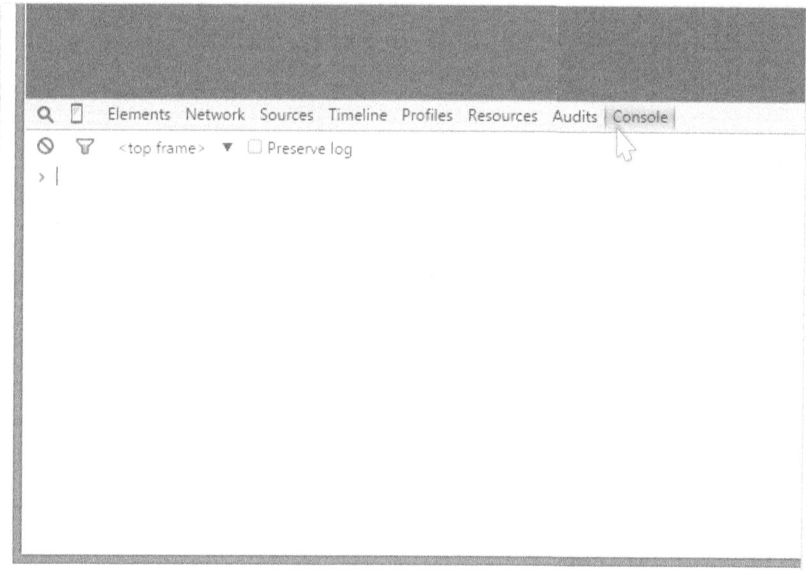

Don't be afraid of the vast emptiness that you see in front of you. Instead, embrace the freedom and fresh air.

Anyway, what the Console provides you with is the ability to inspect or call any object that exists in whatever scope your application is currently running in. With no breakpoints set, launching the console puts you in the global state.

Inspecting Objects

Where your cursor is right now, type in **window** and press Enter:

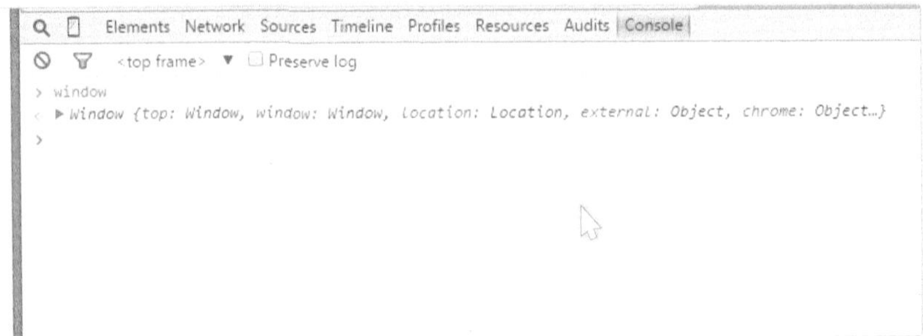

What you will see is an interactive listing of all the things that live in your `window` object. You can start to type in any valid object or property, and if it is in scope, you will be able to access it, inspect its value, or even execute it:

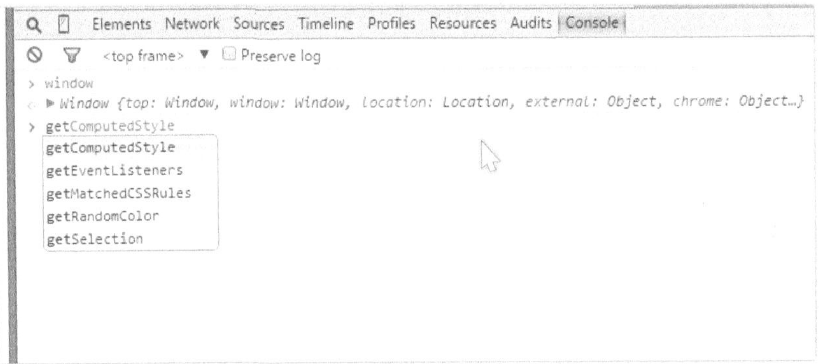

This is by no means a read-only playground. You can cause all sorts of mayhem. For example, if you type in **document.body.remove()** and press Enter, your entire document will just disappear. If you did end up deleting the `body`, just refresh the page to get back to your earlier state. Developer Tools primarily work with the in-memory representation of your page and don't write back to source. Your experimentations will safely stay in the transient realm.

REFRESHER ON THE SCOPE/STATE

On several occasions, I mentioned that your console allows you to inspect the world at whatever scope you are currently in. This is basically just applying what you learned about Variable Scope in **Chapter 6** to the Console's behavior.

Let's say you have a breakpoint set at the following highlighted line:

```
var oddNumber = false;

function calculateOdd(num) {
  if (num % 2 == 0) {
    oddNumber = false;
  } else {
    oddNumber = true;
  }
}
calculateOdd(3);
```

When you run the code and the breakpoint gets hit, the value of `oddNumber` is still **false**. Your breakpointed line hasn't been executed yet, and you can verify this by testing the value of add Number in the Console. Next, let's say you run this code, hit this breakpoint, and step through to the next line.

At this point, your `oddNumber` value is set to **true**. Your Console will now reflect the new value, for that is what the in-memory representation of `oddNumber` states. The main takeaway is that your Console's view of the world is directly tied to where in the code you are currently focusing on. This is especially made obvious when you are stepping through code and the scope you are in changes frequently.

Logging Messages

We are almost done with all of this Developer Tools business. The last thing we will look at is the console's ability to log messages from your code. Remember all those times where we did something like this?

```
function doesThisWork() {
  alert("It works!!!");
}
```

The "this" being where we used an `alert` statement to print some value or prove that the code is being executed. Well, we can stop doing that now. By using the console, you have a far less annoying way of printing messages without interrupting everything with a modal dialog box. You can use the `console.log` function to pass in whatever you want to print into the console:

```
function doesThisWork() {
  console.log("It works!!!")
}
```

When this code executes, you'll see whatever you logged get printed in your Console when you bring it up:

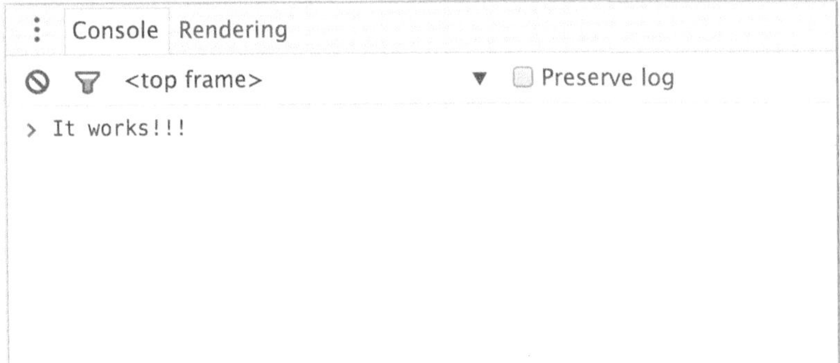

Using the console is, in almost every way, superior to using `alert` for debugging purposes. In future code snippets, you'll start to see me using `console.log` over `alert` in some cases.

THE ABSOLUTE MINIMUM

If you have never used a Developer Tool before, I really REALLY think you should take some time to get familiar with one. JavaScript is one of those languages where things can go wrong even when everything looks right. In the very simple examples you'll encounter in this book, it's easy to spot mistakes. When you start working on larger and more complex applications, having the right tools to diagnose issues will save you many hours of effort.

To learn more about the Developer Tools (aka ***Dev Tools*** as the cool kids call it) in far greater detail than what I've covered here, check out the following resources:

- **Overview of the Chrome Dev Tools: http://bit.ly/kirupaChromeDevTools**
- **Overview of the IE/Edge F12 Dev Tools: http://bit.ly/kirupaIEDevTools**
- **Overview of the Firefox Dev Tools: http://bit.ly/kirupaFFDevTools**
- **Overview of the Safari Web Inspector http://bit.ly/kirupaSafariDevTools**

TIP Just a quick reminder for those of you reading these words in the print or e-book edition of this book: If you go to **www.quepublishing.com** and register this book, you can receive free access to an online Web Edition that not only contains the complete text of this book but also features a short, fun interactive quiz to test your understanding of the chapter you just read.

If you're reading these words in the Web Edition already and want to try your hand at the quiz, then you're in luck – all you need to do is scroll down!

IN THIS CHAPTER

- Understand how communication happens between you and your app
- Learn about events
- Use event arguments to better handle event-related scenarios

28

EVENTS

In case you haven't noticed, most applications and websites are pretty boring when left alone. They launch with great fanfare and gusto, but the excitement they bring to the table goes away very quickly if you don't start interacting with them:

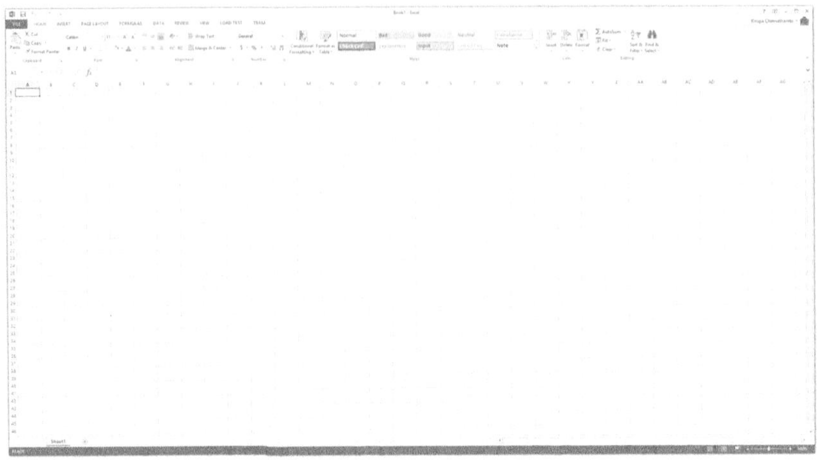

OMG! Just do something...anything!

The reason for this is simple. Your applications exist to react to things that you do to them. They have some built-in motivation when you launch them to get themselves out of bed and ready for the day. Everything else that they do afterwards depends largely on what you tell them to do. This is where things get really interesting.

You tell your applications what to do by having them react to what are known as **events**. In this chapter, we will take an introductory look at what events are and how you can use them.

Onwards!

What Are Events?

At a high level, everything you create can be modeled by the following statement as shown in the following:

When _______ happens, do _______.

You can fill in the blanks in this statement in a bajillion different ways. The first blank calls out *something that happens*. The second blank describes the *reaction to that*. The following are some examples of this statement filled out:

When a page load happens, do play the video of a cat sliding into cardboard.

When a click happens, do submit my online purchase.

When a mouse release happens, do hurl the giant/not-so-happy bird.

When a delete key press happens, do send this file to the Recycle Bin.

When a touch gesture happens, do apply this old timey filter to this photo.

When a file download happens, do update the progress bar.

This generic model applies to all of the code we've written together. This model also applies to all of the code your favorite developer/designer friends wrote for their applications. There is no way of escaping this model, so…there is no point in resisting. Instead, you need to learn to embrace the star of this model, the very talented critter known as the **event**.

An event is nothing more than a signal. It communicates that something has just happened. This something could be a mouse click. It could be a key press on your keyboard. It could be your window getting resized. It could just be your document simply getting loaded. The thing to take away is that your signal could be one of hundreds of somethings that are built in to the JavaScript DOM API…or custom somethings that you created just for your app alone.

Getting back to our model, events make up the first half:

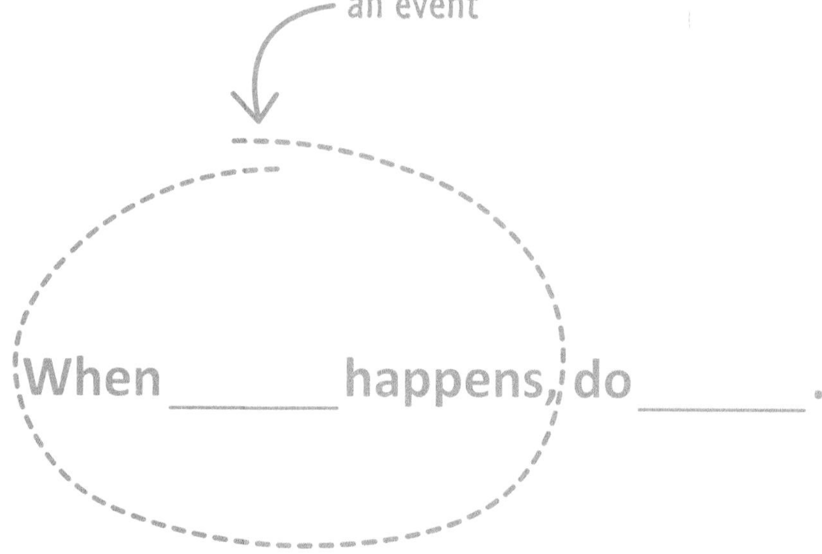

Events define the thing that happens. They fire the signal. The second part of the model is defined by the reaction to the event:

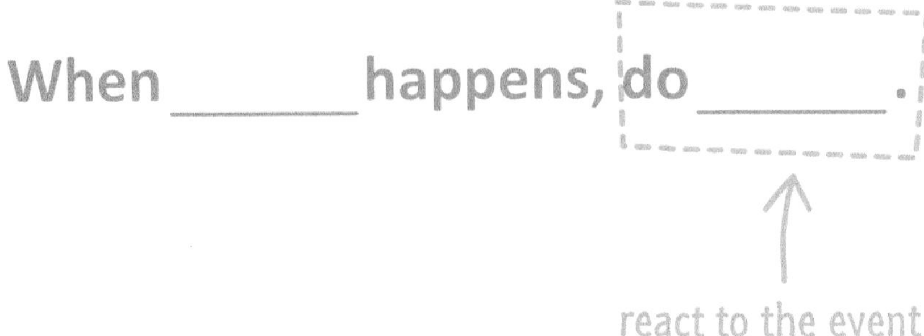

After all, what good is a signal if there isn't someone somewhere that is waiting for it and then takes the appropriate action?! Okay, now that you have a high-level overview of what events are, let's dive into how events live in the nature reserve known as JavaScript.

Events and JavaScript

Given the importance of events, it should be no surprise to you that JavaScript provides you with a lot of great support for working with them. To work with events, there are two things you need to do:

1. Listen for events
2. React to events

These two steps seem pretty simple, but never forget that we are dealing with JavaScript here. The simplicity is just a smokescreen for the deep trauma JavaScript will inflict upon you if you take a wrong step. Maybe I am being overly dramatic here, but we'll find out soon enough.

1. Listening for Events

To more bluntly state what I danced around earlier, almost everything you do inside an application results in an event getting fired. Sometimes, your application will fire events automatically such as when it loads. Sometimes, your application will fire events as a reaction to you actually interacting with it. The thing to note is that your application is bombarded by events constantly whether you intended to have them get fired or not. Our task is to tell your application to listen only to the events we care about.

The thankless job of listening to the right event is handled entirely by a function called `addEventListener`. This function is responsible for being eternally vigilant so that it can notify another part of your application when an interesting event gets fired.

The way you use this function looks as follows:

```
source.addEventListener(eventName, eventHandler, useCapture);
```

That's probably not very helpful, so let's dissect what each part of this function means.

The Source

You call `addEventListener` via an element or object that you want to listen for events on. Typically, that will be a DOM element, but it can also be your `document`, `window`, or any other object that just happens to fire events.

The Event Name

The first argument you specify to the `addEventListener` function is the name of the event you are interested in listening to. The full list of events you have at your disposal is simply too large to list here (go to **http://bit.ly/kirupaEvents** instead), but some of the most common events you will encounter are shown in the following table.

Event	Events Is Fired...
click	...when you press down and release the primary mouse button/trackpad and so on.
mousemove	...whenever your mouse cursor moves
mouseover	...when you move the mouse cursor over an element. This is the event you would use for detecting a hover!
mouseout	...when your mouse cursor moves outside the boundaries of an element.
dblclick	...when you quickly click the mouse button/trackpad twice.
DOMContentLoaded	...when your document's DOM has fully loaded. You will learn more about this event in **Chapter 32**.
load	...when your entire document (DOM, external stuff like images, scripts, and so on) has fully loaded.
keydown	...when you press down on a key on your keyboard
keyup	...when you release a key press on your keyboard
scroll	...when an element is scrolled around
wheel & DOMMouseScroll	...every time you use your mousewheel to scroll up or down

In subsequent chapters, we will look at a lot of these events in greater detail. For now, just take a quick glance at the **click** event, for we will be using that one in a few moments.

The Event Handler

The second argument requires you to specify a function that will get called when the event gets overheard. This function is very affectionately known as the **event handler** by friends and family. You'll learn a whole lot more about this function in a few moments.

To Capture or Not to Capture—That Is the Question!

The last argument is made up of either a **true** or a **false**. To fully help you understand the implications of specifying either value, you are going to have to wait until the the next chapter where we talk about **Event Bubbling and Capturing**.

Putting It All Together

Now that you've seen the **addEventListener** function and what it looks like, let's tie it all up with an example of this function fully decked out:

```
document.addEventListener("click", changeColor, false);
```

Our **addEventListener** in this example is attached to the **document** object. When a **click** event is overheard, it calls the **changeColor** function (aka the event handler) to react to the event. This sets us up nicely for the next section which is all about reacting to events.

2. Reacting to Events

As you saw in the previous section, listening to events is handled by **addEventListener**. What to do after an event is overheard is handled by the event handler. I wasn't joking when I mentioned earlier that an event handler is nothing more than a function:

```
function normalAndBoring() {
    // I like hiking and puppies and other stuff!
}
```

The only distinction between a typical function and one that is designated as the event handler is that your event handler function is specifically called out by name in an **addEventListener** call (and receives an **Event** object as its argument):

```
document.addEventListener("click", changeColor, false);

function changeColor() {
    // I am important!!!
}
```

Any code you place inside your event handler will execute when the event your **addEventListener** function cares about gets overheard. It's all pretty simple!

A Simple Example

The best way to make sense of what we've learned so far is to see all of this actually working. To play along, add the following markup and code to an HTML file:

```
<!DOCTYPE html>
<html>
<head>
    <title>Click Anywhere!</title>
</head>
<body>
    <script>
        document.addEventListener("click", changeColor, false);

        function changeColor() {
            document.body.style.backgroundColor = "#FFC926";
        }
    </script>
</body>
</html>
```

If you preview your document in the browser, you will initially just see a blank page:

Things will change when you click anywhere on the page, though. Once you've completed your click, your page's background will change from white to a yellowish color:

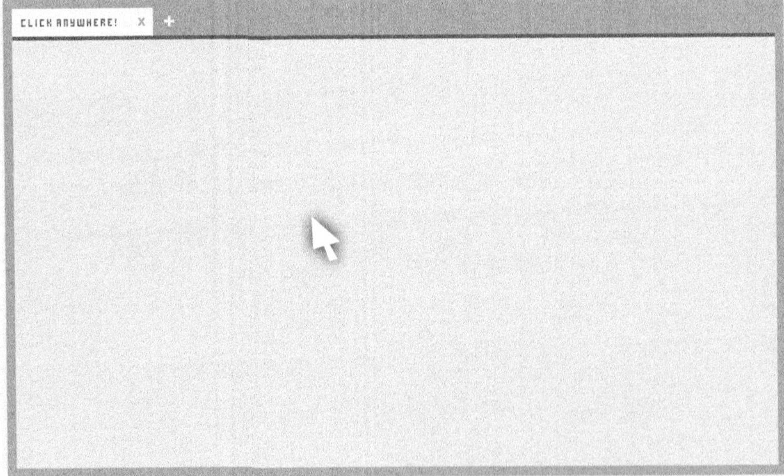

The reason for this is pretty easy to see. Let's take a look at the code:

```
document.addEventListener("click", changeColor, false);

function changeColor() {
    document.body.style.backgroundColor = "#FFC926";
}
```

The **addEventListener** call is identical to what you saw earlier, so let's skip that one. Instead, pay attention to the **changeColor** event handler:

```
document.addEventListener("click", changeColor, false);

function changeColor() {
    document.body.style.backgroundColor = "#FFC926";
}
```

This function gets called when the **click** event on the **document** is overheard. When this function gets called, it sets the background color of the body element to a shade of yellow. Tying this back to the very beginning where we generalized how applications work, this is what this example looks like:

If all of this makes complete sense to you, then that's great! You just learned about one of the most important concepts you'll encounter. We aren't done just yet. We let the event handler off the hook a little too easily, so let's pay it one more visit.

The Event Arguments and the Event Type

Your event handler does more than just get called when an event gets overheard by an event listener. It also provides access to the underlying event object as part of its arguments. To access this event object easily, we need to modify your event handler signature to support this argument.

Here is an example:

```
function myEventHandler(e) {
    // event handlery stuff
}
```

At this point, your event handler is still a plain ol' boring function. It just happens to be a function that takes one argument...the event argument! You can go with any valid identifier for the argument, but I tend to go with **e** because that is what all the cool kids do. There is nothing technically wrong with identifying your event as follows:

```
function myEventHandler(isNyanCatReal) {
    // event handlery stuff
}
```

Anyway, the event argument points to an `Event` object, and this object is passed in as part of the event firing. There is a reason why we are paying attention to what seems like a typical and boring occurrence. This `Event` object contains properties that are *relevant to the event that was fired*. An event triggered by a mouse click will have different properties when compared to an event triggered by your keyboard key press, a page load, an animation, and a whole lot more. Most events will have their own specialized behavior that you will rely on, and the event object is your gateway into all of that uniqueness.

Despite the variety of events and resulting event objects you can get, there are certain properties that are common. This commonality is made possible because all event objects are derived from a base `Event` type (technically, an `Interface`). Some of the popular properties from the `Event` type that you will use are as follows:

1. `currentTarget`
2. `target`
3. `preventDefault`
4. `stopPropagation`
5. `type`

To fully understand what these properties do, we need to go a little deeper into our understanding of events. We aren't there yet, so just know that these properties exist. You'll be seeing them real soon in future chapters.

REMOVING AN EVENT LISTENER

Sometimes, you will need to remove an event listener from an element. The way you do that is by using `addEventListener`'s arch-nemesis, the `removeEventListener` function:

```
something.removeEventListener(eventName, eventHandler, useCapture);
```

As you can see, this function takes the exact number and type of arguments as an `addEventListener` function. The reason for that is simple. When you are listening for an event on an element or object, JavaScript uses an `addEventListener`'s **`eventName`**, **`eventHandler`**, and the **true/false** value to uniquely identify that event listener. To remove this event listener, you need to specify the exact same arguments.

Here is an example:

```
document.addEventListener("click", changeColor, false);
document.removeEventListener("click", changeColor, false);

function changeColor() {
    document.body.style.backgroundColor = "#FFC926";
}
```

The event listener we added in the first line is completely neutralized by the `removeEventListener` call in the highlighted second line. Notice the identical argument values for both of these functions.

THE ABSOLUTE MINIMUM

Well, that's all there is to getting an introduction to events. Just remember that you have your `addEventListener` function that allows you to register an event handler function. This event handler function will get called when the event your event listener is listening for gets fired. While we touched base on a few other topics, they will make more sense when we view them in the context of more advanced event-related examples that you will see in the following chapters!

TIP Just a quick reminder for those of you reading these words in the print or e-book edition of this book: If you go to **www.quepublishing.com** and register this book, you can receive free access to an online Web Edition that not only contains the complete text of this book but also features a short, fun interactive quiz to test your understanding of the chapter you just read.

If you're reading these words in the Web Edition already and want to try your hand at the quiz, then you're in luck – all you need to do is scroll down!

IN THIS CHAPTER

- Learn how events travel through the DOM
- Understand the differences between event capturing and event bubbling
- Interrupt events

29

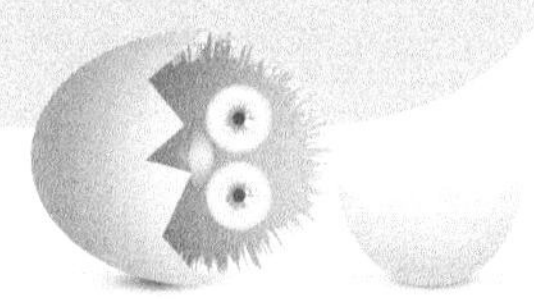

EVENT BUBBLING AND CAPTURING

In the previous chapter, you learned how to use the `addEventListener` function to listen for events that you want to react to. That chapter covered the basics, but it glossed over an important detail about how events actually get fired. An event isn't an isolated disturbance. Like a butterfly flapping its wings, an earthquake, a meteor strike, or a Godzilla visit, many events ripple and affect a bunch of elements that lie in their path.

In this article, I will put on my investigative glasses, a top hat, and a serious British accent to explain what exactly happens when an event gets fired. You will learn about the two phases events live in, why all of this is relevant, and a few other tricks to help you better take control of events.

Event Goes Down. Event Goes Up.

To better help us understand events and their lifestyle, let's frame all of this in the context of a simple example. Here is some HTML we'll refer to.

```
<!DOCTYPE html>
<html>

<head>
  <title>Events!</title>
</head>

<body id="theBody" class="item">
  <div id="one_a" class="item">
    <div id="two" class="item">
      <div id="three_a" class="item">
        <button id="buttonOne" class="item">one</button>
      </div>
      <div id="three_b" class="item">
        <button id="buttonTwo" class="item">two</button>
        <button id="buttonThree" class="item">three</button>
      </div>
    </div>
  </div>
  <div id="one_b" class="item">

  </div>
  <script>

  </script>
</body>

</html>
```

As you can see, there is nothing really exciting going on here. The HTML should look pretty straightforward (as opposed to being shifty and constantly staring at its phone), and its DOM representation looks as shown in Figure 29.1.

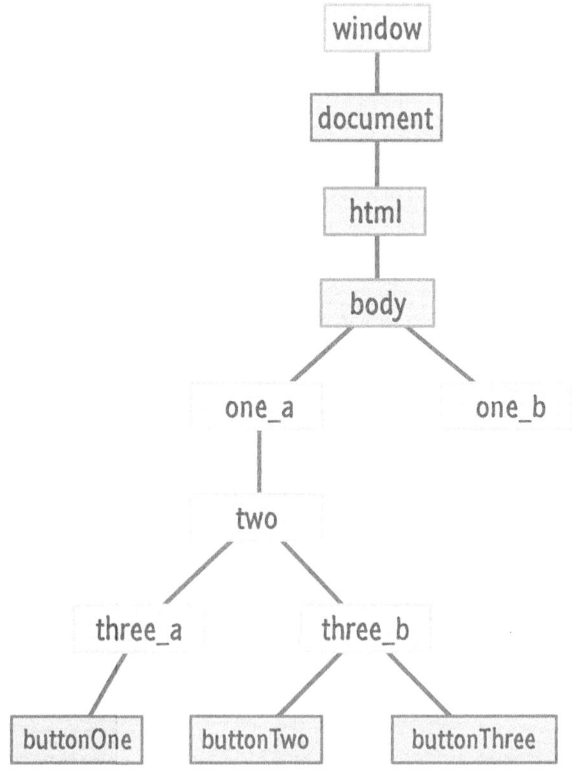

FIGURE 29.1

What the DOM for the markup you saw looks like.

Here is where our investigation is going to begin. Let's say that we click on the **buttonOne** element. From what we saw previously, you know that a click event is going to be fired. The interesting part that I omitted is where exactly the click event is going to get fired from. Your click event (just like almost every other JavaScript event) does not actually originate at the element that you interacted with. That would be too easy and make far too much sense.

Instead, an event starts at the root of your document:

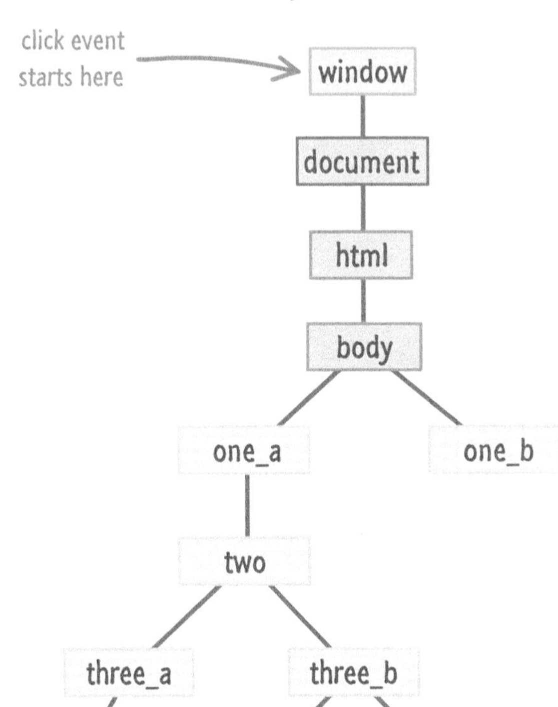

From the root, the event makes its way through the narrow pathways of the DOM and stops at the element that triggered the event, **buttonOne** (also more formally known as the **event target**):

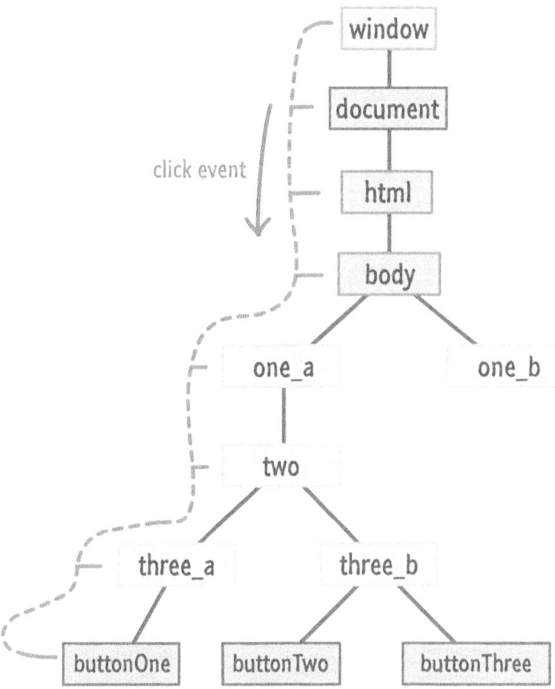

As shown in the diagram, the path your event takes is direct, but it does obnoxiously notify every element along that path. This means that if you were to listen for a click event on **body**, **one_a**, **two**, or **three_a**, the associated event handler will get fired. This is an important detail that we will revisit in a little bit.

Now, once your event reaches its target, it doesn't stop. Like some sort of an energetic bunny for a battery company whose trademarked name I probably can't mention here, the event keeps going by retracing its steps and returning back to the root:

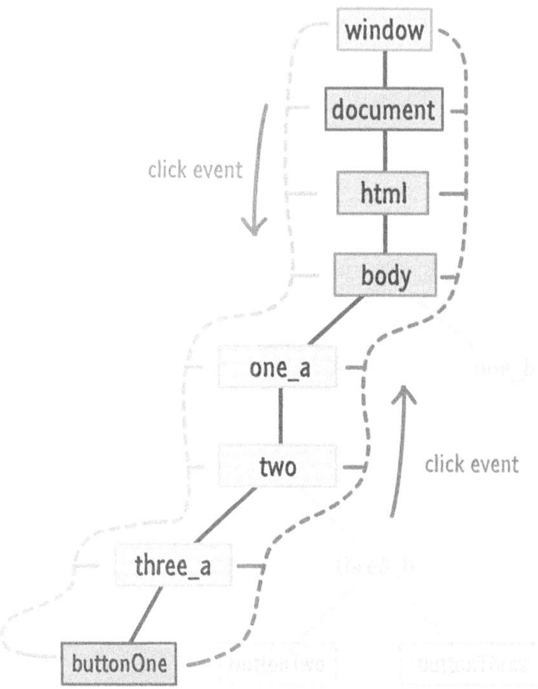

Just like before, every element along the event's path as it is moving on up gets notified about its existence.

Meet the Phases

One of the main things to note is that it doesn't matter where in your DOM you initiate an event. The event always starts at the root, goes down until it hits the target, and then goes back up to the root. This entire journey is very formally defined, so let's look at all of this formalness.

The part where you initiate the event and the event barrels down the DOM from the root is known as the **Event Capturing Phase**:

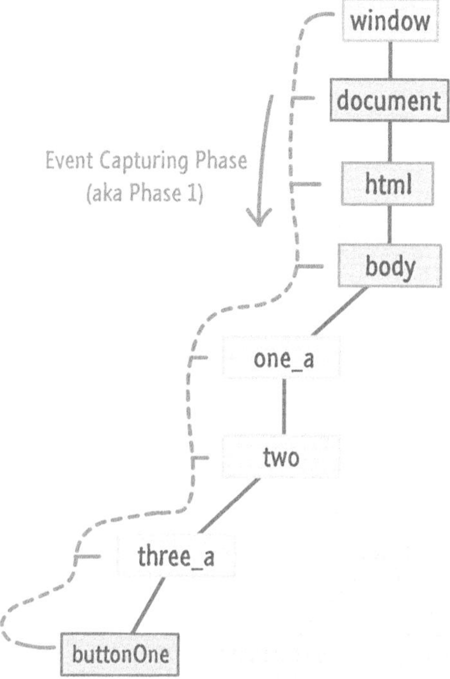

The less learned in the world may just call it **Phase 1**, so be aware that you'll see the proper name and the phase name used interchangeably in event-related content you may encounter in real life. Up next is **Phase 2** where your event bubbles back up to the root:

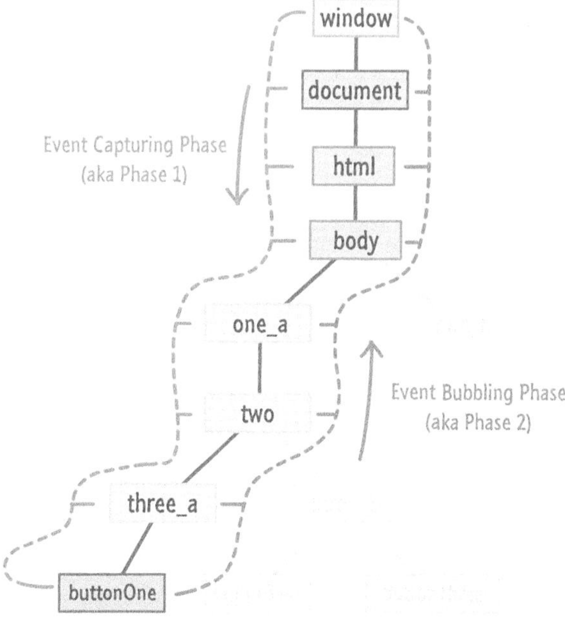

This phase is also known as the **Event Bubbling Phase**. The event "bubbles" back to the top!

Anyway, all of the elements in an event's path are pretty lucky. They have the good fortune of getting notified twice when an event is fired. This kinda sorta maybe affects the code you write, for every time you listen for events, you make a choice on which phase you want to listen for your event on. Do you listen to your event as it is fumbling down in the capture phase? Do you listen to your event as it climbs back up in the bubbling phase?

Choosing the phase is a very subtle detail that you specify with a **true** or **false** as part of your `addEventListener` call:

```
item.addEventListener("click", doSomething, true);
```

If you remember, I glossed over the third argument to `addEventListener` in the previous chapter. This third argument specifies whether you want to listen for this event during the capture phase. An argument of **true** means that you want to listen to the event during the capture phase. If you specify **false**, this means you want to listen for the event during the bubbling phase.

To listen to an event across both the capturing and bubbling phases, you can simply do the following:

```
item.addEventListener("click", doSomething, true);
item.addEventListener("click", doSomething, false);
```

I don't know why you would ever want to do this, but if you ever do, you now know what needs to be done.

NOT SPECIFYING A PHASE

Now, you can be rebellious and choose to not specify this third argument for the phase altogether:

```
item.addEventListener("click", doSomething);
```

When you don't specify the third argument, the default behavior is to listen to your event during the bubbling phase. It's equivalent to passing in a **false** value as the argument.

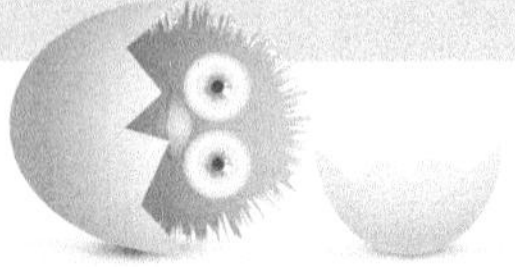

Who Cares?

At this point, you are probably wondering why all of this matters. This is doubly true if you have been happily working with events for a really long time and this is the first time you've ever heard about this. Your choice of listening to an event in the capturing or bubbling phase is mostly irrelevant to what will be doing. Very rarely will you find yourself scratching your head because your event listening and handling code isn't doing the right thing because you accidentally specified **true** instead of **false** in your `addEventListener` call.

With all this said...there will come a time in your life when you need to know and deal with a capturing or bubbling situation. This time will sneak up on your code and cause you many hours of painful head scratching. Over the years, these are the situations where I've had to consciously be aware of which phase of my event's life I am watching for:

1. Dragging an element around the screen and ensuring the drag still happens even if the element I am dragging slips out from under the cursor
2. Nested menus that reveal submenus when you hover over them
3. You have multiple event handlers on both phases, and you want to focus only on the capturing or bubbling phase event handlers exclusively
4. A third party component/control library has its own eventing logic and you want to circumvent it for your own custom behavior
5. You want to override some built-in/default browser behavior such as when you click on the scrollbar or give focus to a text field

In my nearly 105 years of working with JavaScript, these five things were all I was able to come up with. Even this is a bit skewed to the last few years, since various browsers didn't work well with the various phases at all.

Event, Interrupted

The last thing I am going to talk about before re-watching Godzilla is how to prevent your event from propagating. An event isn't guaranteed to live a fulfilling life where it starts and ends at the root. Sometimes, it is actually desirable to prevent your event from growing old and happy.

To end the life of an event, you have the `stopPropagation` method on your `Event` object:

```
function handleClick(e) {
    e.stopPropagation();

    // do something
}
```

As its name implies, the `stopPropagation` method prevents your event from continuing through the phases. Continuing with our earlier example, let's say that you are listening for the `click` event on the **three_a** element and wish to stop the event from propagating. The code for preventing the propagation will look as follows:

```
var theElement = document.querySelector("#three_a");
theElement.addEventListener("click", doSomething, true);

function doSomething(e) {
    e.stopPropagation();
}
```

When you click on **buttonOne**, here is what our event's path will look like:

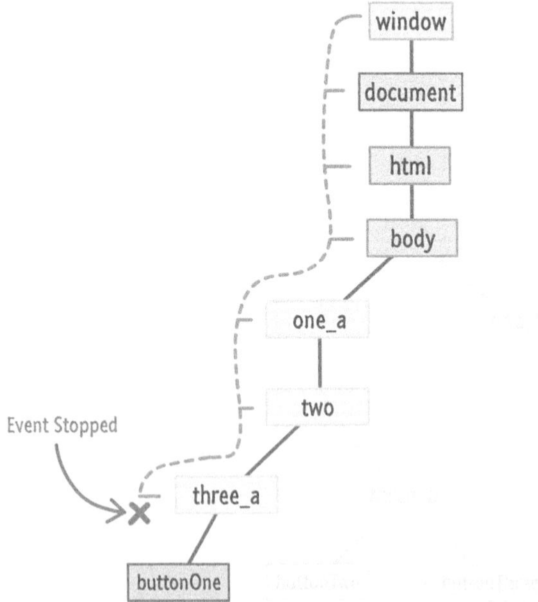

Your `click` event will steadfastly start moving down the DOM tree and notifying every element on the path to **buttonOne**. Because the **three_a** element is listening for the `click` event during the capture phase, the event handler associated with it will get called:

```
function doSomething(e) {
    e.stopPropagation();
}
```

In general, events will not continue to propagate until an event handler that gets activated is fully dealt with. Because **three_a** has an event listener specified to react on a `click` event, the `doSomething` event handler gets called. Your event is in a holding pattern at this point until the `doSomething` event handler executes and returns.

In this case, the event will not propagate further. The `doSomething` event handler is its last client thanks to the `stopPropagation` function that is hiding in the shadows to kill the event right there and then....gangsta' style! The `click` event will never reach the **buttonOne** element nor get a chance to bubble back up. So tragically sad.

TIP Another function that lives on your event object that you may awkwardly run into is `preventDefault`:

```
function overrideScrollBehavior(e) {
    e.preventDefault();

    // do something
}
```

What this function does is a little mysterious. Many HTML elements exhibit a default behavior when you interact with it. For example, clicking in a textbox gives that textbox focus with a little blinking text cursor appearing. Using your mouse wheel in a scrollable area will scroll in the direction you are scrolling. Clicking on a check box will toggle the checked state on or off. All of these are examples of built-in reactions to events your browser instinctively knows how to handle.

If you want to turn off this default behavior, you can call the `preventDefault` function. This function needs to be called when reacting to an event on the element whose default reaction you want to ignore. You can see an example of me using this function in the *Smooth Parallax Scrolling* tutorial online at: **http://bit.ly/kirupaParallax**.

THE ABSOLUTE MINIMUM

So...yeah! How about those events and their bubbling and capturing phases? One of the best ways to learn more about how event capturing and bubbling works is to just write some code and see how your event makes its way around the DOM.

Below is a simple example related to the DOM tree we've been looking at:

```
<!DOCTYPE html>
<html>
<body id="theBody" class="item">
    <div id="one_a" class="item">
        <div id="two" class="item">
            <div id="three_a" class="item">
                <button id="buttonOne" class="item">one</button>
            </div>
            <div id="three_b" class="item">
                <button id="buttonTwo" class="item">two</button>
                <button id="buttonThree" class="item">three</button>
            </div>
        </div>
    </div>
    <div id="one_b" class="item">

    </div>

    <script>
        var items = document.querySelectorAll(".item");

        for (var i = 0; i < items.length; i++) {
            var el = items[i];

            //capturing phase
            el.addEventListener("click", doSomething, true);
```

```
            //bubbling phase
            el.addEventListener("click", doSomething, false);
        }

        function doSomething(e) {
            console.log(e.currentTarget.id);
        }
    </script>
</body>
</html>
```

If you make an HTML document out of this and preview it in your browser, you will see three buttons. If you click on **buttonOne** and inspect your browser's console, you'll see the following path your `click` event takes from beginning to end:

- theBody
- one_a
- two
- three_a
- buttonOne
- buttonOne
- three_a
- two
- one_a
- theBody

If you examine our DOM, it should be no surprise to you that this is the order the `click` event propagates through the elements (with each element represented by the `currentTarget` property).

We are done with the technical part of all this, but if you have a few more minutes to spare, then I encourage you watch (**http://bit.ly/kirupaBubblyTime**) the somewhat related episode of **Comedians Getting Coffee** aptly titled *It's Bubbly Time, Jerry!* In what is probably their ***bestest*** episode, Michael Richards and Jerry Seinfeld just chat over coffee about events, the bubbling phase, and other very important topics. I think.

TIP Just a quick reminder for those of you reading these words in the print or e-book edition of this book: If you go to **www.quepublishing.com** and register this book, you can receive free access to an online Web Edition that not only contains the complete text of this book but also features a short, fun interactive quiz to test your understanding of the chapter you just read.

If you're reading these words in the Web Edition already and want to try your hand at the quiz, then you're in luck – all you need to do is scroll down!

IN THIS CHAPTER

- Learn how to listen to the mouse using the various mouse events
- Understand the MouseEvent object
- Deal with the Mouse Wheel

30

MOUSE EVENTS

One of the most common ways people (and possibly cats) interact with their computers is by using a pointing device known as a **mouse:**

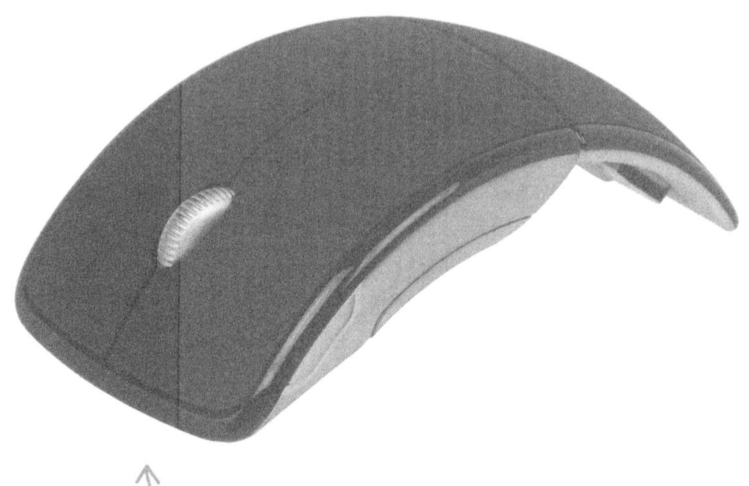

FIGURE 30.1

*Cats probably like them too. (**Image Source**)*

This magical device allows you to accomplish great things by moving it around with your hands and clicking around with your fingers. Using them as a, um... user is one thing. As a developer, trying to make your code work with a mouse is something else. That's where this chapter comes in.

Meet the Mouse Events

In JavaScript, your primary way of dealing with the mouse is through events. There are a boatload of events that deal with the mouse, but we won't be looking at all of them here. Instead, we'll focus on just the cool and popular ones such as the following:

- `click`
- `dblclick`
- `mouseover`
- `mouseout`
- `mouseenter`
- `mouseleave`
- `mousedown`
- `mouseup`
- `mousemove`
- `contextmenu`
- `mousewheel` and `DOMMouseScroll`

The names of these events should give you a good idea of what they do, but we'll take nothing for granted and look at each of these events in some level of greater detail in the following sections. I should warn you that some events are just dreadfully boring to learn about.

Clicking Once and Clicking Twice

Let's start with probably the most popular of all the mouse events that you will use—the `click` event. This event is fired when you `click` on an element. To state this differently in a way that doesn't involve mentioning the thing you are describing as part of your description, the `click` event is fired when you use your mouse to press down on an element and then release the press while still over that same element.

Here is a totally unnecessary visualization of what I am talking about:

1. Normal 2. Press Down 3. Release the Press 4. Win!!!

button button button click!

You've seen the code for working with the click event a few times already, but you can never really get enough of it. Here is another example:

```
var button = document.querySelector("#myButton");
button.addEventListener("click", doSomething, false);

function doSomething(e) {
    console.log("Mouse clicked on something!");
}
```

The way you listen to the **click** event is just like almost any other event that you'll encounter, so I won't unnecessarily bore you with that detail and our old friend **addEventListener**. Instead, I will bore you with details about the somewhat related **dblclick** event.

The **dblclick** event is fired when you quickly repeat a click action a double number of times, and the code for using it looks as follows:

```
var button = document.querySelector("#myButton");
button.addEventListener("dblclick", doSomething, false);

function doSomething(e) {
    console.log("Mouse clicked on something...twice!");
}
```

The amount of time between each click that ends up resulting in a **dblclick** event is based on the OS you are running the code in. It's neither browser specific nor something you can define (or read) using JavaScript.

DON'T OVERDO IT

If you happen to listen to both the `click` and `dblclick` event on an element, your event handlers will get called three times when you double-click. You will get two `click` events to correspond to each time you clicked. After your second click, you will also get a `dblclick` event.

Mousing Over and Mousing Out

The classic hover over and hover out scenarios are handled by the appropriately titled `mouseover` and `mouseout` events respectively:

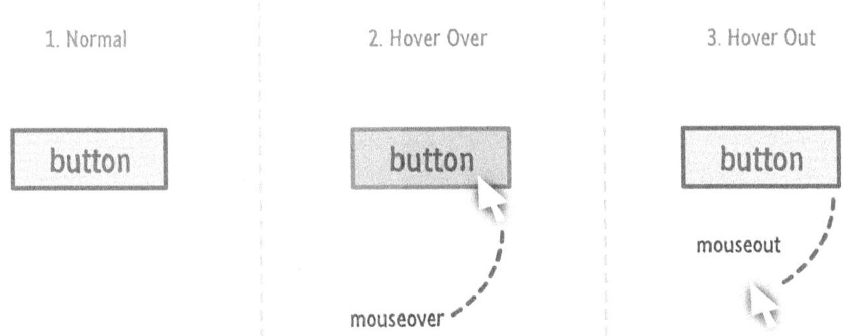

Here is a snippet of these two events in action:

```
var button = document.querySelector("#myButton");
button.addEventListener("mouseover", hovered, false);
button.addEventListener("mouseout", hoveredOut, false);

function hovered(e) {
    console.log("Hovered!");
}
```

```
function hoveredOut(e) {
    console.log("Hovered Away!");
}
```

That's all there is to these two events. They are pretty boring overall...which, as you've probably found out by now, is actually a good thing when it comes to programming concepts.

WHAT ABOUT THE OTHER TWO SIMILAR-LOOKING EVENTS?

We just looked at two events (`mouseover` and `mouseout`), which are all about hovering over something and hovering away from something. As it turns out, you have two more events that pretty much do the exact same thing. These are your `mouseenter` and `mouseleave` events. There is one important detail to know about these events that makes them unique. The `mouseenter` and `mouseleave` events do not bubble.

This detail only matters if the element you are interested in hovering over or out from has child elements. All four of these events behave identically when there are no child elements at play. If there are child elements at play:

- `mouseover` and `mouseout` will get fired each time you move the mouse over and around a child element. This means that you could be seeing many unnecessary event fires even though it seems like you are moving your mouse within a single region.
- `mouseenter` and `mouseleave` will get fired only once. It doesn't matter how many child elements your mouse moves through.

For 90% of what you will do, `mouseover` and `mouseout` will be good enough. For the other times, often involving slightly more complex UI scenarios, you'll be happy that the non-bubbling `mouseenter` and `mouseleave` events are available.

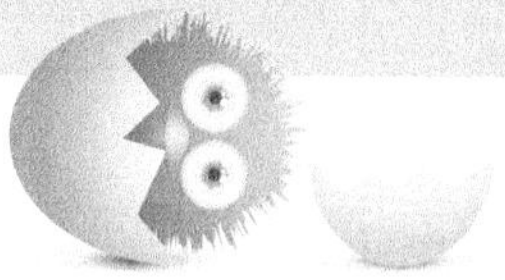

The Very Click-like Mousing Down and Mousing Up Events

Two events that are almost subcomponents of the `click` event are the `mousedown` and `mouseup` ones. From the following diagram, you'll see why:

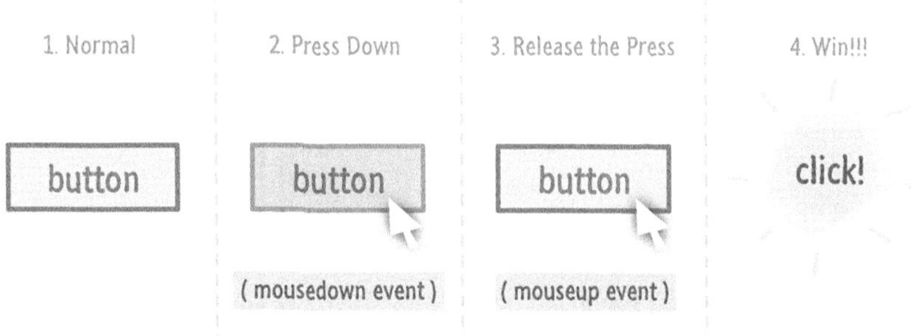

When you press down with your mouse, the `mousedown` event is fired. When you release the press, the `mouseup` event is fired. If the element you pressed down on and released from are the same element, the `click` event will also fire.

You can see all of this from the following snippet:

```
var button = document.querySelector("#myButton");
button.addEventListener("mousedown", mousePressed, false);
button.addEventListener("mouseup", mouseReleased, false);
button.addEventListener("click", mouseClicked, false);

function mousePressed(e) {
    console.log("Mouse is down!");
}

function mouseReleased(e) {
    console.log("Mouse is up!");
}

function mouseClicked(e) {
    console.log("Mouse is clicked!");
}
```

You may be wondering, "Why bother with these two events?" The `click` event seems perfectly suited for most cases where you may want to use `mousedown` and `mouseup`. If you are spending sleepless nights wondering about this, the answer is...**Yes!** A more helpful (and sensible) answer is that the `mousedown` and `mouseup` events simply give you more control in case you need it. Some interactions (such as drags...or awesome moves in video games where you press and hold to charge a lightning bolt of doom!) need you to act only when the `mousedown` event has happened but the `mouseup` event hasn't.

The Event Heard Again...and Again...and Again!

One of the most chatty events that you'll ever encounter is the very friendly `mousemove` event. This event fires a whole lotta times as your mouse moves over the element you are listening for the `mousemove` event on:

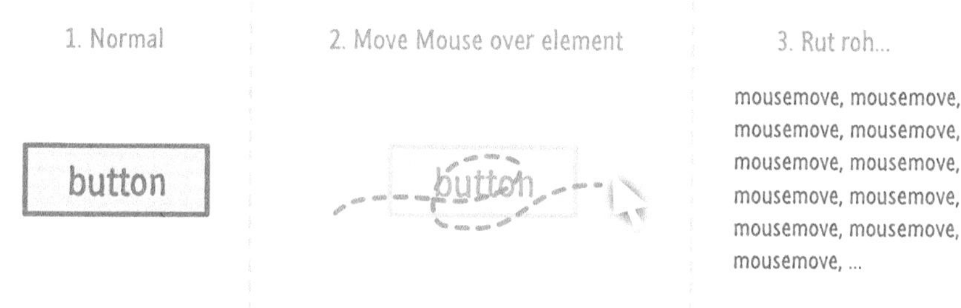

What follows is an example of the `mousemove` event in code:

```
var button = document.querySelector("#myButton");
button.addEventListener("mousemove", mouseIsMoving, false);

function mouseIsMoving(e) {
    console.log("Mouse is on the run!");
}
```

Your browser controls the rate at which the `mousemove` event gets fired, and this event gets fired if your mouse moves even a single pixel. This event is great for many interactive scenarios where your mouse's current position is relevant to keep track of, for example.

The Context Menu

The last mouse-related event we are going to look at is affectionately called `contextmenu`. As you probably know very well, when you commonly right-click in various applications, you will see a menu:

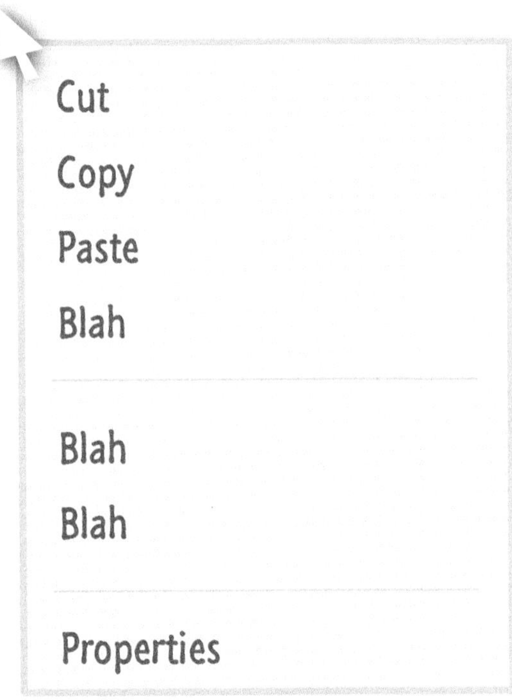

This menu is known as the **context menu**. The `contextmenu` event is fired just before this menu appears.

Now, you may be wondering why anybody would want an event for this situation. To be completely honest with you (as opposed to all of the other times when I've been lying), there is only one primary reason to listen for this event. That reason has to do with preventing this menu from appearing when you right-click or use a context menu keyboard button or shortcut.

Here is an example of how you can **prevent** the **default** behavior where the context menu appears:

```
document.addEventListener("contextmenu", hideMenu, false);

function hideMenu(e) {
    e.preventDefault();
}
```

The `preventDefault` property on any type of `Event` stops whatever the default behavior is from actually happening. Because the `contextmenu` event is fired before the menu appears, calling `preventDefault` on it ensures the context menu never shows up. The default behavior has been prevented from running. Yes, this is also the second time I'm mentioning this property. As you know, I am being paid by the word :P

With all of this said, I can think of a billion other ways you could prevent the context menu from appearing without using an event for dealing with all of this, but that's the way things are...for now <insert evil, maniacal laughter>!

The MouseEvent Properties

Let's get a little bit more specific. All of the mouse events we've seen so far are based around `MouseEvent`. Normally, this is the kind of factoid you keep under your hat for trivia night and ignore. This time around, though, this detail is important because `MouseEvent` brings with it a number of properties that make working with the mouse easier. Let's look at some of them.

The Global Mouse Position

The `screenX` and `screenY` properties return the distance your mouse cursor is from the top-left location of your primary monitor:

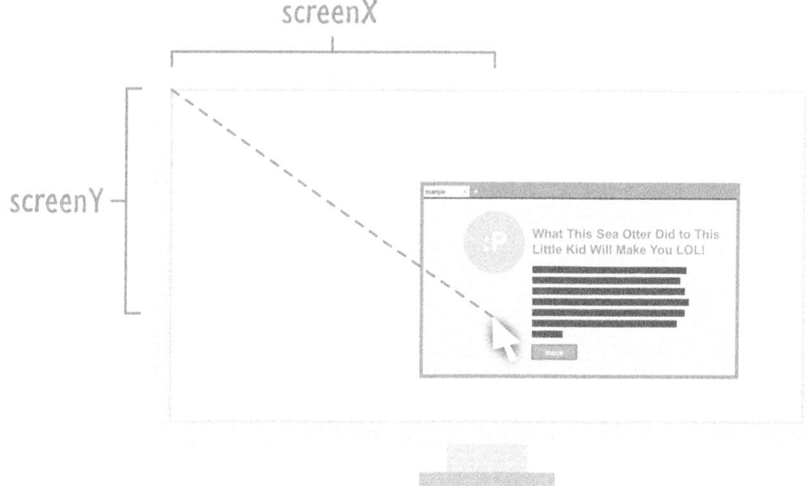

Here is a very simple example of the **screenX** and **screenY** properties at work:

```
document.addEventListener("mousemove", mouseMoving, false);

function mouseMoving(e) {
    console.log(e.screenX + " " + e.screenY);
}
```

It doesn't matter what other margin/padding/offset/layout craziness you may have going on in your page. The values returned are always going to be the distance between where your mouse is now and where the top-left corner of your primary monitor is.

The Mouse Position Inside the Browser

The **clientX** and **clientY** properties return the x and y position of the mouse relative to your browser's (technically, the browser viewport's) top-left corner:

The code for this is nothing exciting:

```
var button = document.querySelector("#myButton");
button.addEventListener("mousemove", mouseMoving, false);

function mouseMoving(e) {
    console.log(e.clientX + " " + e.clientY);
}
```

You just call the clientX and clientY properties of the event argument that got passed in to our event handler to get the values.

Detecting Which Button Was Clicked

Your mice often have multiple buttons or ways to simulate multiple buttons. The most common button configuration involves a left button, a right button, and a middle button (often a click on your mouse wheel). To figure out which mouse button was pressed, you have the button property. This property returns a **0** if the left mouse button was pressed, a **1** if the middle button was pressed, and a **2** if the right mouse button was pressed:

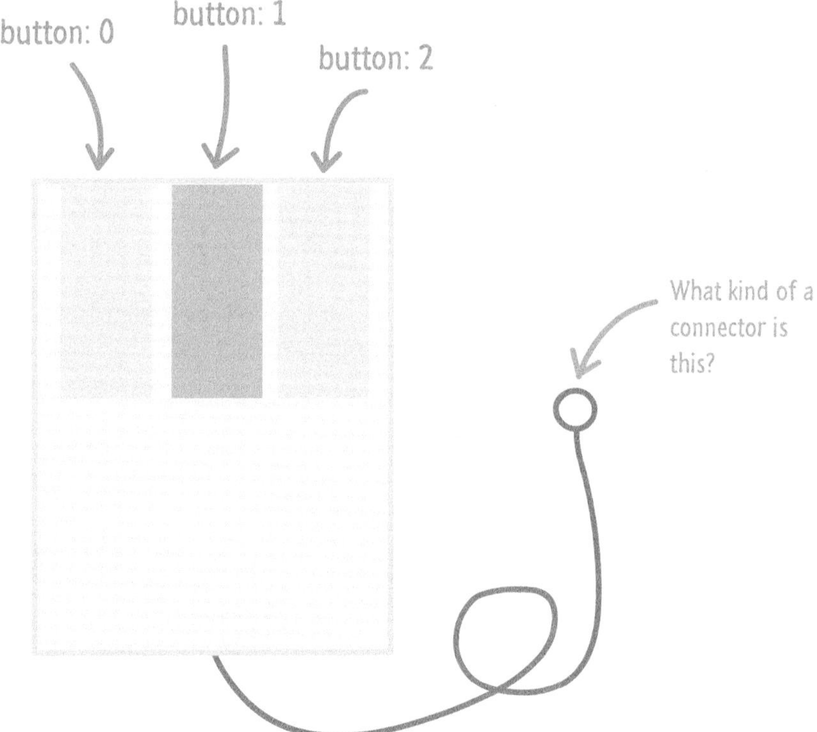

The code for using the button property to check for which button was pressed looks exactly as you would expect:

```
document.addEventListener("mousedown", buttonPress, false);

function buttonPress(e) {
    if (e.button == 0) {
        console.log("Left mouse button pressed!");
```

```
    } else if (e.button == 1) {
        console.log("Middle mouse button pressed!");
    } else if (e.button == 2) {
        console.log("Right mouse button pressed!");
    } else {
        console.log("Things be crazy up in here!!!");
    }
}
```

In addition to the `button` property, you also have the `buttons` and `which` properties that sorta do similar things to help you figure out which button was pressed. I'm not going to talk too much about those two properties, but just know that they exist. You can Google them if you want to know more.

Dealing with the Mouse Wheel

The mouse wheel is special compared to everything else we've seen so far. The obvious difference is that we are dealing with a wheel as opposed to a button. The less obvious, yet probably more relevant, detail is that you have two events to deal with. You have the `mousewheel` event that is used by Internet Explorer and Chrome and the `DOMMouseScroll` event used by Firefox.

The way you listen for these mouse wheel-related events is just the usual:

```
document.addEventListener("mousewheel", mouseWheeling, false);
document.addEventListener("DOMMouseScroll", mouseWheeling, false);
```

It's what happens afterwards where things get interesting. The `mousewheel` and `DOMMouseScroll` events will fire the moment you scroll the mouse wheel in any direction. For all practical purposes, the direction you are scrolling the mousewheel is important. To get that information, we'll need to go spelunking in the event handler to find the event argument.

The event arguments for a `mousewheel` event contain a property known as `wheelDelta`. For the `DOMMouseScroll` event, you have the detail property on the event argument. Both of these properties are similar in that their values change from positive or negative depending on what direction you scroll the mouse wheel. The thing to note is that they are inconsistent in what sign they go with. The `wheelDelta` property associated with the `mousewheel` event is positive when you scroll up on the mouse wheel. It is negative when you scroll down. The exact opposite holds true for `DOMMouseScroll's detail` property. This property is negative when you scroll up, and it is positive when you scroll down.

Handling this `wheelDelta` and `detail` inconsistency is pretty simple...as you can see in the following snippet:

```
function mouseWheeling(e) {
    var scrollDirection = e.wheelDelta || -1 * e.detail;

    if (scrollDirection > 0) {
        console.log("Scrolling up! " + scrollDirection);
    } else {
        console.log("Scrolling down! " + scrollDirection);
    }
}
```

The `scrollDirection` variable stores the value contained by the `wheelData` property or the `detail` property. Depending on whether this value is positive or negative, you can then special case the behavior.

THE ABSOLUTE MINIMUM

Generally, it is true that if you know how to just work with one event, you pretty much know how to work with all other events. The only thing you need to know is which event corresponds to what you are trying to do. The mouse events are a good introduction to working with events because they are very easy to play with. They aren't very fussy, and the things you learn about them you will use in almost all apps that you build.

Some additional resources and examples that you may want to check out:

- **Move Element to Click Position: http://bit.ly/kirupaElementClickPosition**
- **Are You On a Touch-Enabled Device: http://bit.ly/kirupaTouchEnabled**

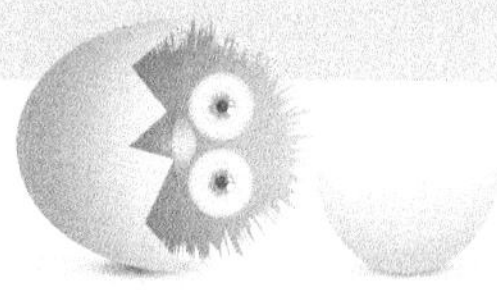

TIP Just a quick reminder for those of you reading these words in the print or e-book edition of this book: If you go to **www.quepublishing.com** and register this book, you can receive free access to an online Web Edition that not only contains the complete text of this book but also features a short, fun interactive quiz to test your understanding of the chapter you just read.

If you're reading these words in the Web Edition already and want to try your hand at the quiz, then you're in luck – all you need to do is scroll down!

IN THIS CHAPTER

- Listen and react to the keyboard
- Understand how to work with the various keyboard-related events
- See some examples that highlight how common keyboard scenarios work

31

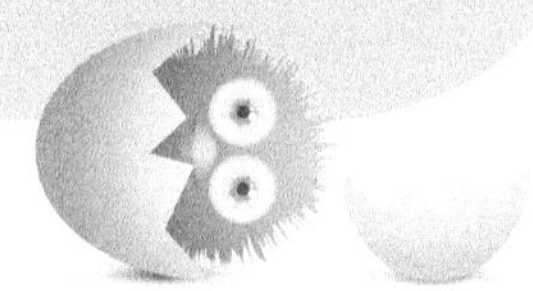

KEYBOARD EVENTS

We spend a lot of time in various applications tapping away at our keyboards. In case you are wondering what a keyboard looks like, Figure 31.1 features a sweet one from I think about a hundred years ago:

FIGURE 31.1

What a keyboard might look like…in a museum probably. (***Image Source***)

Anyway, our computers (more specifically, the applications that run on them) just know how to deal with our board of plastic depressible keys. You never really think about it. Sometimes, depending on what you are doing, you will have to think about them. In fact, you'll have to deal with them and make them work properly. Better cancel any plans you have, for this chapter is going to be pretty intense!

By the end of this chapter, you will learn all about how to listen to the keyboard events, what each of those events do, and see a handful of examples that highlight some handy tricks that may come in…um…handy.

Onwards!

Meet the Keyboard Events

To work with keyboards in an HTML document, there are three events that you will need to familiarize yourself with. Those events are

- `keydown`
- `keypress`
- `keyup`

Given what these events are called, you probably already have a vague idea of what each event does. The `keydown` event is fired when you press down on a key on your keyboard. The `keyup` event is fired when you release a key that you just pressed. Both of these events work on any key that you interact with.

The `keypress` event is a special bird. At first glance, it seems like this event is fired when you press down on any key. Despite what the name claims, the `keypress` event is fired only when you press down on a key that displays a character (letter, number, and the like). What this means is somewhat confusing, but it makes sense in its own twisted way.

If you press and release a character key such as the letter **y**, you will see the `keydown`, `keypress`, and `keyup` events fired in order. The `keydown` and `keyup` events fire because the **y** key is simply a key to them. The `keypress` event is fired because the **y** key is a character key. If you press and release a key that doesn't display anything on the screen (such as the spacebar, arrow key, or function keys), all you will see are the `keydown` and `keyup` events fired.

This difference is subtle but very important when you want to ensure your key presses are actually overheard by your application.

SAY WHAT?

It is weird that an event called `keypress` doesn't fire when any key is pressed. Maybe this event should be called something else like `characterkeypress`, but that is probably a moo point. (What is a "moo point"? Well… **http://bit.ly/kirupaMoo**)

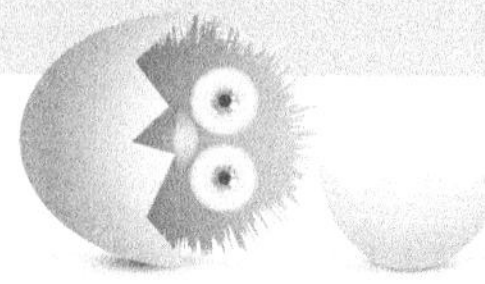

Using These Events

The way you listen to the `keydown`, `keypress`, and `keyup` events is similar to any other event you may want to listen and react to. You call `addEventListener` on the element that will be dealing with these events, specify the event you want to listen for, specify the event handling function that gets called when the event is overheard, and a **true/false** value indicating whether you want this event to bubble.

Here is an example of me listening to our three keyboard events on the `window` object:

```
window.addEventListener("keydown", dealWithKeyboard, false);
window.addEventListener("keypress", dealWithKeyboard, false);
window.addEventListener("keyup", dealWithKeyboard, false);

function dealWithKeyboard(e) {
    // gets called when any of the keyboard events are overheard
}
```

If any of these events are overheard, the `dealWithKeyboard` event handler gets called. In fact, this event handler will get called three times if you happen to press down on a character key. This is all pretty straightforward, so let's kick everything up a few notches and go beyond the basics in the next few sections.

The Keyboard Event Properties

When an event handler that reacts to a keyboard event is called, a `Keyboard` event argument is passed in. Let's revisit our `dealWithKeyboard` event handler that you saw earlier. In that event handler, the keyboard event is represented by the `e` argument that is passed in:

```
function dealWithKeyboard(e) {
    // gets called when any of the keyboard events are overheard
}
```

This argument contains a handful of properties:

- `KeyCode`
  Every key you press on your keyboard has a number associated with it. This read-only property returns that number.
- `CharCode`
  This property only exists on event arguments returned by the keypress event, and it contains the ASCII code for whatever character key you pressed.
- `ctrlKey, altKey, shiftKey`
  These three properties return a **true** if the Ctrl key, Alt key, or Shift key are pressed.

- `MetaKey`
  The **metaKey** property is similar to the **ctrlKey**, **altKey**, and **shiftKey** properties in that it returns a **true** if the Meta key is pressed. The Meta key is the Windows key on Windows keyboards and the Command key on Apple keyboards.

The **Keyboard** event contains a few other properties, but the ones you see above are the most interesting ones. With these properties, you can check for which key was pressed and react accordingly. In the next couple of sections, you'll see some examples of this.

CAUTION The `charCode` and `keyCode` properties are currently marked as deprecated by the web standards people at the W3C. It's replacement might be the mostlyunsupported `code` property. Just be aware of this, and be ready to update your code in the future when whichever successor to `charCode` and `keyCode` has taken his/her rightful place on the throne.

Some Examples

Now that you've seen the horribly boring basics of how to work with Keyboard events, let's look at some examples that clarify (or potentially confuse!) everything you've seen so far.

Checking That a Particular Key Was Pressed

The following example shows how to use the **keyCode** property to check if a particular key was pressed:

```
window.addEventListener("keydown", checkKeyPressed, false);

function checkKeyPressed(e) {
    if (e.keyCode == "65") {
        console.log("The 'a' key is pressed.");
    }
}
```

The particular key I check is the **a** key. Internally, this key is mapped to the **keyCode** value of **65**. In case you never memorized all of them in school, you can find a handy list of all key and character codes at the following link: **http://bit.ly/kirupaKeyCode** Please do not memorize every single code from that list. There are far more interesting things to memorize instead.

Some things to note. The **charCode** and **keyCode** values for a particular key are not the same. Also, the **charCode** is only returned if the event that triggered your event handler was a **keypress**. In our example, the **keydown** event would not contain anything useful for the **charCode** property.

If you wanted to check the **charCode** and use the **keypress** event, here is what the above example would look like:

```
window.addEventListener("keypress", checkKeyPressed, false);

function checkKeyPressed(e) {
    if (e.charCode == 97) {
        alert("The 'a' key is pressed.");
    }
}
```

The **charCode** for the **a** key is **97**. Again, refer to the table of key and character codes I listed earlier for such details.

Doing Something When the Arrow Keys Are Pressed

You see this most often in games where pressing the arrow keys does something interesting. The following snippet of code shows how that is done:

```
window.addEventListener("keydown", moveSomething, false);

function moveSomething(e) {
    switch(e.keyCode) {
        case 37:
            // left key pressed
            break;
        case 38:
            // up key pressed
            break;
        case 39:
            // right key pressed
            break;
        case 40:
            // down key pressed
            break;
    }
}
```

Again, this should be pretty straightforward as well. And, would you believe it—an actual use for the `switch` statement that you learned about forever ago in **Chapter 4, "Conditional Statements: if, else, and switch."**

Detecting Multiple Key Presses

Now, this is going to be epic! An interesting case revolves around detecting when you need to react to multiple key presses. What follows is an example of how to do that:

```
window.addEventListener("keydown", keysPressed, false);
window.addEventListener("keyup", keysReleased, false);

var keys = [];

function keysPressed(e) {
    // store an entry for every key pressed
    keys[e.keyCode] = true;

    // Ctrl + Shift + 5
    if (keys[17] && keys[16] && keys[53]) {
        // do something
    }

    // Ctrl + f
    if (keys[17] && keys[70]) {
        // do something

        // prevent default browser behavior
        e.preventDefault();
    }
}

function keysReleased(e) {
    // mark keys that were released
    keys[e.keyCode] = false;
}
```

Going into great detail about this will require another chapter by itself, but let's just look at how this works very briefly.

First, we have a keys array that stores every single key that you press:

```
var keys = [];
```

As keys get pressed, the `keysPressed` event handler gets called:

```
function keysPressed(e) {
    // store an entry for every key pressed
    keys[e.keyCode] = true;
}
```

When a key gets released, the `keysReleased` event handler gets called:

```
function keysReleased(e) {
    // mark keys that were released
    keys[e.keyCode] = false;
}
```

Notice how these two event handlers work with each other. As keys get pressed, an entry gets created for them in the `keys` array with a value of **true**. When keys get released, those same keys are marked with a value of **false**. The existence of the keys you press in the array is superficial. It is the values they store that is actually important.

As long as nothing interrupts your event handlers from getting called properly such as an alert window, you will get a one-to-one mapping between keys pressed and keys released as viewed through the lens of the `keys` array. With all of this said, the checks for seeing which combination of keys have been pressed is handled in the `keysPressed` event handler. The following highlighted lines show how this works:

When a key gets released, the `keysReleased` event handler gets called:

```
function keysPressed(e) {
    // store an entry for every key pressed
    keys[e.keyCode] = true;

    // Ctrl + Shift + 5
    if (keys[17] && keys[16] && keys[53]) {
        // do something
    }
```

```
        // Ctrl + f
        if (keys[17] && keys[70]) {
            // do something

            // prevent default browser behavior
            e.preventDefault();
        }
    }
```

There is one thing you need to keep in mind. Some key combinations result in your browser doing something. To avoid your browser from doing its own thing, use the `preventDefault` method as I show when checking to see if **Ctrl + F** is being used:

```
function keysPressed(e) {
    // store an entry for every key pressed
    keys[e.keyCode] = true;

    // Ctrl + Shift + 5
    if (keys[17] && keys[16] && keys[53]) {
        // do something
    }

    // Ctrl + f
    if (keys[17] && keys[70]) {
        // do something

        // prevent default browser behavior
        e.preventDefault();
    }
}
```

The `preventDefault` method prevents an event from triggering a default behavior. In this case, it was preventing the browser from showing the Find dialog box. Different key combinations will trigger different reactions by the browser, so keep this method handy to put a stop to those reactions.

Anyway, looking at the code in aggregate, you have a basic blueprint for how to check for multiple key presses easily.

THE ABSOLUTE MINIMUM

The keyboard is pretty important when it comes to how people interact with their computer-like devices. Despite its importance, you often won't have to deal with them directly. Your browser, the various text-related controls/elements, and everything in-between just handle it as you would expect by default. There are certain kinds of applications where you may want to deal with them, though, which is why you have this chapter.

This chapter started off in the most boring way possible by explaining how to work with the `Keyboard` events and their event arguments. Along the way, things (hopefully) got more interesting as you saw several examples that address common things you would do when dealing with the keyboard in code. One thing to note is that all of our examples listened for the keyboard events on the `window` object. You don't have to use `window`. You can listen for your keyboard events on any DOM element...that it makes sense to listen for keyboard events on :P

TIP Just a quick reminder for those of you reading these words in the print or e-book edition of this book: If you go to **www.quepublishing.com** and register this book, you can receive free access to an online Web Edition that not only contains the complete text of this book but also features a short, fun interactive quiz to test your understanding of the chapter you just read.

If you're reading these words in the Web Edition already and want to try your hand at the quiz, then you're in luck – all you need to do is scroll down!

IN THIS CHAPTER

- Learn about all the events that fire as your page is getting loaded
- Understand what happens behind the scenes during a page loads
- Fiddle with the various `script` element attributes that control exactly when your code runs

32

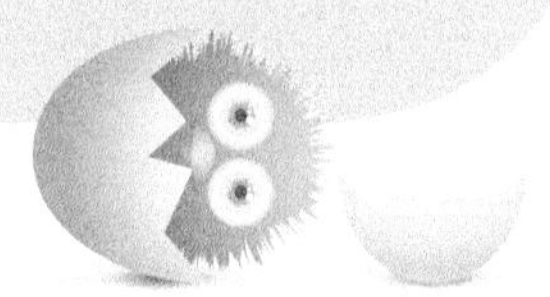

PAGE LOAD EVENTS AND OTHER STUFF

An important part of working with JavaScript is ensuring that your code runs at the right time. Things aren't always as simple as putting your code at the bottom of your page and expecting everything to work once your page has loaded. Yes, we are going to revisit some things we looked at in **Chapter 9, "Where Should Your Code Live."** Every now and then, you may have to add some extra code to ensure your code doesn't run before the page is ready. Sometimes, you may even have to put your code at the top of your page...like an animal!

There are many factors that affect what the "right time" really is to run your code, and in this chapter, we're going to look at those factors and narrow down what you should do to a handful of guidelines.

Onwards!

The Things That Happen During Page Load

Let's start at the very beginning. You click on a link or press Enter after typing in a URL and, if the stars are aligned properly, your page loads. All of that seems pretty simple and takes up a very tiny sliver of time to complete from beginning to end:

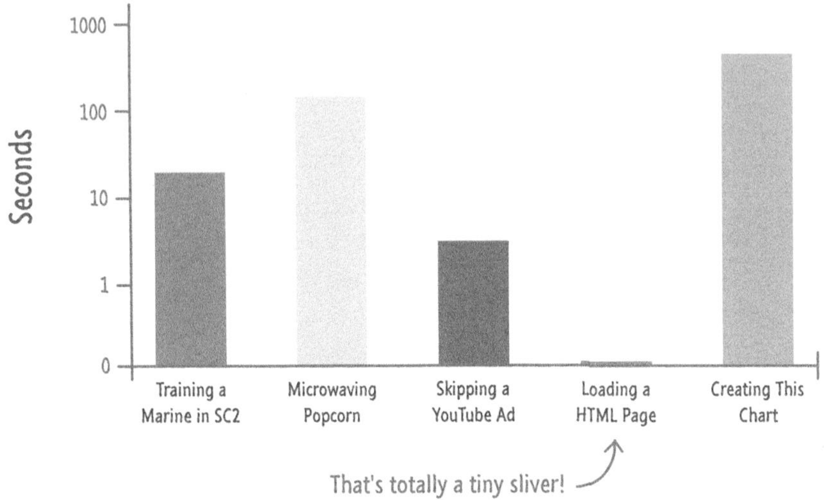

In that short period of time between you wanting to load a page and your page loading, a lot of relevant and interesting stuff happen that you need to know more about. One example of the relevant and interesting stuff that happens is that any code specified on the page will run. When exactly the code runs depends on a combination of the following things that all come alive at some point while your page is getting loaded:

- The `DOMContentLoaded` event
- The `load` Event

- The `async` attribute for script elements
- The `defer` attribute for script elements
- The location your scripts live in the DOM

Don't worry if you don't know what these things are. You'll learn (or re-learn) what all of these things do and the effect they have when your code runs really soon. Before we get there, though, let's take a quick detour and look at the three stages of a page load.

Stage Numero Uno

The first stage is when your browser is about to start loading a new page:

Stage #1: Nothing Much Going On

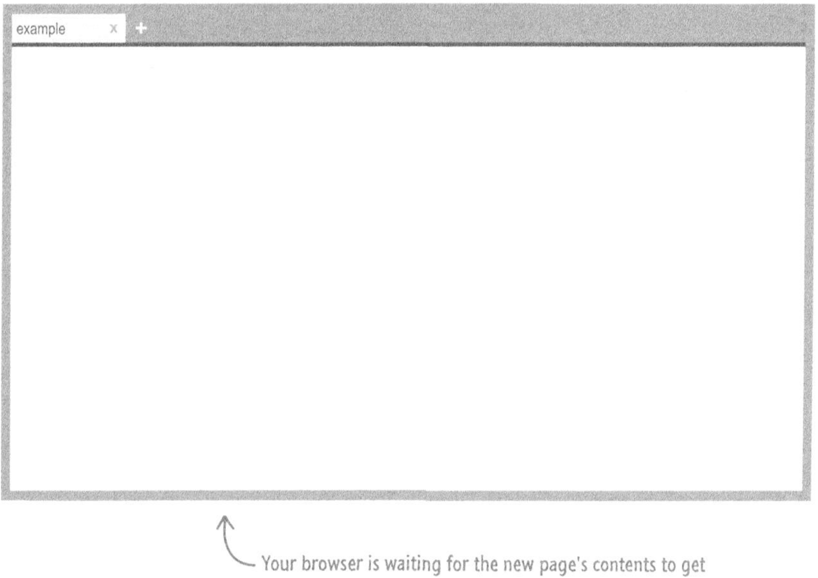

Your browser is waiting for the new page's contents to get downloaded

At this stage, there isn't anything interesting going on. A request has been made to load a page, but nothing has been downloaded yet.

Stage Numero Dos

Things get a bit more exciting with the second stage where the raw markup and DOM of your page has been loaded and parsed:

Stage #2: The DOM is Ready

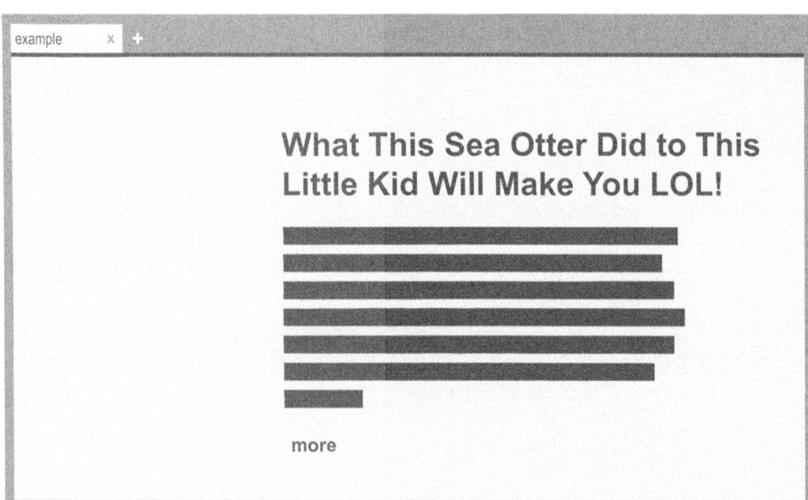

The thing to note about this stage is that external resources like images and linked stylesheets have not been parsed. You only see the raw content specified by your page/document's markup.

Stage Numero Three

The final stage is where your page is fully loaded with any images, stylesheets, scripts, and other external resources making their way into what you see:

Stage #3: Page is Fully Loaded

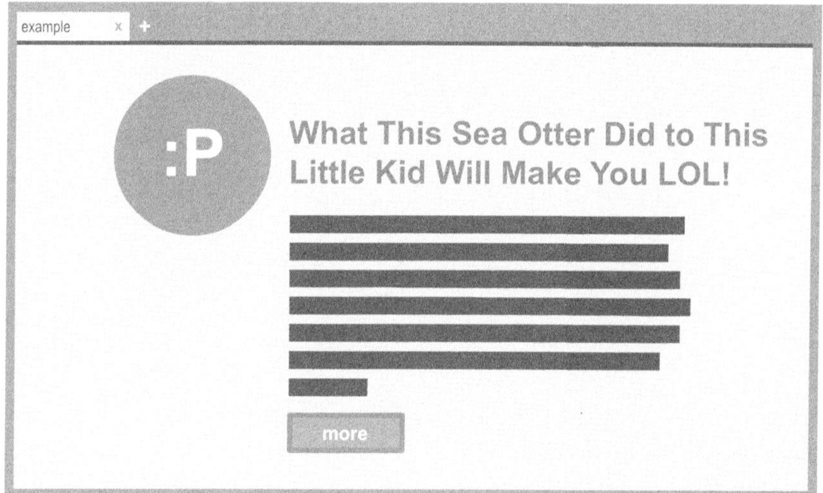

This is the stage where your browser's loading indicators stop animating, and this is also the stage you almost always find yourself in when interacting with your HTML document. That said, sometimes you'll find yourself in an in-between state where 99% of your page has loaded with only some random thing taking forever to load. If you've been to one of those viral/buzz/feedy sites, you'll totally know what I am talking about :P

Now that you have a basic idea of the three stages your document goes through when loading content, let's move forward to the more interesting stuff. Keep these three stages at the tip of your fingers (or under your hat if you are wearing one while reading this), as we'll refer back to these stages a few times in the following sections.

The `DOMContentLoaded` and `load` Events

There are two events that represent the two important milestones while your page loads: `DOMContentLoaded` and `load`. The `DOMContentLoaded` event fires at the end of Stage #2 when your page's DOM is fully parsed. The `load` event fires at the end of Stage #3 once your page has fully loaded. You can use these events to time when exactly you want your code to run.

Below is a snippet of these events in action:

```
document.addEventListener("DOMContentLoaded", theDomHasLoaded, false);
window.addEventListener("load", pageFullyLoaded, false);

function theDomHasLoaded(e) {
    // do something
}

function pageFullyLoaded(e) {
    // do something again
}
```

You use these events just like you would any other event, but the main thing to note about these events is that you need to listen to them from the document element. You can technically listen to these events on other elements, but for page loading scenarios, you want to stick with the document element.

Now that we've got the boring technical details out of the way, why are these events important? Simple. If you have any code that relies on working with the DOM such as anything that uses the querySelector or querySelectorAll functions, you want to ensure your code runs only after your DOM has been fully loaded. If you try to access your DOM before it has fully loaded, you may get incomplete results or no results at all.

Here is an awesome extreme example from **Kyle Murray** that should help you never forget this:

```
<!DOCTYPE html>
<html>
<head>
  <script>
    // try to analyze the book's meaning here
  </script>
</head>

<body>
  [INSERT ENTIRE COPY OF /WAR AND PEACE/ HERE]
</body>

</html>
```

A sure-fire way to ensure you never get into a situation where your code runs before your DOM is ready is to listen for the `DOMContentLoaded` event and let all of the code that relies on the DOM to run only after that event is overheard:

```
document.addEventListener("DOMContentLoaded", theDomHasLoaded, false);

function theDomHasLoaded(e) {
    var images = document.querySelectorAll("img");

    // do something with the images
}
```

For cases where you want your code to run only after your page has fully loaded, use the `load` event. In my years of doing things in JavaScript, I never had too much use for the `load` event at the document level outside of checking the final dimensions of a loaded image or creating a crude progress bar to indicate progress. Your mileage may vary, but...I doubt it :P

Scripts and Their Location in the DOM

In **Chapter 7, "Variable Scope,"** we looked at the various ways in which you can have scripts appear in your document. You saw that your script elements' position in the DOM affects when they run. In this section, we are going to re-emphasize that simple truth and go a few steps further.

To review, a simple script element can be some code stuck inline somewhere:

```
<script>
var number = Math.random() * 100;
alert("A random number is: " + number);
</script>
```

A simple script element can also be something that references some code from an external file:

```
<script src="/foo/something.js"></script>
```

Now, here is the important detail about these elements. Your browser parses your DOM sequentially from the top to the bottom. Any script elements that are found along the way will get parsed in the order they appear in the DOM.

Below is a very simple example where you have many script elements:

```
<!DOCTYPE html>
<html>
<body>
    <h1>Example</h1>
    <script>
        console.log("inline 1");
    </script>
    <script src="external1.js"></script>
    <script>
        console.log("inline 2");
    </script>
    <script src="external2.js"></script>
    <script>
        console.log("inline 3");
    </script>
</body>
</html>
```

It doesn't matter if the script contains inline code or references something external. All scripts are treated the same and run in the order in which they appear in your document. Using the above example, the order in which the scripts will run is as follows: **inline 1**, **external 1**, **inline 2**, **external 2**, and **inline 3**.

Now, here is a really REALLY important detail to be aware of. Because your DOM gets parsed from top to bottom, your script element has access to all of the DOM elements that were already parsed. Your script has no access to any DOM elements that have not yet been parsed. Say what?!

Let's say you have a script element that is at the bottom of your page just above the closing body element:

```
<!DOCTYPE html>
<html>
<body>
    <h1>Example</h1>

    <p>
        Quisque faucibus, quam sollicitudin pulvinar dignissim,
        nunc velit sodales leo, vel vehicula odio lectus vitae
```

```
        mauris. Sed sed magna augue. Vestibulum tristique cursus
        orci, accumsan posuere nunc congue sed. Ut pretium sit amet
        eros non consectetur. Quisque tincidunt eleifend justo,
        quis molestie tellus venenatis non. Vivamus interdum urna
        ut augue rhoncus, eu scelerisque orci dignissim. In commodo
        purus id purus tempus commodo.
    </p>

    <button>Click Me</button>

    <script src="something.js"></script>
</body>
</html>
```

When **something.js** runs, it has the ability to access all of the DOM elements that appear just above it such as the `h1`, `p`, and `button` elements. If your script element was at the very top of your document, it wouldn't have any knowledge of the DOM elements that appear below it:

```
<!DOCTYPE html>
<html>
<body>
    <script src="something.js"></script>

    <h1>Example</h1>

    <p>
        Quisque faucibus, quam sollicitudin pulvinar dignissim,
        nunc velit sodales leo, vel vehicula odio lectus vitae
        mauris. Sed sed magna augue. Vestibulum tristique cursus
        orci, accumsan posuere nunc congue sed. Ut pretium sit amet
        eros non consectetur. Quisque tincidunt eleifend justo,
        quis molestie tellus venenatis non. Vivamus interdum urna
        ut augue rhoncus, eu scelerisque orci dignissim. In commodo
        purus id purus tempus commodo.
    </p>

    <button>Click Me</button>

</body>
</html>
```

By putting your script element at the bottom of your page as shown earlier, the end behavior is identical to what you would get if you had code that explicitly listened to the `DOMContentLoaded` event. If you can guarantee that your scripts will appear toward the end of your document after your DOM elements, you can avoid following the whole `DOMContentLoaded` approach described in the previous section. Now, if you really want to have your script elements at the top of your DOM, ensure that all of the code that relies on the DOM runs after the `DOMContentLoaded` event gets fired.

Here is the thing. I'm a huge fan of putting your script elements at the bottom of your DOM. There is another reason besides easy DOM access why I recommend having your scripts live toward the bottom of the page. When a script element is being parsed, your browser stops everything else on the page from running while the code is executing. If you have a really long-running script or your external script takes its sweet time in getting downloaded, your HTML page will appear frozen. If your DOM is only partially parsed at this point, your page will also look incomplete in addition to being frozen. Unless you are Facebook, you probably want to avoid having your page look frozen for no reason.

Script Elements—Async and Defer

In the previous section, I explained how a script element's position in the DOM determines when it runs. All of that only applies to what I call **simple** script elements. To be part of the non-simple world, script elements that point to external scripts can have the `defer` and `async` attributes set on them:

```
<script async src="myScript.js"></script>
<script defer src="somethingSomethingDarkSide.js"></script>
```

These attributes alter when your script runs independent of where in the DOM they actually show up, so let's look at how they end up altering your script.

async

The `async` attribute allows a script to run asynchronously:

```
<script async src="someRandomScript.js"></script>
```

If you recall from the previous section, if a script element is being parsed, it could block your browser from being responsive and usable. By setting the `async` attribute on your script element, you avoid that problem altogether. Your script will run whenever it is able to, but it won't block the rest of your browser from doing its thing.

This casualness in running your code is pretty awesome, but you must realize that your scripts marked as **async** will not always run in order. You could have a case where several scripts marked as async will run in an order different from what was specified in your markup. The only guarantee you have is that your scripts marked with **async** will start running at some mysterious point before the `load` event gets fired.

defer

The **defer** attribute is a bit different from **async**:

```
<script defer src="someRandomScript.js"></script>
```

Scripts marked with **defer** run in the order in which they were defined, but they only get executed at the end just a few moments before the `DOMContentLoaded` event gets fired. Take a look at the following example:

```
<!DOCTYPE html>
<html>
<body>
    <h1>Example</h1>
    <script defer src="external3.js"></script>
    <script>
        console.log("inline 1");
    </script>
    <script src="external1.js"></script>
    <script>
        console.log("inline 2");
    </script>
    <script defer src="external2.js"></script>
    <script>
        console.log("inline 3");
    </script>
</body>
</html>
```

Take a second and tell the nearest human/pet the order in which these scripts will run. It's okay if you don't provide them with any context. If they love you, they'll understand.

Anyway, your scripts will execute in the following order: **inline 1**, **external 1**, **inline 2**, **inline 3**, **external 3**, and **external 2**. The **external 3** and **external 2** scripts are marked as `defer`, and that's why they appear at the very end despite being declared in different locations in your markup.

THE ABSOLUTE MINIMUM

In the previous sections, we looked at all sorts of factors that influence when your code will execute. The following diagram summarizes everything you saw into a series of colorful lines and rectangles:

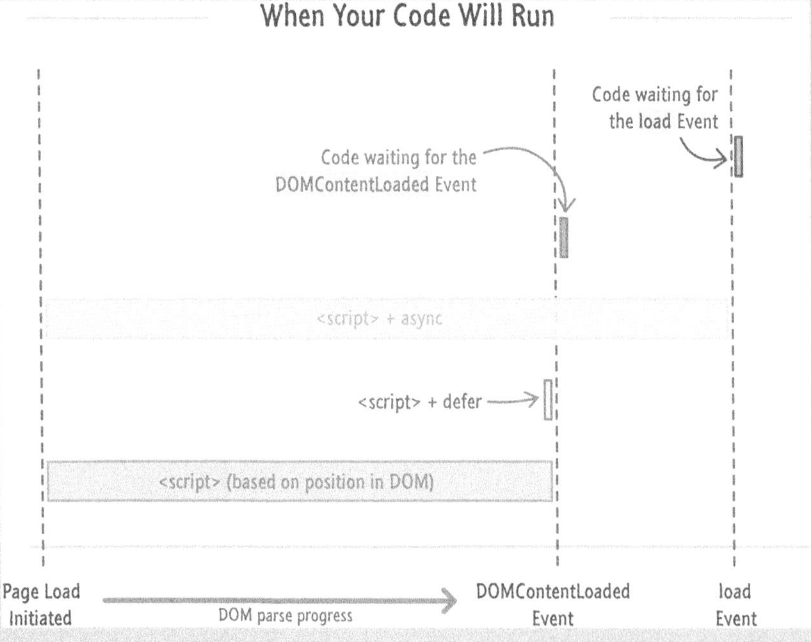

Now, here is probably what you are looking for. When is the right time to load your JavaScript? The answer is...

1. Place your script references below your DOM directly above your closing `body` element.
2. Unless you are creating a library that others will use, don't complicate your code by listening to the `DOMContentLoaded` or `load` events. Instead, see the previous point.

3. Mark your scripts referencing external files with the `async` attribute.
4. If you have code that doesn't rely on your DOM being loaded and runs as part of teeing things off for other scripts in your document, you can place this script at the top of your page with the `async` attribute set on it.

That's it. I think those four steps will cover almost 90% of all your cases to ensure your code runs at the right time. For more advanced scenarios, you should definitely take a look at a third-party library like **require.js**, which gives you greater control over when your code will run.

Some additional resources and examples:

- **Module Loading with RequireJS: http://bit.ly/kirupaRequireJS**
- **Preloading Images: http://bit.ly/kirupaPreloadImages**

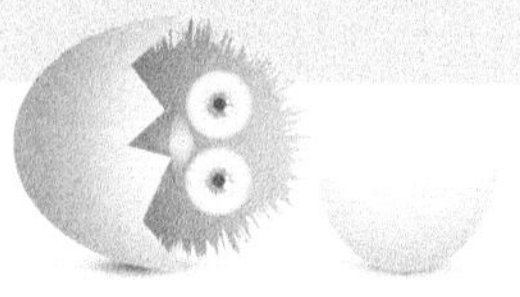

TIP Just a quick reminder for those of you reading these words in the print or e-book edition of this book: If you go to **www.quepublishing.com** and register this book, you can receive free access to an online Web Edition that not only contains the complete text of this book but also features a short, fun interactive quiz to test your understanding of the chapter you just read.

If you're reading these words in the Web Edition already and want to try your hand at the quiz, then you're in luck – all you need to do is scroll down!

IN THIS CHAPTER

- Learn to efficiently react to multiple events
- Revisit how events work for one last time

33

HANDLING EVENTS FOR MULTIPLE ELEMENTS

In its most basic case, an event listener deals with events fired from a single element:

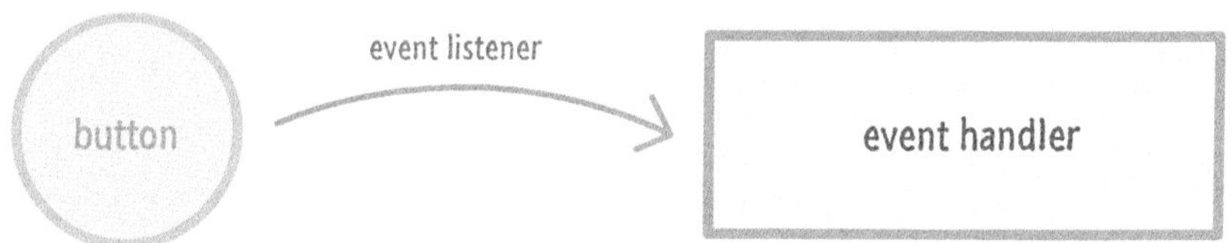

As you build more complicated things, the "one event handler for one element" mapping starts to show its limitation. The most common reason revolves around you creating elements dynamically using JavaScript. These elements you are creating can fire events that you may want to listen and react to, and you can have anywhere from a handful of elements that need eventing support to many MANY elements that need to have their events dealt with.

What you don't want to do is this:

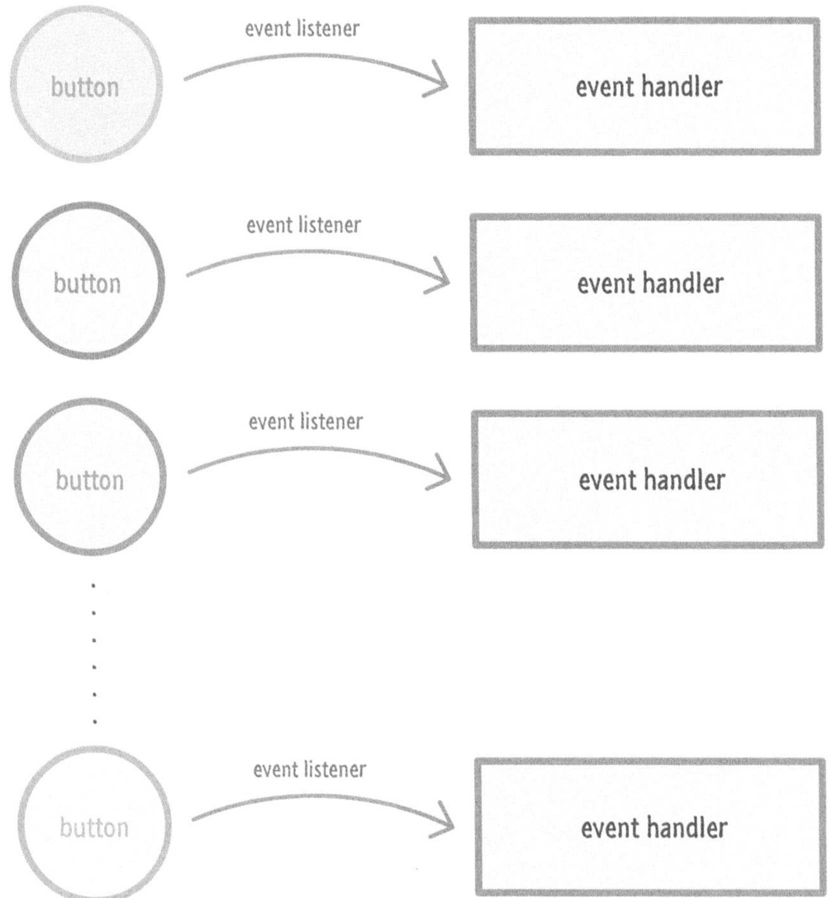

You don't want to create an event listener for each element. The reason is because your parents told you so. The other reason is because it is inefficient. Each of these elements carries around data about an event listener and its properties that can really start adding up the memory usage when you have a lot of content. Instead, what you want is a clean and fast way of handling events on multiple elements with minimal duplication and unnecessary things. What you want will look a little bit like this:

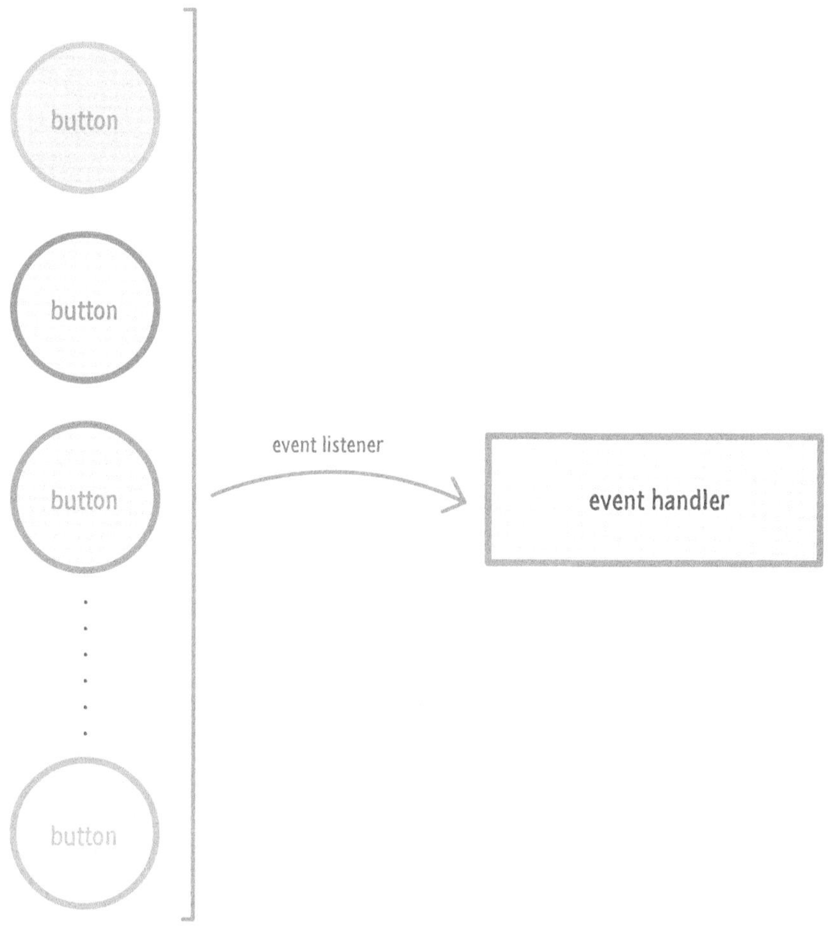

All of this may sound a bit crazy, right? Well, in this chapter, you will learn all about how non-crazy this is and how to implement this using just a few lines of JavaScript.

Onwards!

How to Do All of This

Okay - at this point, you know how simple event handling works where you have one element, one event listener, and one event handler. Despite how different the case with multiple elements may seem, by taking advantage of the disruptiveness of events, solving it is actually quite easy.

Imagine we have a case where you want to listen for the click event on any of the sibling elements whose id values are one, two, three, four, and five. Let's complete our imagination by picturing the DOM as follows:

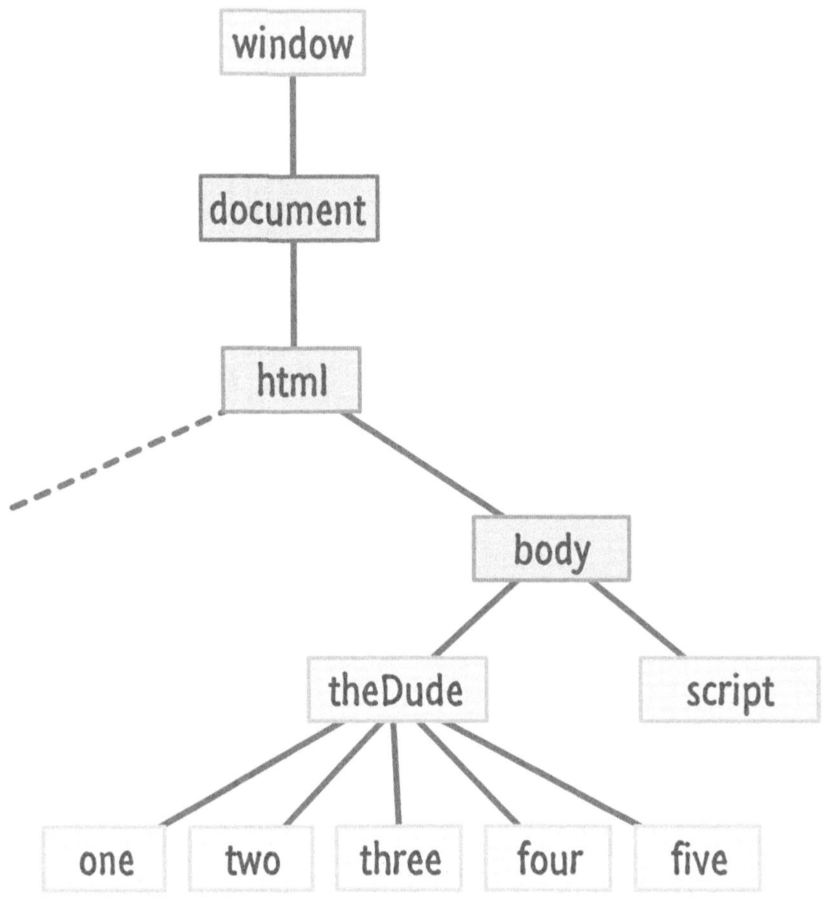

At the very bottom, we have the elements we want to listen for events on. They all share a common parent with an element whose id value is theDude. To solve our event handling problems, let's look at a terrible solution followed by a good solution.

A Terrible Solution

Here is what we don't want to do. We don't want to have five event listeners for each of these buttons:

```
var oneElement = document.querySelector("#one");
var twoElement = document.querySelector("#two");
```

```
var threeElement = document.querySelector("#three");
var fourElement = document.querySelector("#four");
var fiveElement = document.querySelector("#five");

oneElement.addEventListener("click", doSomething, false);
twoElement.addEventListener("click", doSomething, false);
threeElement.addEventListener("click", doSomething, false);
fourElement.addEventListener("click", doSomething, false);
fiveElement.addEventListener("click", doSomething, false);

function doSomething(e) {
    var clickedItem = e.target.id;
    alert("Hello " + clickedItem);
}
```

To echo what I mentioned in the intro, the obvious reason is that you don't want to duplicate code. The other reason is that each of these elements now has their `addEventListener` property set. This is not a big deal for five elements. It starts to become a big deal when you have dozens or hundreds of elements each taking up a small amount of memory. The other OTHER reason is that your number of elements, depending on how adapative or dynamic your UI really is, can vary. It may not be a nice fixed number of five elements like we have in this contrived example.

A Good Solution

The good solution for this mimics the diagram you saw much earlier where we have just one event listener. I am going to confuse you first by describing how this works. Then I'll hopefully un-confuse you by showing the code and explaining in detail what exactly is going on. The simple and confusing solution to this is:

1. Create a single event listener on the parent **theDude** element.
2. When any of the **one**, **two**, **three**, **four**, or **five** elements are clicked, rely on the propagation behavior that events possess and intercept them when they hit the parent **theDude** element.
3. (Optional) Stop the event propagation at the parent element just to avoid having to deal with the event obnoxiously running up and down the DOM tree.

I don't know about you, but I'm certainly confused after having read those three steps! Let's start to unconfuse ourselves by starting with a diagram that explains those steps more visually:

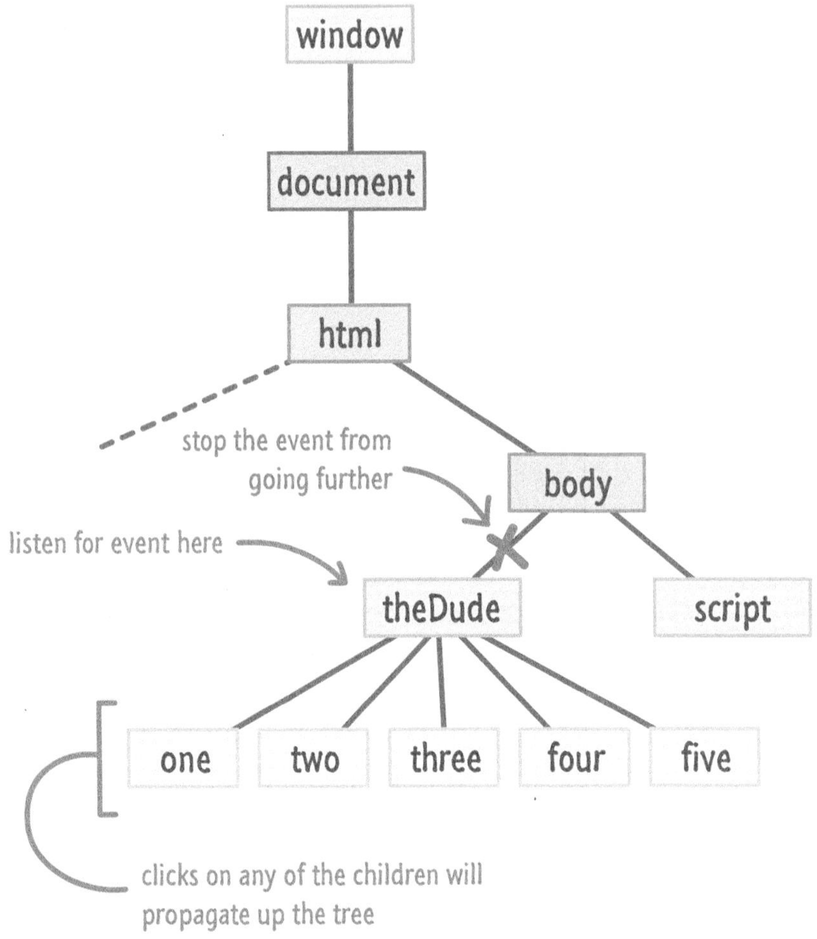

The last step in our quest for complete unconfusedness is the code that translates what the diagram and the three steps represent:

```
var theParent = document.querySelector("#theDude");
theParent.addEventListener("click", doSomething, false);

function doSomething(e) {
    if (e.target !== e.currentTarget) {
        var clickedItem = e.target.id;
```

```
        alert("Hello " + clickedItem);
    }
    e.stopPropagation();
}
```

Take a moment to read and understand the code you see here. It should be pretty self-explanatory after seeing our initial goals and the diagram. We listen for the event on the parent **theDude** element:

```
var theParent = document.querySelector("#theDude");
theParent.addEventListener("click", doSomething, false);
```

There is only one event listener to handle this event, and that lonely creature is called `doSomething`:

```
function doSomething(e) {
    if (e.target !== e.currentTarget) {
        var clickedItem = e.target.id;
        alert("Hello " + clickedItem);
    }
    e.stopPropagation();
}
```

This event listener will get called each time **theDude** element is clicked along with any children that get clicked as well. We only care about click events relating to the children, and the proper way to ignore clicks on this parent element is to simply avoid running any code if the element the click is from (aka the event target) is the same as the event listener target (aka **theDude** element):

```
function doSomething(e) {
    if (e.target !== e.currentTarget) {
        var clickedItem = e.target.id;
        alert("Hello " + clickedItem);
    }
    e.stopPropagation();
}
```

The target of the event is represented by `e.target`, and the target element the event listener is attached to is represented by `e.currentTarget`. By simply checking that these values not be equal, you can ensure that the event handler doesn't react to events fired from the parent element that you don't care about.

To stop the event's propagation, we simply call the `stopPropagation` method:

```
function doSomething(e) {
    if (e.target !== e.currentTarget) {
        var clickedItem = e.target.id;
        alert("Hello " + clickedItem);
    }
    e.stopPropagation();
}
```

Notice that this code is actually outside of my `if` statement. This is because I want the event to stop traversing the DOM under all situations once it gets overheard.

Putting It All Together

The end result of all of this code running is that you can click on any of the Dude's children and listen for the event as it propagates up:

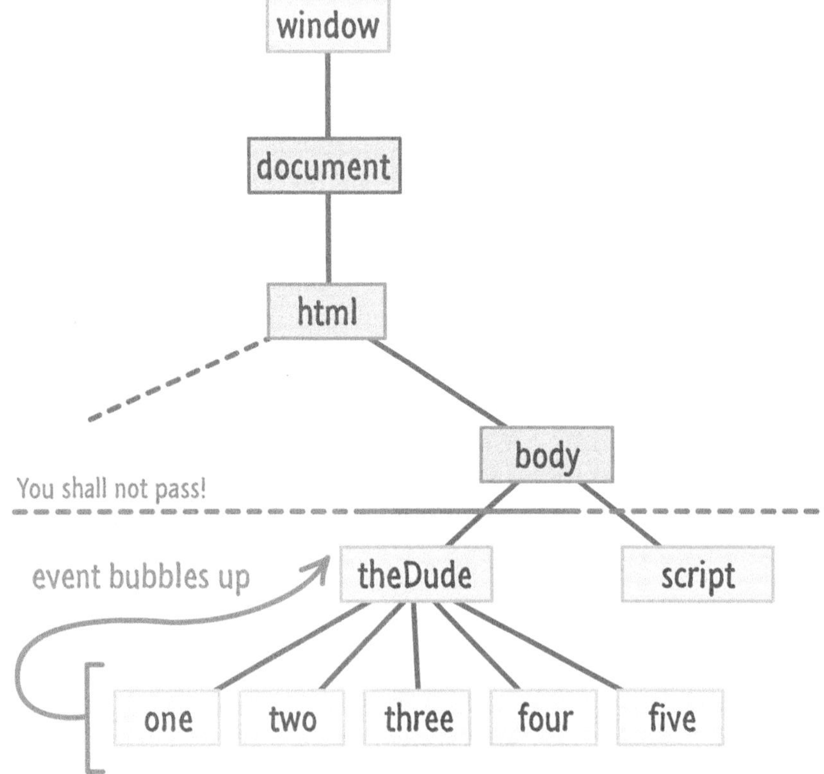

Because all of the event arguments are still tied to the source of the event, you can target the clicked element in the event handler despite calling `addEventListener` on the parent. The main thing to call out about this solution is that it satisfies the problems we set out to avoid. You only created one event listener. It doesn't matter how many children **theDude** ends up having. This approach is generic enough to accommodate all of them without any extra modification to your code. This also means that you should do some strict filtering if your **theDude** element ends up having children besides buttons and other elements that you care about.

THE ABSOLUTE MINIMUM

For some time, I actually proposed a solution for our Multiple Element Eventing Conundrum (**MEEC** as the cool kids call it!) that was inefficient but didn't require you to duplicate many lines of code. Before many people pointed out the inefficiences of it, I thought it was a valid solution.

The way this solution worked was by using a `for` loop to attach event listeners to all the children of a parent (or an array containing HTML elements). Here is what that code looked like:

```
var theParent = document.querySelector("#theDude");

for (var i = 0; i < theParent.children.length; i++) {
    var childElement = theParent.children[i];
    childElement.addEventListener('click', doSomething, false);
}

function doSomething(e) {
    var clickedItem = e.target.id;
    alert("Hello " + clickedItem);
}
```

The end result was that this approach allowed us to listen for the click event directly on the children. The only code I wrote manually was this single event listener call that was parameterized to the appropriate child element based on where in the loop the code was in:

```
childElement.addEventListener('click', doSomething, false);
```

The reason this approach isn't great is because each child element has an event listener associated with it. This goes back to our efficiency argument where this approach unnecessarily wastes memory.

Now, if you do have a situation where your elements are spread throughout the DOM with no nearby common parent, using this approach on an array of HTML elements is not a bad way of solving our MEEC problem.

Anyway, as you start working with larger quantities of UI elements for games, data-visualization apps, and other HTMLElement-rich things, you'll end up having to use everything you saw here at least once. I hope. If all else fails, this chapter still served an important purpose. All of the stuff about event tunneling and capturing you saw earlier clearly came in handy here. That's something!

TIP Just a quick reminder for those of you reading these words in the print or e-book edition of this book: If you go to **www.quepublishing.com** and register this book, you can receive free access to an online Web Edition that not only contains the complete text of this book but also features a short, fun interactive quiz to test your understanding of the chapter you just read.

If you're reading these words in the Web Edition already and want to try your hand at the quiz, then you're in luck – all you need to do is scroll down!

IN THIS CHAPTER

- Pat ourselves on the back for a job well done
- Pat ourselves on the back one more time just for kicks

34

CONCLUSION

Well, now you've done it! You just couldn't stop binge reading and now you are nearing the end. How does it feel knowing that you won't have any more new content to look forward to until the next season?

Anyway, if you've been following along from the very beginning, you'll agree that we covered a lot of ground. We started with this:

```
<script>
alert("hello, world!");
</script>
```

We ended up with this:

```
var theParent = document.querySelector("#theDude");
theParent.addEventListener("click", doSomething, false);

function doSomething(e) {
    if (e.target !== e.currentTarget) {
        var clickedItemId = e.target.id;
        alert("Hello " + clickedItemId);
    }
    e.stopPropagation();
}
```

These lines of code are probably not very impressive, but they hide a great deal of conceptual knowledge that you've learned along the way - knowledge about variables, basic types, objects, the DOM, dealing with events, and a whole lot more spread across 32 chapters that are now too basic to even bother mentioning.

The thing you should remember is that writing code is easy. Writing ***elegant*** code that actually solves a problem is hard. This was best captured by one of my favorite lines from **Scarface** where Tony Montana delivered the following line (exact wording may be off a bit...it's hard to understand him sometimes, as you know if you've seen the film):

This book is all about the basics. The way you go from the basics to the next step is by continuing to write code, trying out new things, and learning more along the way. This book described all the various tools and provided short examples of how they fit together help you build small things. It's up to you to take this knowledge and apply it towards building all the cooler non-small things that you often see associated with JavaScript.

So with that...see you all later, and feel free to drop me a line at **kirupa@kirupa.com** or find me on Facebook and Twitter (**@kirupa**). Like I mentioned in the introduction, I enjoy hearing from readers such as you, so don't be shy about contacting me.

Also, I know you have a lot of choices in books for learning JavaScript. Thank you for choosing this book and allowing me to live vicariously through your code editor :P

Cheers,

Kirupa

Glossary

A very casual look at the various terms you will encounter in this book and beyond.

A

Arguments The values you provide (or pass in) to a function.

Array A data structure that allows you to store and access a sequence of values.

B

Boolean A data structure that represents true or false.

C

Cascading Style Sheets (CSS) A styling language used primarily for changing how the content in your HTML page looks.

Closure An inner function that has access to an outer function's variables (in addition to its own and any global variables).

Comments Human readable text (often separated by // or /* and */ characters) in your code that is completely ignored by JavaScript.

D

Developer Tools In the context of browsers, they are extensions that help you inspect, debug, and diagnose what is going on inside your web page.

Do...While Loop A control statement that executes some code until a condition you specify returns false. (This is great if you don't know how many times you want to loop!)

Document Object Model (DOM) The JavaScript representation (often in a tree-like structure) of your HTML page and all the things inside it.

E

Event Bubbling The phase where an event starts at the element that initiated the event and climbs the DOM back to the root.

Event Capturing The phase where an event starts at the root and traverses down the DOM until it reaches the element that initiated the event.

Event Listener A function that listens for an event and then executes some code when that event is overheard.

Event Target The element that is responsible for having initiated (aka fired) an event.

Event A signal that travels through your DOM to indicate something has happened.

F

For Loop A control statement that executes some code a finite number of times.

Functions A reusable block of code that takes arguments, groups statements together, and can be called on to execute the code contained inside it.

G

Global Scope Something declared outside of a function that is accessible to the entire app.

I

If Statement A conditional statement that executes some code if the condition is true.

If/Else Statement A conditional statement that executes different pieces of code depending on whether a condition is true or false.

IIFE (Immediately Invoked Function Expression) A way of writing JavaScript that allows you to execute some code in its own scope without leaving behind any trace of its existence.

Invoke A fancy way of saying the same thing as calling a function.

J

JavaScript A fussy and (often) inconsistent scripting language that, to everyone's surprise over the years, has grown to be quite popular for building apps on the web and the server.

L

Local Scope Something that is accessible only to the enclosing function or block.

Loop A control statement that allows you to execute code repeatedly.

N

Node A generic name for an item in the DOM.

O

Object A very flexible and ubiquitous data structure you can use to store properties and their values and...even other objects.

Operators A built-in function such as your friendly +, -, *, /, `for`, `while`, `if`, `do`, =, etc. words.

P

Primitives A basic type that isn't composed of other types.

R

Return A keyword that exits a function or block. In the case of functions, it is often used to return some data back to whatever called the function.

S

Scope A term indicating the visibility of something. In the real world, it is also a brand of mouthwash.

Strict Equality (===) Comparison Checks whether value and type of two things is equal.

Strict Inequality (!==) Comparison Checks whether the value and type of two things is not equal.

String A sequence of characters that make up what we think of as text. It is also the name of formal type for dealing with text in JavaScript.

Switch Statement A conditional statement that checks a particular condition against a list of cases. If one of the cases matches the condition, the code associated with that case executes.

T

Timer Functions Functions that execute code at a periodic interval. The most common timer functions are `setTimeOut`, `setInterval`, and `requestAnimationFrame`.

Type A classification that helps identify your data and the values you can use.

V

Values The formal name for the various types of data you'll encounter.

Variable Scope The term for describing the visibility of a variable in a section of code.

Variables A named bucket for storing some data.

W

Weak Equality (==) Comparison Checks only whether the value of two things is equal.

Weak Inequality (!=) Comparison Checks only whether the value of two things is unequal.

Web Browser A complex application that, at its bare minimum, helps you browse the internet and display web pages.

While Loop A control statement that continually executes some code until a condition you specify returns false.

Index

Symbols

A

B

C

D

E

F

N

How can we make this index more useful? Email us at indexes@quepublishing.com

Q

R

S

T

U

V

W